1 d4 d5 2 c4 c6 3 ♘f3 ♘f6 4 ♘c3 e6

To my grandfather, the man who started it all.

# The Semi-Slav

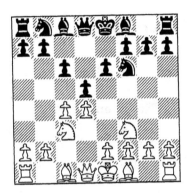

# CHESS PRESS OPENING GUIDES

Other titles in this series include:

| | | |
|---|---|---|
| 1 901259 05 6 | Caro-Kann Advance | Byron Jacobs |
| 1 901259 06 4 | Closed Sicilian | Daniel King |
| 1 901259 03 X | Dutch Leningrad | Neil McDonald |
| 1 901259 10 2 | French Advance | Tony Kosten |
| 1 901259 02 1 | Scandinavian | John Emms |
| 1 901259 01 3 | Sicilian Taimanov | James Plaskett |
| 1 901259 00 5 | Slav | Matthew Sadler |
| 1 901259 04 8 | Spanish Exchange | Andrew Kinsman |
| 1 901259 09 9 | Trompowsky | Joe Gallagher |

Chess Press Opening Guides

# The Semi-Slav

Matthew Sadler

The Chess Press, Brighton

First published in 1998 by Chess Press, a division of First Rank Publishing

Reprinted 2003

**British Library Cataloguing-in-Publication Data**
A catalogue record for this book is available from the British Library.

ISBN 1 901259 08 0

Distributed in North America by The Globe Pequot Press, P.O Box 480, 246 Goose Lane, Guilford, CT 06437-0480.

All other sales enquiries should be directed to Everyman Chess, Gloucester Publishers plc, Gloucester Mansions, 140A Shaftesbury Avenue, London WC2H 8HD
tel: 020 7539 7600  fax: 020 7379 4060
email: info@everymanchess.com
website: www.everymanchess.com

Everyman is the registered trade mark of Random House Inc. and is used in this work under license from Random House Inc.

Cover design by Ray Shell Design.
Production by Navigator Guides.

Printed by Lightning Source

# CONTENTS

1 d4 d5 2 c4 c6 3 ♘f3 ♘f6
4 ♘c3 e6

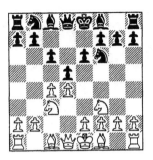

# BIBLIOGRAPHY

**Books**

*Encyclopaedia of Chess Openings vol.D*, Sahovski Informator, 1987
*The Complete Semi-Slav*, Peter Wells (Batsford, 1994)
*D44*, Alexander Beliavsky and Adrian Mikhalchishin (Sahovski Informator, 1993)

**Periodicals**

*Informator*
*ChessBase MegaBase CD-ROM*
*New In Chess Yearbook*
*British Chess Magazine*
*Chess Monthly*

# INTRODUCTION

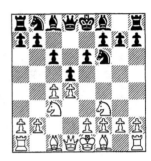

Every chessplayer is both fascinated and appalled by the Semi-Slav: fascinated by the sheer romance of this opening where the double-rook sacrifices and king hunts seem to recall the golden years of the 'Immortal' and 'Evergreen' games; but appalled by the number of complicated variations and the volume of analysis surrounding it. Often an initial burst of enthusiasm to learn the opening is followed by profound despair at the confusion that such fantasy and complexity brings!

Witness the following example, the game Topalov-Kramnik, Dortmund 1996 (analysed in full in Game 7 of this book). Topalov and Kramnik have had many great fights over the years but this clash has to be my favourite. I just can't see it often enough.

**1 d4 d5 2 c4 c6 3 ♘f3 ♘f6 4 ♘c3 e6 5 ♗g5 dxc4 6 e4 b5 7 e5 h6 8 ♗h4 g5 9 ♘xg5 hxg5 10 ♗xg5 ♘bd7 11 exf6 ♗b7 12 g3 c5 13 d5 ♕b6 14 ♗g2 0-0-0 15 0-0 b4 16 ♖b1**

16...♕a6 17 dxe6 ♗xg2 18 e7

18...♗xf1 19 ♕d5 ♗xe7 20 fxe7 ♗d3 21 ♘e4 ♗xb1

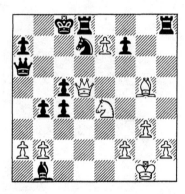

**22 ♘d6+ ♔c7 23 ♗f4 ♔b6 24 ♘xc4+ ♔b5 25 ♘d6+ ♔b6 26 exd8♗+**

**26...♖xd8 27 ♘c4+ ♔b5 28 ♘d6+ ♔b6 29 ♘c4+ ♔b5 ½-½**

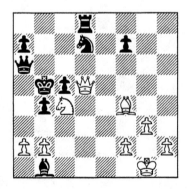

Since the theory of the Semi-Slav is

so well developed, the 'real' game may sometimes only begin after move 18 or 19. A common approach when preparing such an opening is to learn these theoretical moves by rote in a few minutes, and to concentrate only on what comes after. This is a major error; before one can play the early middlegame well, it is necessary to grasp the logic of the opening. This is achieved not by detailed and time-consuming analysis, but by describing the conflict of ideas in the opening in words: the positional aims of both sides, the territory they seek, the squares they weaken.

*Question 1:* What purpose does this approach serve?

*Answer:* Positional themes from the opening – the weakening of the opponent's dark squares, the creation of a queenside majority, etc. – shape and define the early middlegame. Positional understanding of the opening is the foundation of good play in the early middlegame. By highlighting the essentials of the position, this method ensures that our middlegame analysis will focus only on the important factors.

After 1 d4 d5 2 c4 c6 3 ♘f3 ♘f6 4 ♘c3, 4...e6 introduces the Semi-Slav.

*see following diagram*

The move 4...e6 locks the light-squared bishop on c8 inside the pawn chain. However, by freeing the dark-squared bishop, Black threatens to win a pawn with 5...dxc4 as the typical 6 a4, preventing ...b7-b5 can be met by 6...♗b4! 7 e3 (intending ♗xc4) 7...b5! when 8 axb5 cxb5 9 ♘xb5 is impossible as the knight is pinned to the king. White has two basic reactions:

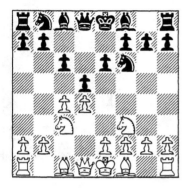

1) He can place the dark-squared bishop outside the pawn chain with 5 ♗g5, intending to defend c4 on the next move with 6 e3. After the consistent 5...dxc4, White can set up an 'ideal' centre with 6 e4 (threatening ♗xc4 regaining the pawn) when 6...b5 (protecting c4) 7 e5 plunges into the complications of the Botvinnik system (Chapters 1-6)

2) He can forestall ...d5xc4 by calmly protecting the c4-pawn with 5 e3. However, this has the disadvantage of blocking White's dark-squared bishop inside his pawn chain. A full discussion of the Meran variation and other possibilities after 5 e3 can be found in Chapters 7-14.

# CHAPTER ONE

## Botvinnik Variation:
## Main Line with 15...b4

**1 d4 d5 2 c4 c6 3 ♘f3 ♘f6 4 ♘c3 e6 5 ♗g5 dxc4 6 e4 b5 7 e5 h6 8 ♗h4 g5 9 ♘xg5 hxg5 10 ♗xg5 ♘bd7 11 exf6 ♗b7 12 g3 c5 13 d5 ♕b6 14 ♗g2 0-0-0 15 0-0 b4**

In this chapter we shall consider the main line of the Botvinnik system. However, let us start with an explanation of the opening moves that lead to the main line position.

With

**5 ♗g5**

White seeks to 'have it all': before defending against Black's threat of ...d5xc4 with e2-e3, White wants to develop his dark-squared bishop outside the pawn chain in order to obtain the maximum activity for his pieces. However, the drawback to 5 ♗g5 is that it does not defend the c-pawn, so

**5...dxc4**

is Black's most consistent response.

**6 e4**

then grabs the central space that Black conceded by taking on c4, after which

**6...b5**

is practically forced: if White is allowed to recapture the pawn with 7 ♗xc4, then Black will have given up the centre for nothing. However, now White can use his central control and the activity of his bishop on g5 to attack the knight on f6 with

**7 e5**

Now the knight cannot move as this would lose the queen to 8 ♗xd8. Black must use tactics to stay alive:

**7...h6**

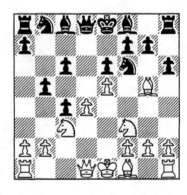

counterattacks against the bishop on g5. White usually then retreats his bishop along the h4-d8 diagonal with

**8 ♗h4**

again threatening to win a piece with 9 exf6.

Black's reply is forced:

**8...g5**

attacks the bishop again so that 9 exf6 can be met by 9...gxh4, regaining the piece. This move also blocks the h4-d8 diagonal so that a retreat of the bishop with 9 ♗g3 can be met by 9...♘d5, leaving Black a pawn up. Therefore White strikes with

**9 ♘xg5 hxg5 10 ♗xg5**

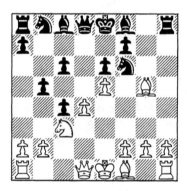

By sacrificing his knight for Black's g- and h-pawns, White has destroyed the barrier on the h4-d8 diagonal and now threatens 11 ♗xf6, forking the queen on d8 and the rook on h8.

**10...♘bd7**

defends the knight on f6 and starts to develop the queenside pieces. This is important since Black's king will only find a safe(ish!) home on the queenside – castling kingside would require a supreme effort of faith! Now

**11 exf6**

regains the piece.

Although 5 ♗g5 began as a pawn sacrifice, White is now a pawn up! The extra pawn on f6 is a strange one:

Black can easily recapture it, but this would expose weaknesses in his position. For example 11...♘xf6 gives White an unpleasant pin on the knight on f6 by the bishop on g5. Consequently, Black usually prefers

**11...♗b7**

intending the central break ...c6-c5, which will attack the two points most weakened by White's tactical efforts to maintain the pin on the knight on f6: Black's light-squared bishop now attacks g2, which would usually be shielded by a knight on f3, and the pawn on c5 attacks d4 which now lacks the support of the knight on f3. White also needs a safe place for his king: he would like to castle kingside, but with the removal of the h- and g-pawns, Black has two half-open files against the white kingside. Thus White usually plays

**12 g3**

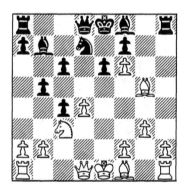

to protect his kingside. This shields h2 against a combined attack by a rook on h8 and a queen on c7, and protects g2 against a combination of a bishop on b7 and a rook on g8. It looks cheeky to play g2-g3 when Black has just played his bishop on b7,

but the logical

**12...c5**

threatening ...♗xh1, meets with

**13 d5**

By maintaining the pawn on d5, White checks his opponent's d-file play and finds a cunning use for the f6-pawn. If Black undermines d5 with 13...b4 then 14 dxe6!! is very strong, as 14...fxe6 loses to 15 f7+, discovering an attack on the queen.

**13...♕b6**

side-steps this, protecting e6 and b5 while allowing the black king to castle queenside. After

**14 ♗g2**

both sides put their kings to safety:

**14...0-0-0 15 0-0**

and now

**15...b4**

undermines the d5-pawn by attacking the knight on c3, its most important defender

Now we have arrived at the starting position of this chapter. Black intends to win the pawn on d5 and overwhelm his opponent with his central control; whereas White will try to open lines on the queenside against Black's king – since Black's queenside

pawns are so far advanced, he has plenty of targets!

The first six games in this chapter deal with the most common move in this position, 16 ♘a4. 16 ♖b1 is considered in Games 7-10.

> ## Game 1
> ## Ivanchuk-Shirov
> ### *Wijk aan Zee 1996*

**1 d4 d5 2 c4 c6 3 ♘c3 ♘f6 4 ♘f3 e6 5 ♗g5 dxc4 6 e4 b5 7 e5 h6 8 ♗h4 g5 9 ♘xg5 hxg5 10 ♗xg5 ♘bd7 11 exf6 ♗b7 12 g3 c5 13 d5 ♕b6 14 ♗g2 0-0-0 15 0-0 b4 16 ♘a4 ♕b5**

*Question 1:* Why does the queen go here?

*Answer:* Black has tried three moves in this position: 16...♕a6 (see Game 6), 16...♕d6 (see the notes to Game 6) and 16...♕b5. The latter seems the best all-round positional move. The queen protects c4 and attacks White's loose knight on a4, preventing the white queen from leaving the a4-d1 diagonal. The queen also stays in contact with the bishop on b7, which allows him to transfer the queen rapidly to the a8-h1 diagonal if White exchanges bishops with d5xe6 and ♗xb7. Finally, on b5 the queen is relatively safe from the white pieces!

**17 a3**

Now White will open the a-file with a3xb4 and Black will respond with ...c5xb4 to prevent the knight on a4 from returning to c3. This has the effect of 'diluting' the central black pawn mass, which makes it much harder for Black to achieve his desired idea of ...d5-d4, once he has taken the pawn on d5 with his e-pawn.

*Question 2:* Why does Black wish to play ...d5-d4?

*Answer:* The advance ...d5-d4 activates Black's pawn mass, which is his major positional trump. It also invites the exchange of light-squared bishops, which generally weakens White's kingside more than Black's queenside. (See Game 3 for a graphic illustration of this.)

17 dxe6 is discussed in Game 5.

**17...exd5**

The text wins back the sacrificed pawn as 18 ♗xd5 is impossible due to 18...♘e5! 19 ♗xb7+ ♕xb7 20 ♕e2 ♘f3+ 21 ♔h1 ♖xh2+ mate.

17...♘e5 and 17...♘b8 (which may transpose to one another) are the subject of Game 4.

**18 axb4 cxb4**

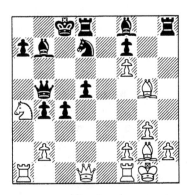

Black has regained the pawn that he sacrificed on the kingside by taking the white central d5-pawn. This has resulted in a lopsided pawn structure: White has a 4-1 kingside majority and a useful passed h-pawn, and Black has a 4-1 queenside majority and a passed d-pawn. Black's plan is simple: ...d5-

d4. White's plan is less obvious and requires some thought:

1) White wants to make it hard for Black to achieve his own plan. For example, he may blockade the d-pawn by occupying d4 either with his bishop or queen. (Note that after ...d5-d4, the black queen on b5 will attack the bishop on g5.)

2) White can try to take advantage of Black's weak dark squares: his central structure leaves the dark squares around it rather weak, while the f6-pawn takes control of e7 and g7 away from Black's pieces.

3) White can open up the black queenside with b2-b3.

4) The f6-pawn provides two outposts for the white pieces: g7, and most usually, e7. By placing a rook on e7, White occupies the seventh rank from a central position, giving him targets on both wings. This move is often played as a sacrifice, offering to trade the rook for Black's dark-squared bishop on f8. After ...♗xe7, f6xe7, White gets a passed pawn on the seventh rank, just one step away from queening, and removes the black piece best suited to defending his weak dark squares: the dark-squared bishop.

5) The black king looks quite safe on c8, but if the knight were diverted from d7, the king could be caught in an unpleasant crossfire with a bishop on f4 taking b8 from the king and a queen on g4 or a bishop on h3 delivering a nasty check. Note that, for now at least, the rook on h8 prevents ♗h3+.

6) Finally, the most important target for White: the a7-pawn. This pawn

is a very useful defensive unit, covering b6 and therefore helping to stop White's knight from becoming active. It allows Black's knight to move from d7 when it desires and also provides a haven on a8 for the black king. However, it is also a natural target for White's pieces: White can play the positionally desirable moves ♕d4 or ♗e3, preventing ...d5-d4 and at the same time attacking a key black defensive unit. Black will nearly always seek to shield it from attack or defend it, as moving the a-pawn weakens another dark square: b6.

**19 ♗e3**

The major continuation. On g5 all the bishop seemed to do was defend the f6-pawn, whereas on e3 the bishop attacks the a-pawn and helps to prevent the ...d5-d4 push. For 19 ♖e1 see Game 3.

**19...♘c5**

Shielding the a7-pawn, unmasking the support of the rook on d8 for the pawn on d5, and eyeing the outposts on b3 and d3. By exchanging White's knight, Black frees c5 for his bishop to support ...d5-d4.

**20 ♕g4+!**

A rather awkward check since the natural 20...♔b8 21 ♕d4! ♘xa4 22 ♕xa7+ and 20...♕d7 21 ♕xd7+ ♘xd7 22 ♖fd1 ♘xf6 23 ♗xa7!, intending ♗d4 and ♘b6+ (Agzamov) are both dodgy for Black. However, 20...♔c7! was suggested by Ivanchuk. Black is threatening simply ...♘xa4, so White must react rapidly. Then 21 ♗f4+ conceals a cunning trap: 21...♗d6 blocks the check, but 22 ♘xc5 ♕xc5 23 ♗e3! wins the a-pawn. So 21...♔c6! is best.

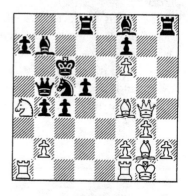

*Question 3:* Well hang on a minute, I...

*Answer:* I know it looks suicidal, but it may well be okay! I have a theory that in positions where the pawns in front of your king have moved far forward, your king is safest not on the back rank, but on the third or fourth rank, close to the pawn wall that shields the king! Black does indeed have a large number of pieces on the queenside to protect his king in this position, so White will have to sacrifice substantially if he is to breach his opponent's position. After 22 ♘xc5 ♗xc5, Black intends ...♔b6 and ...d5-d4!

**20...Ξd7**

After this move the rook on d7 is pinned to the king by the queen on g4. White will look to exploit this either by playing ♗h3 or by opening up the position to make this tactical detail count for more. However, Black's rook is a strong defensive piece, covering Black's seventh rank.

**21 ♕g7!!**

I told you that White had an outpost on g7!

**21...♗xg7 22 fxg7 Ξg8 23 ♘xc5**

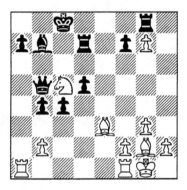

Black has a queen for knight and bishop. However, the a7-pawn is likely to fall, while the rook on d7 can be attacked further by a bishop on h3, so White will gain further material for the queen. Several positional factors are important:

1) White has a passed h-pawn.

2) White's king is very safe whereas Black's is not.

3) White can blockade the d-pawn with ♗d4, which stops Black from activating his queenside majority and leaves him with a passive bishop on b7.

*Question 4:* What should Black do?

*Answer:* Black wants to play ...d5-d4 to activate his queenside majority and his bishop on b7, but it is hard to achieve this. He should exchange a pair of rooks to reduce the danger to his king and give his queen more room to enter the white position.

**23...d4?**

This devilish idea is actually a tactical blunder. 23...Ξxg7 is considered in the next game.

**24 ♗xb7+ Ξxb7 25 ♘xb7!**

Threatening to fork the king and queen with 26 ♘d6+.

**25...♕b6!**

This was Shirov's idea; 25...♔xb7 would simply have allowed 26 ♗xd4, protecting the g7-pawn and attacking a7. Shirov's move defends the d4-pawn and parries the fork on d6. Unfortunately...

**26 ♗xd4!**

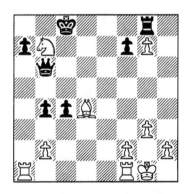

**26...♕xd4 27 Ξfd1 ♕xb2 28 ♘d6+ ♔b8 29 Ξdb1! ♕xg7**

Ivanchuk points out that 29...♕d2, attempting to keep hold of the b4-pawn, is cleverly met by 30 ♘xc4 ♕c3 31 Ξa4! b3 32 ♘a5! b2 33 Ξb4+!, picking up the b-pawn, as 33...♕xb4 loses the queen to 34 ♘c6+, forking the king and queen.

30 罝xb4+ 含c7 31 罝a6 罝b8 32 罝xa7+ 含xd6 33 罝xb8 豐g4 34 罝d8+ 含c6 35 罝a1 1-0

A magnificent game!

1 d4 d5 2 c4 c6 3 ᐃf3 ᐃf6 4 ᐃc3 e6 5 ᐃg5 dxc4 6 e4 b5 7 e5 h6 8 ᐃh4 g5 9 ᐃxg5 hxg5 10 ᐃxg5 ᐃbd7 11 g3 ᐃb7 12 ᐃg2 豐b6 13 exf6 0-0-0 14 0-0 c5 15 d5 b4 16 ᐃa4 豐b5 17 a3 exd5 18 axb4 cxb4 19 ᐃe3 ᐃc5 20 豐g4+! 罝d7 21 豐g7!! ᐃxg7 22 fxg7 罝g8 23 ᐃxc5

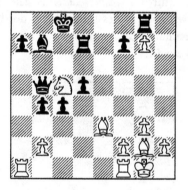

**23...罝xg7 24 ᐃd4**

In the notes to his game against Shirov, Ivanchuk mentioned 24 罝xa7, but now Lalic's 24...d4!! seems good. For example:

a) 25 罝xb7 豐xc5!

b) 25 ᐃxb7+ 罝xb7! 26 ᐃxb7 (threatening to fork king and queen with ᐃd6+) 26...豐b6!! Now after 27 ᐃxd4 豐xd4 28 罝fa1 罝g6! the white knight on b7 is very short of squares.

c) 25 ᐃxd7 ᐃxg2 26 ᐃxd4!? just leads to a draw after 26...ᐃxf1! (greedy

and correct – the best sort of move!) 27 ᐃb6+ 含b8 28 ᐃd7+ 含c8, as 27...含d8 allows a lovely mate in two: 28 ᐃf6+ 含e8 29 罝a8 mate.

Ivanchuk also mentions 24 ᐃh3 f5! 25 ᐃxf5 d4! (seizing the opportunity to open the a8-h1 diagonal) 26 ᐃxd4

26...罝gf7 'retaining definite counter-chances'. I think it is clear that White has lost control of this position.

The text is the right idea, stopping any tricks with ...d5-d4 and threatening to win material with ᐃxb7 and then ᐃxg7.

**24...f5 25 ᐃh3?**

The bishop on d4 is White's most important piece; and removing the bishop from the h1-a8 diagonal allows Black to dislodge it by playing a major piece to e4. 25 ᐃxd7 罝xd7 26 罝xa7 was better, with a mess, although it may be a little easier for White to play this position than Black.

The game illustrates what I mean by this. Although Black gets a good version of this line, he still has to be accurate or his weak king and vulnerable pawns will lose him the game. As we shall see, the pressure very quickly became too much for Black.

25...Rgf7 26 Rxa7 Rc7 27 Ne6 Rce7 28 Ng5 We8 29 Nxf7 Wxf7 30 Rfa1 Wh5! 31 Bg2 f4 32 R7a5 f3 33 Bf1 Rh7?

Black misses his chance! 33...Re4! (Lalic) was best, and would have been very awkward for White to meet. Now, however, Black is in trouble.

34 h4 Wf5 35 Be3! Wc2 36 Bf4 Rf7 37 Bh3+ Kd8 38 Bd6 Rf5 39 Ra7 Bc8 40 Rg7 Wxb2 41 Raa7 Wb1+ 42 Kh2 Rf8 43 Bxf8 Bxh3 44 Bc5 Be6 45 Ra8+ Bc8 46 Bb6+ 1-0

Mate follows on the next move. There is plenty of scope for practical tests here, but, in general, I feel that White has the easier task in a practical game, even if I cannot say that he is 'theoretically' better.

*Game 3*
## Stean-Rivas
*Marbella 1982*

1 d4 d5 2 c4 c6 3 Nf3 Nf6 4 Nc3 e6 5 Bg5 dxc4 6 e4 b5 7 e5 h6 8 Bh4 g5 9 Nxg5 hxg5 10 Bxg5 Nbd7 11 exf6 Bb7 12 g3 c5 13 d5 Wb6 14 Bg2 0-0-0 15 0-0 b4 16 Na4 Wb5 17 a3 exd5 18 axb4 cxb4

## 19 Re1

With this move White takes control of the e-file and dreams of playing Re7.

## 19...Bh6

I was suspicious when I first saw 19...Bh6: Black allows his opponent access to e7 and the seventh rank without even having to sacrifice the exchange! This is, however, a typical idea in the Botvinnik variation: by exchanging off the dark-squared bishop, Black undermines the defence of the f6-pawn and virtually assures himself of winning it. He also removes one of the best pieces for blockading on d4 and attacking a7, the queen being the other.

The alternative 19...d4!? 20 Wxd4 Bxg2 21 Kxg2 Wxg5 22 Wxc4+ Kb8 23 Red1! gave White a huge attack in Van Wely-Piket, Wijk aan Zee 1994.

## 20 Bxh6 Rxh6 21 Wd4 Rxf6

Black deals with the threat to his a-pawn tactically: 22 Wxa7 is met by 22...Ra6, winning the knight on a4.

## 22 Bh3!

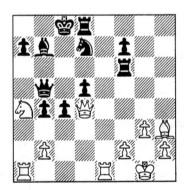

White uses the absence of the black rook from the h-file to play this annoying move, pinning the knight on d7 to the king, and threatening ♕xf6.

**22...♖d6 23 ♘c5**

The next few moves are critical. Black is threatening to unpin with ...♔b8, solving all his problems, so White must take purposeful action.

**23...♕b6!**

Black does not mind losing the exchange on two conditions:

1) He can keep his other rook on the board to help push his own pawns and stop White's outside passed pawn.

2) He can exchange queens to remove the last piece capable of actively blockading the d-pawn.

**24 ♖ed1**

24 ♖e7, to increase pressure on d7, should be met by 24...♔c7 intending, yes you've guessed it, 25...♔c6, unpinning and putting pressure on the c5-knight. Remember that this knight cannot capture on d7 while the queen on d4 is unprotected. Now 25 ♗xd7 ♖8xd7 26 ♖xd7+ ♖xd7 26 ♕e5+ ♖d6 27 ♕e7+ ♔c6! (27...♔c8 28 ♘xb7 ♖d7 29 ♕e8+ wins) gives Black a good position, while 25 ♖d1, defending the queen on d4, is met by 25...♗c8, when Black is a little tied up but after 26 ♖xf7 ♔c6 27 ♘e6 ♕xd4 (27...♖xe6 28 ♕xd5+) 28 ♘xd8+ ♔c5 29 ♖xd4 (29 ♘e6+ ♖xe6! 30 ♖xd4 ♖e1+ wins) 29...♔xd4 30 ♘e6+ ♔d3, he escapes!

**24...♔c7 25 ♗xd7 ♖8xd7 26 ♘xd7 ♕xd4 27 ♖xd4 ♔xd7**

Such unbalanced material endings are very typical of the Semi-Slav. Black will try to create a passed pawn on the queenside by playing his king to c5 to chase the rook from d4. This will allow the black d5-pawn to advance to d4 with two effects: first, the

pawn can go 'all the way' with the support of the rook on d6; and second, the advance activates the bishop on b7. From f3, it can remove a blockader on d1, and from e4 it can prevent the passed h-pawn from advancing to h7. White cannot hold d4 by doubling rooks on the d-file, as Black will just create another passed pawn either on the c-file (...c4-c3) or the a-file (...a5-a4-a3); and he cannot support the rook on d4 with his king on e3, since Black will just check and drive it away. White's task is the more difficult, particularly in a practical game. Passed pawns win endings and White has just one while his opponent has several!

**28 h4 ♔c6! 29 h5 ♔c5 30 ♖h4 ♖h6!**

Necessary to prevent h5-h6.

**31 g4 d4 32 g5 ♖h8 33 ♖xa7**

33 ♖a5+ ♔b6 34 ♖f5 ♖d8! 35 ♔f1 c3 36 bxc3 b3! is very good for Black.

**33...♗c6 34 ♖a5+ ♔b5**

After the text move the game quickly peters out to a draw. Black could still have played for a win with 34...♔b6!?

**35 ♖xd4 ♔xd4 36 ♖xb5 ♖xh5 37 ♖xb4 ½-½**

Black's two other possibilities on move 17 are linked in a very spectacular way.

**1 d4 d5 2 c4 c6 3 ♘c3 ♘f6 4 ♘f3 e6 5 ♗g5 dxc4 6 e4 b5 7 e5 h6 8 ♗h4 g5 9 ♘xg5 hxg5 10 ♗xg5 ♘bd7 11 exf6 ♗b7 12 g3 c5 13 d5 ♛b6 14 ♗g2 0-0-0 15 0-0 b4 16 ♘a4 ♛b5 17 a3 ♘e5**

Very logical. Black unmasks the attack of the rook on the d5-pawn and intends to win it without blocking his bishop on b7 with ...e6xd5. From e5, the knight aims for the defensive square c6 as well as d3. However, White has a wonderful tactical possibility that makes this move unplayable.

**18 axb4 cxb4 19 ♛d4!**

Attacking the knight on e5 and the pawn on a7.

**19...♘c6**

This position can also be reached via a different move order: 17...♘b8 18 axb4 cxb4 19 ♛d4 and now

19...♘c6.

**20 dxc6!! ♖xd4 21 cxb7+**

White's compensation for the queen is 'two pieces, a passed pawn on the seventh and a host of tricks', to quote Peter Wells.

**21...♔c7 22 ♗e3 e5 23 ♘c3!! bxc3 24 bxc3 ♗c5!?**

This was Kramnik's attempt to rehabilitate this line after the crushing White win in Salov-Illescas, Madrid 1993, which continued 24...♖d6 25 ♖ab1! a6 26 ♖xb5 axb5 27 ♖a1 ♖d8 28 ♗e4 ♗h6 29 ♗c5 ♗f8 30 ♗a7 with an overwhelming position for White.

**25 cxd4 ♗xd4**

25...exd4 loses to 26 ♗f4+ ♗d6 27 ♗xd6+ ♔xd6 and 28 ♖fb1 followed by 29 b8♛+.

**26 ♖fb1!**

The start of a magnificent series of moves.

**26...♛c5 27 ♖a6! ♖b8**

27...♗xe3 28 ♖c6+ ♛xc6 29 ♗xc6 is clearly better for White according to Kramnik.

**28 ♗c1!!**

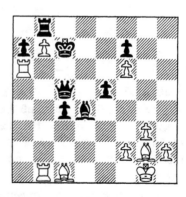

Quite superb, bringing the bishop round to the sensitive d6-square via a3.

**28...c3 29 ♗a3! ♛c4 30 ♗d6+ ♔d7**

**31 ♗c6+!!**

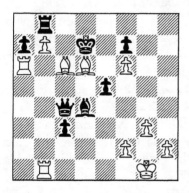

**31...♔e6**

31...♔xd6 loses the queen to 32 ♗b5+.

**32 ♗b5! ♗xf2+ 33 ♔xf2 ♕d4+ 34 ♔f1 ♕e4 35 ♖e1 ♕h1+ 36 ♔f2 ♕xh2+ 37 ♔f3 ♖xb7 38 ♗xe5+ ♖b6 39 ♗c4+ ♔d7 40 ♖xa7+ ♔c8 41 ♖c7+ 1-0**

A magical performance that destroyed two lines – 17...♘e5 and 17...♘b8 – in one game!

Now we turn to the old line: 16 ♘a4 ♕b5 17 dxe6.

**Game 5**
**Nikolic-Shirov**
*Wijk aan Zee (match) 1993*

**1 d4 d5 2 c4 c6 3 ♘f3 ♘f6 4 ♘c3 e6 5 ♗g5 dxc4 6 e4 b5 7 e5 h6 8 ♗h4 g5 9 ♘xg5 hxg5 10 ♗xg5 ♘bd7 11 g3 ♗b7 12 ♗g2 ♕b6 13 exf6 0-0-0 14 0-0 c5 15 d5 b4 16 ♘a4 ♕b5 17 dxe6**

Instead of opening the queenside with 17 a3, White takes on e6, denying his opponent the chance to form a massive queenside pawn chain and

keeping his extra pawn. The drawback, however, is the activity that Black receives and that White forgoes. First, without the open a-file and a3xb4 to create holes in Black's queenside structure, White lacks a target on the queenside. Second, d5xe6 opens the d-file for Black's rook and allows him to weaken White's kingside light squares by exchanging the light-squared bishops.

**17...♗xg2 18 ♔xg2 ♕c6+! 19 f3**

19 ♕f3 loses the queen to the deflection 19...♖xh2+! 20 ♔xh2 ♕xf3.

**19...♕xe6**

Threatening ...♕h3+, winning the h-pawn.

**20 ♕c2**

A dual-purpose move: White protects the second rank to meet 20...♕h3+ with 21 ♔g1, and gets the queen off the d-file so that ...♘e5 no longer comes with tempo.

**20...♘e5 21 ♖ae1 ♖d4!!**

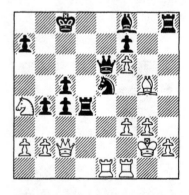

Savchenko's superb discovery introduces the optimal set-up for the black pieces. Black wants to develop his dark-squared bishop to its most active square on d6, but first brings the queen's rook to d4 so that the bishop does not block the rook's path on the d-file. On d4 the rook defends c4, leaves the d3-outpost free for the knight, and prevents White from using e4 for his queen to trouble Black's queenside light squares. White cannot win a piece with 22 f4 due to the unpleasant 22...♕d5+!

**22 h4**

Stopping Black from playing ...♕h3+, but weakening the g3-square.

**22...♗d6**

Eyeing g3 and completing Black's development.

**23 a3**

This was Nikolic's improvement over the stem game Rublevsky-Savchenko, Helsinki 1992, where 23 ♗e3? showed another brutal point to Black's set-up: 23...♖dxh4!! 24 gxh4 ♖xh4

25 ♔g1 (25 ♖h1 ♘xf3!! 26 ♔xf3 ♕g4+ wins) 25...♘d3! 26 ♕g2 ♗h2+ 27 ♕xh2 ♖xh2 28 ♔xh2 ♘xe1 29 ♖xe1 ♕xf6, threatening ...♕h4+, when Black had a clear advantage (analysis by Savchenko).

23 a3 aims to weaken Black's control of d4 by swapping off his useless a-pawn for Black's c-pawn with a3xb4,

...c5xb4. White players may like to investigate Shirov's suggestion of 23 ♖e2 ♕d5 24 ♕f5+ ♔c7 25 ♖fe1 (25 ♗f4 ♖e8 is unclear) 25...♘d3 26 ♕xd5 ♔xd5 27 ♖e7+ ♗xe7 28 ♖xe7+ ♔c6 29 ♖xf7 with a mess, as 23 a3 does not seem to work.

**23...♕d5**

Centralising and increasing Black's influence along the d-file, while eyeing the f3-pawn.

**24 ♕f5+ ♔c7 25 ♖e2 ♔c6!!**

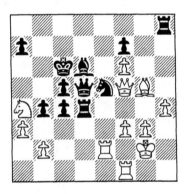

Not a surprise to us now!! This superb idea prepares to exchange off queens with ...♘d3 and allows the king to recapture on d5 after ♕xd5, in order to support the queenside pawns. Shirov evaluates the position as slightly better for Black.

**26 b3! c3 27 axb4 cxb4 28 ♖a1! ♘d3 29 ♕xd5+ ♖xd5 30 ♖e4! ♔b5 31 ♖c4! ♖e8! 32 ♖a2! ♘e1+ 33 ♔h3 ♘xf3 34 ♖xc3 ♘xg5+ 35 hxg5 ♖h8+ 36 ♔g2 bxc3 37 ♘xc3+ ♔c6 38 ♘xd5 ♔xd5 39 ♖xa7 ♔e6 40 ♖a4?**

40 ♔f3 ♖h3 41 ♔g4 ♖xg3+ 42 ♔h5 ♖h3+ 43 ♔g4 ♖xb3 44 ♖a6 would have allowed White to squeak a draw according to Shirov. The text allows Black to win the crucial g5-pawn.

**40...♖g8 41 ♖g4 ♗e5 0-1**

After 42...♔f5, Black will win both the g5- and f6-pawns.

---

*Game 6*
**Ivanchuk-Shirov**
*Novgorod 1994*

---

**1 d4 d5 2 c4 c6 3 ♘c3 ♘f6 4 ♘f3 e6 5 ♗g5 dxc4 6 e4 b5 7 e5 h6 8 ♗h4 g5 9 ♘xg5 hxg5 10 ♗xg5 ♘bd7 11 exf6 ♗b7 12 g3 c5 13 d5 ♕b6 14 ♗g2 0-0-0 15 0-0 b4 16 ♘a4 ♕a6**

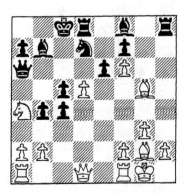

On a6 the queen attacks the knight on a4, keeps in touch with the bishop on b7 and hence the a8-h1 diagonal, and protects the pawn on c4. In contrast to 16...♕b5, this move also keeps in touch with e6 so that after d5xe6 or ...e6xd5 the queen can transfer to e6, eyeing h3 and the white light squares on the kingside. The drawback is that a3xb4, opening the a-file, will be more dangerous as the queen is in the line of fire of the rook on a1.

16...♕d6!? 17 ♗f4 ♕a6 aims for a 16...♕a6 line with the white bishop on f4. Although f4 is a more attacking post than g5 – taking c7 and b8 away

from the black king – it does leave the f6-pawn unprotected, enabling Black to recapture on f6 put extra pressure on the d5-pawn. Ionov-Bjerring, El Vendrell 1996, continued 18 dxe6 fxe6 19 ♗xb7+ ♕xb7 20 ♕g4 ♗h6 21 ♗d6! ♕c6 22 ♖fd1! with an initiative for White.

**17 a3 ♗xd5!?**

This imaginative idea is attributed to Alexander Shabalov.

**18 ♗xd5 ♘e5 19 ♕e2 ♖xd5 20 axb4 cxb4 21 ♘c3 ♕c6!?**

There is another interesting idea here, which Piket played in a TV game against Lutz in Germany: 21...♖a5!? After 22 ♖xa5 ♕xa5 23 ♘e4, Piket played 23...♘d3 24 b3 ♕e5!? (Lutz mentions 24...♕f5!?, aiming for h3), when 25 ♖c1? ♘xc1 26 ♕xc4+ was easily countered by 26...♕c7 27 ♕xc1 ♕xc1 28 ♗xc1 a5 with a clear advantage to Black. This so impressed Lutz that when he got the chance a little later against Korchnoi, he decided to play it as Black (Horgen 1994). Unfortunately, he was once again on the wrong side of the board! Korchnoi found the much stronger 25 ♖d1!, and sacrificed a piece for a vicious attack after 25...♘c5 26 ♕xc4 ♕xe4 27 ♕b5!, aiming for the e8-square.

**22 ♘xd5 ♕xd5**

Threatening ...♘f3+.

**23 f3 ♗c5+ 24 ♔g2 ♘d3**

Unfortunately, as Kharitonov points out, the lovely 24...♘g4 25 h4 ♕xg5, to meet 26 hxg5 with 26...♖h2+ mate, fails to simply 26 fxg4!

**25 h4 ♔b7!**

The active king again! Black's idea is

to play ...♗b6 and allow the a-pawn to join in the fun with ...a7-a5.

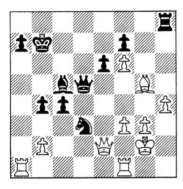

**26 ♖a5**

The right idea but not the best execution. White's idea is to challenge the knight on d3 by undermining its support with b2-b3, attacking the pawn on c4. After Black has taken on b3 or played ...c4-c3, White has two ways to put pressure on the black position:

1) ♖fd1, attacking the knight on d3 which is pinned to the queen on d5.

2) ♖a5, attacking the bishop on c5 which is pinned to the queen on d5.

In a later game Kharitonov-Sabanov, Moscow 1995, White played the immediate 26 b3!, which seems to give Black a lot of problems. In the game, Black chose 26...c3 27 ♖fd1 ♖d8 28 ♖a5! (threatening 29 ♖xc5 ♕xc5 30 ♖xd3, winning a piece) 28...♔b6 and now instead of the violent 29 ♖xc5, Kharitonov claims an initiative with 29 ♕a2!, and this does indeed seem very strong for White. If Black wishes to try this line, he therefore must find an improvement on this game – which is beyond me for the moment!

**26...♕d4 27 b3 ♗b6!**

In comparison with 26 b3, Black gains a tempo to put his bishop on the safe b6-square.

**28 ♖a2 c3 29 ♖d1 ♖d8 30 h5! a5 31 g4 ♘f4+ 32 ♗xf4 ♕xd1 33 ♕xd1 ♖xd1 34 h6 ♔a6?**

A blunder. 34...e5! 35 h7 (35 ♗xe5 ♖d2+ 36 ♔h3 ♖xa2 37 h7 c2 38 ♗f4 ♗c7! wins, as 39 ♗e3 c1♕ 40 ♗xc1 ♖h2 is checkmate) 35...♖d8 36 ♗xe5 ♖h8 would have favoured Black according to Shirov. Suddenly, White is winning.

**35 g5 ♖d8 36 ♔f1 ♗d4 37 ♔e2 e5 38 ♗e3 ♔b5 39 h7 ♖h8 40 ♗xd4 exd4 41 g6! fxg6 42 f7 ♔c6 43 ♔d3 ♔d7 44 ♖e2 a4 45 ♖e8 axb3 46 ♖xh8 b2 47 ♖d8+ 1-0**

Now we move on to the other branch of the main line: 16 ♖b1.

---

### Game 7
### Topalov-Kramnik
### *Dortmund 1996*

---

**1 d4 d5 2 c4 c6 3 ♘f3 ♘f6 4 ♘c3 e6 5 ♗g5 dxc4 6 e4 b5 7 e5 h6 8 ♗h4 g5 9 ♘xg5 hxg5 10 ♗xg5 ♘bd7 11 exf6 ♗b7 12 g3 c5 13 d5 ♕b6 14 ♗g2 0-0-0 15 0-0 b4 16 ♖b1**

By placing his queen's rook on the b-file, White meets the threat of 16...bxc3, as 17 bxc3 ♕a6 18 ♖xb7! ♕xb7 19 dxe6! is clearly better for White.

*Question 5:* Why does White want to keep his knight on c3?

*Answer:* By holding his knight on c3, White maintains his support of the d5-pawn, blocking Black's play along the d-file and the a8-h1 diagonal. White avoids committing his knight to the rim, and hopes to transfer it later to a central post such as e4 or d5.

**16...♕a6!**

Black renews the threat of ...b4xc3, as b2xc3 will now not come with gain of tempo. He wants to force matters and not to let his opponent consolidate behind the barrier on d5.

After 16...♗h6 17 ♗xh6 ♖xh6 18 b3! cxb3 19 ♘a4 ♕b5 20 axb3 exd5 21 ♖c1 Black's position was very loose in Piket-Illescas, Dos Hermanas 1985.

**17 dxe6 ♗xg2!**

17...fxe6 18 ♘e4! (centralising the knight) is good for White, while 17...♕xe6 allows 18 ♗xb7+ ♔xb7 19 ♕f3+ with dangerous play against the black king. Kramnik's move exploits the fact that 18 exd7+ loses to 18...♖xd7, attacking the white queen on d1, while after 18 ♔xg2 Black can play 18...♕xe6, threatening both 19...bxc3 and 19...♕h3+.

**18 e7!**

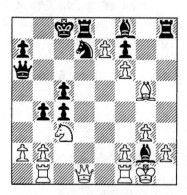

An amazing intermediate move, forking the rook on d8 and bishop on f8.

**18...♗xf1**

Black can also play 18...♗a8, keeping the bishop on the h1-a8 diagonal

and hoping to play the queen to c6 and deliver mate on g2 or h1. Peter Wells considers that 19 ♘d5 ♕b7 20 exf8♕ ♖hxf8 21 ♘e7+ ♔c7 22 ♗f4+ ♘e5 23 ♗xe5+ ♔b6 24 f3! (preventing...♕g2 or ...♕h1 mate) 24...♖xd1 25 ♖bxd1 is fairly promising for White and I am in full agreement. Certainly, none of the top players have tried this for Black.

**19 ♕d5!?**

An astonishing idea of Yermolinsky's. White, a rook and a piece down, ignores the material on offer and instead creates another threat: 20 ♕a8+ ♘b8 21 exd8♕+ ♔xd8 22 ♕xb8+.

19 ♔xf1 is considered in Games 9 and 10.

**19...♗xe7!**

A typical idea, lessening the impact of ♕a8+ by defending the back rank.

**20 fxe7**

Black has protected the back rank with gain of tempo: now 21 ♕a8+ ♘b8 22 exd8♕+ ♖xd8 23 ♗xd8 will win material, but will create no threats against the black king. Black can therefore use his 'spare move' before this happens to attack the white rook.

**20...♗d3!**

This also gives Black the threat of ...b4xc3, which will no longer open the b-file, as Black can then take the rook with ...♗xb1!

In fact 20...♗d3! was Kramnik's remarkable improvement on his own 20...♖dg8 (see the next game).

**21 ♘e4**

Since 21 ♕a8+ ♘b8 and 21 ♗f4 (threatening 22 ♕a8+) 21...♕b7! achieve nothing, White must bring another unit into the attack. From e4, the knight can move to the dangerous d6-square.

**21...♗xb1!**

Greedy but good! White must hurry as his oppoenent threatens ...♗xe4, removing the attacking white knight.

**22 ♘d6+ ♔c7**

This is the critical position. Now 23 ♘xc4 threatens the unpleasant 24 ♗f4+, but then 23...f6 meets 24 ♗f4+ with 24...♘e5, blocking out the check and discovering an attack on the white queen, which is winning for Black. 23 ♘xf7 also looks interesting, intensifying the attack on the rook on d8, while also threatening the check on f4, but the calm 23...♖dc8 24 ♗f4+ ♔b6 wins after 25 ♕xd7 ♕b7! or 25 ♕d6+ ♖c6! 26 ♕xd7 ♕c8. Yermolinsky suggests 23 exd8♕+ ♖xd8 24 ♘xf7; and this looks like the most critical test, as 24...♖e8 25 ♗f4+ ♔b6 26 ♕d6+ ♔a5 27 ♕xd7 gives White good play.

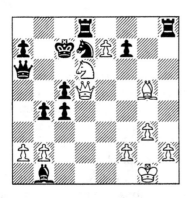

**23 ♗f4!? ♔b6!**

Avoiding the discovered check.

**24 ♘xc4+ ♔b5 25 ♘d6+ ♔b6 26 exd8♗!? ♖xd8 27 ♘c4+ ♔b5 28 ♘d6+ ♔b6**

Neither side can avoid the draw by repetition!

**29 ♘c4+ ♔b5 ½-½**

*Game 8*
**Kasparov-Kramnik**
*New York (rapidplay) 1994*

**1 d4 d5 2 c4 c6 3 ♘f3 ♘f6 4 ♘c3 e6 5 ♗g5 dxc4 6 e4 b5 7 e5 h6 8 ♗h4 g5 9 ♘xg5 hxg5 10 ♗xg5 ♘bd7 11 exf6 ♗b7 12 g3 c5 13 d5 ♕b6 14 ♗g2 0-0-0 15 0-0 b4 16 ♖b1 ♕a6 17 dxe6 ♗xg2 18 e7 ♗xf1 19 ♕d5!? ♗xe7! 20 fxe7 ♖dg8 21 ♘e4!**

We've seen this idea before! White brings the knight to an attacking position from where it aims to give an extremely unpleasant check on d6.

**21...♖g6**

Preventing the knight check on d6, and intending to challenge the white queen on d5 with ...♕c6.

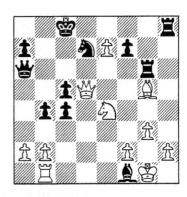

**22 ♖xf1?!**

Natural, but as Kasparov shows, he missed an opportunity to win brilliantly here: 22 ♕a8+ ♘b8 23 ♖xf1, when 23...♕c6 24 ♖d1!! ♕xa8 25 ♖d8+ ♔c7 (25...♔b7 26 ♖xh8 ♖e6 27 ♘xc5+ followed by ♘xe6 and e7-e8♕

wins) 26 ♗f4+ ♔b6 27 ♖xh8 ♖e6 28 e8♕ ♖xe8 29 ♖xe8 wins for White – he will pick up the knight on b8, leaving him with too much material for the queen.

**22...♕c6 23 ♕xc6+ ♖xc6 24 ♖d1 ♖e8 25 ♘d6+ ♖xd6 26 ♖xd6 f6 27 ♗xf6?**

As Kasparov points out, 27 ♗e3, to push the kingside pawns, was much stronger, as with the minor pieces on, Black's queenside majority has a much harder task advancing.

**27...♔c7 28 ♖e6 ♘xf6 29 ♖xf6 ♖xe7 30 ♔f1 ♖e4**

Threatening the unpleasant ...c4-c3.

**31 ♖f4 ♖xf4 32 gxf4 ♔d6 33 ♔e2 a5 34 a4 c3! 35 bxc3 b3! ½-½**

After 36 ♔d2 c4, White's king cannot leave the queenside due to Black's protected passed pawn, while White's kingside pawns restrict his opponent's king to the kingside after 37 h4 ♔e6 38 h5 ♔f5 39 ♔c1 ♔f6!

---

### Game 9
### Kramnik-Shirov
*Monaco (blindfold) 1996*

---

**1 ♘f3 d5 2 d4 ♘f6 3 c4 c6 4 ♘c3 e6 5 ♗g5 dxc4 6 e4 b5 7 e5 h6 8 ♗h4 g5 9 ♘xg5 hxg5 10 ♗xg5 ♘bd7 11 g3 ♗b7 12 ♗g2 ♕b6 13 exf6 0-0-0 14 0-0 c5 15 d5 b4 16 ♖b1 ♕a6 17 dxe6 ♗xg2 18 e7 ♗xf1 19 ♔xf1!**

The only winning attempt. This quiet move prevents the light-squared bishop from causing a nuisance and intends ♕d5.

**19...♕c6!**

An extremely fine move, activating

the black queen along the a8-h1 diagonal while preventing White from doing the same. 19...bxc3 20 bxc3!! leaves Black helpless, as 20...♕c6 (to stop ♕d5) is met by 21 ♖b8+!!, when both 21...♘xb8 and 21...♔xb8 lose to 22 exd8♕+!

The alternative 19...♗xe7 is considered in the next game.

**20 exd8♕+ ♔xd8 21 ♘d5 ♖xh2! 22 ♔g1 ♖h8**

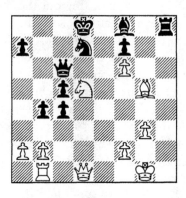

Here is where the mastery of such sharp systems lies. First, it is necessary to calculate the initial flurry of tactics; but the real skill lies in playing the extremely unbalanced positions that then arise. Material is now equal: the f6-pawn is no longer an extra pawn, and with ...♖xh2, Black has eliminated White's passed h-pawn. White's king is rather weak as only the knight on d5 prevents Black from giving mate on h1. However, Black also has his problems: his loose c4-pawn, inappropriately centralised king and inactive bishop.

**23 ♗f4!?**

This prevents the knight from moving to the dangerous e5-square.

**23...♗d6?!**

This solves the problem of Black's bishop, but the exchange on d6 distracts the black queen from the a8-h1 diagonal, allowing White to unravel and coordinate his pieces. In Nikolic-Shirov, Linares 1997, Black tried to improve with 23...♕e6 24 ♕f3 ♕h3 25 ♖d1 b3?! 26 a4 ♕h2+ 27 ♔f1 ♕h1+ 28 ♔e2 ♕xf3+ 29 ♔xf3, but it was clear that this was not the correct path! 23...♔c8! is an improvement, intending to solve the more important problem of Black's king by transferring it to b7, where it protects the queen on c6. By stepping off the d-file, Black also sets up the threat of ...♘b6, removing the knight from d5.

**24 ♗xd6 ♕xd6 25 ♕f3 ♘e5 26 ♕e4 ♖e8 27 ♘e3!**

Highlighting the weakness of c4.

**27...♘c6 28 ♕f3 ♔c7 29 ♘xc4 ♕d4 30 b3 ♕e4 31 ♕xe4 ♖xe4 32 ♔g2 ♘e5 33 ♘e3 ♔d7 34 ♖h1 ♔e6 35 ♖h8 ♔xf6 36 ♖c8 ♘d3 37 ♖a8 ♖d4 38 ♖xa7 ♔g6 39 f4 ♘c1 40 ♘c4 f6 41 ♖a6 ♖e4 42 ♔f3 ♖e2 43 ♘e5+ ♔g7 44 ♖a7+ ♔h6 45 ♘d3 ♖c2 46 ♘xc1 ♖xc1 47 ♔e4 ♔g6 48 f5+ ♔h5 49 ♖h7+ ♔g4 50 ♖g7+ ♔h3 51 ♔d5 ♖c2 52 ♖g6 ♖xa2 53 ♖xf6 ♖b2 54 ♖h6+ ♔xg3 55 f6 ♖xb3 56 ♖g6+ ♔h4 57 f7 ♖f3 58 ♔e6 b3 59 ♖f6 ½-½**

We shall now examine another attempt that Black has made in this line.

*Game 10*
**Kamsky-Kramnik**
*Dos Hermanas 1996*

**1 d4 d5 2 c4 c6 3 ♘c3 ♘f6 4 ♘f3 e6 5 ♗g5 dxc4 6 e4 b5 7 e5 h6 8 ♗h4 g5 9 ♘xg5 hxg5 10 ♗xg5 ♘bd7 11 exf6 ♗b7 12 g3 c5 13 d5 ♕b6 14 ♗g2 0-0-0 15 0-0 b4 16 ♖b1 ♕a6 17 dxe6 ♗xg2 18 e7 ♗xf1 19 ♔xf1 ♗xe7 20 fxe7 ♖dg8**

Kramnik had already tried this sort of idea against Kasparov after 19 ♕d5 (Game 8). In annotating the present game, he described it as dubious.

**21 ♘e4! ♕c6 22 ♘d6+ ♔b8 23 ♗f4 ♖xh2 24 ♔e2! ♕a8 25 ♕c2 ♘b6 26 ♕f5 ♘c8 27 e8♕ ♖xe8+ 28 ♘xe8 ♕xe8+ 29 ♗e3**

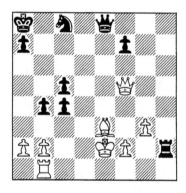

Kramnik considers White to be clearly better here. Resolute endgame defence however, saves a valuable half-point!

**29...♘b6 30 ♖d1 ♔b7 31 ♕xc5 ♕a4 32 ♖d2 c3 33 bxc3 bxc3 34 ♖d4 ♕xa2+ 35 ♔f3 c2 36 ♖d2 ♖h8 37 ♖xc2 ♕d5+ 38 ♕xd5+ ♘xd5 39 ♖b2+ ♘b6 40 ♔e4 ♖c8 41 g4 ♖c6 42 g5 ♖e6+ 43 ♔f5 a5 44 ♖b5 a4 45 ♖a5 ♘c4 46 ♖xa4 ♘xe3+ 47 fxe3 ♖xe3 48 ♖a5 ♔c6 49 ♔f6 ♖f3+ 50 ♔e7 ♖f1 51 ♖a6+ ♔d5 52 ♖f6 ♖g1 53 ♖f5+ ♔e4 54 ♔f6 ♖g4 55 ♖e5+ ♔d4 ½-½**

## Summary

Against 16 ♘a4, 16...♕b5 is my recommendation for Black players, meeting the main line, 17 a3 exd5 18 axb4 cxb4 19 ♗e3 ♘c5 20 ♕g4+, with either 20...♖d7 and Ivanchuk's untried 20...♚c7. In fact, this is also my recommendation for White players as my analysis shows there is plenty of scope for both sides!

16 ♖b1 ♕a6 17 dxe6 ♗xg2 18 e7 ♗xf1 19 ♕d5 is best met by 19...♗xe7 20 fxe7 ♗d3!, as in Kramnik-Topalov, while 19 ♚xf1 leads to a balanced position after 19...♕c6 20 exd8♕+ ♚xd8 21 ♘d5 ♖xh2 22 ♚g1 ♖h8 23 ♗f4 ♚c8! However, White should try this: although he is not better there is still plenty of play!

**1 d4 d5 2 c4 c6 3 ♘f3 ♘f6 4 ♘c3 e6 5 ♗g5 dxc4 6 e4 b5 7 e5 h6 8 ♗h4 g5 9 ♘xg5 hxg5 10 ♗xg5 ♘bd7 11 exf6 ♗b7 12 g3 c5 13 d5 ♕b6 14 ♗g2 0-0-0 15 0-0 b4**

**16 ♘a4**

      16 ♖b1 ♕a6 17 dxe6 ♗xg2 18 e7 ♗xf1 *(D)*

           19 ♕d5 ♗xe7 20 fxe7

                 20...♗d3 – *Game 7*; 20...♖dg8 – *Game 8*

           19 ♚xf1

                 19...♕c6 – *Game 9*; 19...♗xe7 – *Game 10*

**16...♕b5**

      16...♕a6 – *Game 6*

**17 a3 *(D)***

      17 dxe6 – *Game 5*

**17...exd5**

      17...♘e5 – *Game 4*

**18 axb4 cxb4 19 ♗e3**

      19 ♖e1 – *Game 3*

**19...♘c5 20 ♕g4+ ♖d7 21 ♕g7 ♗xg7 22 fxg7 ♖g8 23 ♘xc5 *(D)* d4**

      23...♖xg7 – *Game 2*

**24 ♗xb7+ – *Game 1***

*18...♗xf1*

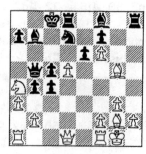
*17 a3*

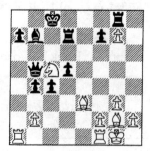
*23 ♘xc5*

# CHAPTER TWO

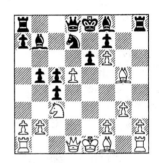

## Botvinnik Variation: Black's 13th Move Alternatives

1 d4 d5 2 c4 c6 3 ♘f3 ♘f6 4 ♘c3 e6 5 ♗g5 dxc4 6 e4 b5 7 e5 h6 8 ♗h4 g5 9 ♘xg5 hxg5 10 ♗xg5 ♘bd7 11 exf6 ♗b7 12 g3 c5 13 d5

In this chapter, we analyse Black's alternatives to the main line. The popularity of these lines peaked in 1993 when all the leading Semi-Slav players played one of these as their main weapon. My feeling is that they renounced these ideas not because of tactical problems, but because the positional risks that Black takes become less attractive once White players developed a good understanding of the appropriate tactical motifs.

The first three games consider 13...♘xf6, restoring material parity, Games 14-16 deal with 13...♗h6 and Games 17 and 18 with 13...♘b6 and 13...♘e5 respectively.

Game 11
**Van Wely-Dreev**
Bern Open 1993

1 d4 d5 2 c4 c6 3 ♘c3 ♘f6 4 ♘f3 e6 5 ♗g5 dxc4 6 e4 b5 7 e5 h6 8 ♗h4 g5 9 ♘xg5 hxg5 10 ♗xg5 ♘bd7 11 exf6 ♗b7 12 g3 c5 13 d5 ♘xf6

13...♘xf6 re-establishes material equality by capturing White's extra pawn on f6, and coordinates substantial pressure against White's d-pawn. The move's boldness lies in the fact that it reactivates the pin on the f6-knight, thereby keeping the black queen tied to the knight's protection and thus preventing Black from moving the queen to prepare queenside castling. Finally, the b5-pawn is still hanging which gives Black another loose point to worry about.

**14 ♗g2 ♗e7**

Breaking the pin on the knight on f6 along the h4-d8 diagonal and thereby increasing the pressure on d5. The alternative 14...♗h6!? is considered in Game 13.

**15 0-0**

This puts the king to safety and protects the bishop on g2, breaking the pin on the d5-pawn.

**15...♘xd5 16 ♗xe7 ♔xe7 17 ♘xb5**

Although material is equal and Black has a large number of files for his major pieces, his pawn structure is very weak and his king is rather draughty in comparison to White's. Black has to play actively or his positional weaknesses will cost him the game.

**17...♕b6 18 ♘a3**

Attacking c4.

**18...c3**

The bizarre 18...♖h4 is considered in the next game.

**19 ♘c4 ♕c7 20 bxc3! ♘xc3 21 ♕d2 ♗xg2 22 ♔xg2**

Wells also suggests 22 ♕g5+!?

**22...♘e4 23 ♕e3 ♘f6 24 ♕f3**

After this move, taking control of the h1-a8 diagonal, White stands slightly better due to his better pawn structure.

**24...♖ab8 25 ♖ab1**

Van Wely suggests 25 ♖fe1 ♖h5 26 ♖ad1 followed by h2-h4. The ending, though not objectively losing, is of course not very inspiring for Black and Van Wely makes it look much easier for White to win than Black to hold!

**25...♘d7 26 h4 ♖b4 27 ♖fc1 ♖hb8 28 ♖b3 ♖xb3 29 axb3 ♕b7 30 ♕xb7 ♖xb7 31 ♖a1 ♘b6 32 ♖a5! ♖c7 33 g4 ♔f8 34 h5 ♔g7 35 ♘d6 ♖d7 36 ♘e8+ ♔h6 37 ♘f6 ♖b7 38 ♖xc5 ♘d5 39 ♘xd5 exd5 40 ♖xd5 ♖xb3 41 ♖a5 a6 42 ♖xa6+ ♔g5 43 f3 ♔h4 44 ♖f6 1-0**

*Game 12*
**Van Wely-Kramnik**
*Biel Interzonal 1993*

**1 d4 d5 2 ♘f3 c6 3 c4 ♘f6 4 ♘c3 e6 5 ♗g5 dxc4 6 e4 b5 7 e5 h6 8 ♗h4 g5 9 ♘xg5 hxg5 10 ♗xg5 ♘bd7 11 exf6 ♗b7 12 g3 c5 13 d5 ♘xf6 14 ♗g2 ♗e7 15 0-0 ♘xd5 16**

♗xe7 ♔xe7 17 ♘xb5 ♕b6 18 ♘a3 ♖h4!?!?

A quite stunning move! Kramnik makes the maximum use of the open files created by Black's fractured pawn structure.

**19 ♕d2!**

A masterful and strong reply. 19 gxh4 ♖g8! wins for Black.

**19...♖d4?**

In a later round of the same tournament, Topalov tried the astounding 19...♘f4 against Oll but was rapidly defeated after 20 ♘xc4 ♕c7 21 f3! ♘xg2 22 ♕g5+ ♔f8 23 gxh4. In response to 20...♕a6 Oll recommended 21 ♘e3 as slightly better for White, but in Ehlvest-Onischuk, Philadelphia Open 1994, White preferred 21 ♗xb7 ♘h3+ 22 ♔g2 ♕xb7+ 23 f3 ♖d8 24 ♕c3, when 24...♖xc4 25 ♕xc4 ♕xb2+ gives Black sufficient play for the draw. There may still be life in this line yet!

20 ♕g5+ ♘f6 21 ♗xb7 ♖g8 22 ♕e5 ♘d7 23 ♕e2 ♕xb7 24 ♘xc4 ♖h4?! 25 f3 ♕c7 26 ♘e3 ♔f8 27 ♘g4 ♖h5 28 ♖ad1 ♖d5 29 ♕e4 ♕d6 30 ♘e3 ♖d4 31 ♖xd4 ♕xd4 32 ♖d1 ♕xe4 33 fxe4 ♔e7 34 ♘c4 ♘b8 35 ♔f2 ♘c6

36 ♖d3! ♖g4 37 ♘d2 a5 38 ♖c3 ♔d6 39 h3 ♖g8 40 ♘c4+ ♔e7 41 ♖b3 ♖d8 42 ♖b5 ♖d4 43 ♖xc5 ♘b4 44 a3 1-0

---

### Game 13
### Kasparov-Ivanchuk
*Linares 1994*

---

1 d4 ♘f6 2 c4 c6 3 ♘c3 d5 4 ♘f3 e6 5 ♗g5 dxc4 6 e4 b5 7 e5 h6 8 ♗h4 g5 9 ♘xg5 hxg5 10 ♗xg5 ♘bd7 11 exf6 ♗b7 12 g3 c5 13 d5 ♘xf6 14 ♗g2 ♗h6!?

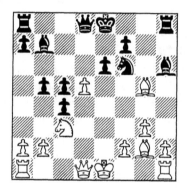

With this move Black seeks to exchange the dark-squared bishops and, by breaking the pin on the knight on f6, to increase the pressure on White's d5-pawn.

**15 ♗xf6**

This removes the knight on f6 and deflects the black queen to f6, thus removing a great deal of pressure from the d5-pawn. 15 ♗xh6 ♖xh6 16 0-0 ♗xd5 was fine for Black in Sherbakov-Korneev, Elista 1996, but 15 ♗h4!? is worth a thought.

**15...♕xf6 16 0-0**

16 ♘xb5 is less good according to Kasparov, as 16...♕e5+ 17 ♕e2 ♕xe2+

(17...♗d2+ 18 ♔f1) 18 ♔xe2 0-0-0 19
♘xa7+ ♔b8 20 ♘c6+ (20 ♘b5 seems
worth a try) 20...♗xc6 21 dxc6 ♖d2+
gives Black counterplay. 16 ♘e4!? is
also worthy of attention.

With 16 0-0, White not only puts
his king to safety, but also protects the
bishop on g2, thus unpinning the
pawn on d5 and threatening d5xe6.
Both sides have several dynamic factors in their favour: White has a
passed h-pawn and is threatening
♘xb5, winning the b-pawn; whereas
Black has the two bishops and two
open files against the white king – the
g- and h-files.

**16...0-0-0 17 ♘xb5 exd5 18 ♘xa7+!
♔b8 19 ♘b5**

Although White is a pawn up,
Black's position looks quite promising
– he has the two bishops, a trio of central pawns, and two open files against
White's king. However, the removal
of the a7-pawn has not only weakened
Black's king position but also provided a secure outpost for the white
knight on b5, from where it eyes a7
and c7. This spells danger for Black's
king: if White can reach a5 with his
queen both ♕a7+ and ♕c7+ will be
dangerous. Furthermore, the bishop
on h6 blocks the h-file and this ob-
structs Black's plan of doubling on the
h-file and attacking h2. He will have
to waste time redirecting this bishop
before he can strike at White's position.

**19...♗g7**

Komljenovic-Lupu, Andorra Open
1994, continued 19...♗g5 20 f4 ♕h6!
21 fxg5 ♕xh2+ 22 ♔f2 d4!
(threatening ...♕xg2+) 23 ♖g1 ♖h4!!

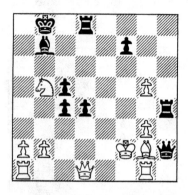

A sensational move which threatens
to expose the white king still further
with ...♖f4+! and also has the threat of
...♖e8, increasing the strength of ...♖f4
by cutting the king from its flight
squares on the e-file. 24 gxh4 fails to
24...♕xh4+! 25 ♔f1 (25 ♔e2 ♖e8+ 26
♔d2 ♕f2+) 25...♕f4+ 26 ♔e1 ♖e8+ 27
♕e2 ♖xe2+ 28 ♔xe2 ♕e3+ 29 ♔f1 c3!?
30 bxc3 d3! 31 ♖e1 ♕f4+! However,
we should borrow from Kasparov and
instead of 20 f4 play 20 ♕e1, eyeing a5
and e5: 20...♕h6 21 ♕e5+ ♔a8 22 h3!,
intending ♕c7, looks rather unpleasant for Black.

**20 a4**

20 ♕e1 immediately was also possible, as after 20...♖xh2 21 ♔xh2 ♖h8+
22 ♔g1 ♕h6 23 f3 ♕h2+ 24 ♔f2 ♖h3
25 ♕e8+ ♗c8 26 ♖g1 Black must still
prove that he has enough for the sacrificed rook.

**20...♕h6?!**

Kasparov suggests a different line up
on the h-file with 20...♖h6, intending
21...♖dh8.

**21 h4 ♗f6 22 ♕e1!**

The culmination of White's opening plan. It is impressive how Kasparov managed to find such a strong

method of coordinating his pieces over the board: giving up the bishop pair, using his queen's knight to grab a pawn on a7 at great cost in time and anticipating that this would give him such a strong attacking set-up on the queenside. It shows visionary attacking talent!

**22...♗xh4 23 ♕a5**

Strong, but 23 ♕e5+ ♔a8 24 ♕c7 would have been even better according to Kasparov.

**23...♗e7 24 ♕c7+ ♔a8 25 ♕a5+ ♔b8 26 ♕c7+ ♔a8 27 ♖fe1 ♗d6 28 ♕b6 ♗b8 29 a5 ♖d7 30 ♖e8!**

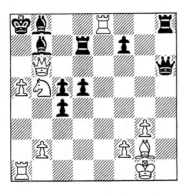

**30...♕h2+ 31 ♔f1 ♕xg2+ 32 ♔xg2 d4+ 33 ♕xb7+ ♖xb7 34 ♖xh8 ♖xb5 35 a6 ♔a7 36 ♖f8 ♖xb2 37 ♖xf7+ ♔a8 38 a7 c3 39 ♖f8 1-0**

A magnificent game.

---

*Game 14*
### Bareev-Filippov
*Russia 1995*

---

**1 d4 d5 2 c4 c6 3 ♘f3 ♘f6 4 ♘c3 e6 5 ♗g5 dxc4 6 e4 b5 7 e5 h6 8 ♗h4 g5 9 ♘xg5 hxg5 10 ♗xg5 ♘bd7 11 exf6 ♗b7 12 g3 c5 13 d5 ♗h6**

**14 ♗xh6 ♖xh6**

By forcing the exchange of the dark-squared bishops, Black removes White's protection of f6. He intends to capture on f6 with the knight, without allowing the pin that arises in the 13...♘xf6 line. Moreover, Black frees f8 for his king, which allows him to consider ...e6xd5 since a check on the e-file is no longer devastating. However, the exchange of the dark-squared bishops costs Black some control over the central dark squares; d6 in particular is a tempting target for White's queen's knight, either via e4 or via the unprotected pawn on b5. Finally, 14 ♗xh6 ♖xh6 draws Black's king's rook to an exposed position and White can use this to gain tempi for his development.

**15 ♕d2**

This move attacks the exposed rook on h6 and achieves several positional ideas with tempo. First, it tempts Black to recapture the sacrificed pawn on f6 with the queen or with the rook, thus depriving the knight on d7 of its ideal square. Second, it covers the e1-a5 diagonal and enables ♘xb5 without fear of ...♕a5+. Finally, it prepares rapid queenside castling.

**15...♕xf6 16 0-0-0 ♔f8**

Now that White has castled his king to safety on the queenside, ♘e4, attacking the queen and threatening ♘d6+ forking king and bishop, was a big threat and ♘xb5, threatening ♘d6+ or ♘c7+, is also possible. After 16...♔f8, neither ♘d6 nor ♘c7 will come with check and this reduces the power of ♘e4 and ♘xb5. Moreover, by removing the king from the e-file, Black makes it safe to take on d5 and open the e-file.

16...0-0-0, for example, would have led to disaster: 17 ♘e4! ♕e5 18 ♕xh6 ♕xe4 19 dxe6 ♕xh1 20 ♗h3! as in Quist-Thiesing, Dieren Open 1988.

**17 f3!?**

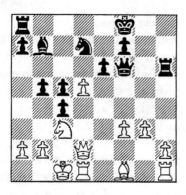

This blocks the h1-a8 diagonal, breaking the pin on the d5-pawn (18 dxe6 is now the threat), and covers e4, supporting the white queen's knight when it arrives there. Its drawback is that it is now hard to find an active square for the white light-squared bishop – it is restricted by the b5- and c4-pawns and f2-f3 blocks the h1-a8 and e2-h5 diagonals, while the h3-c8 diagonal is covered by the rook on h6.

17 h4 is discussed in the next game, while 17 f4 is met by 17...♘b6, with tremendous pressure on the white d-pawn.

**17...exd5 18 ♘xd5 ♕d6 19 ♕g5!?**

20 ♘c7 is a threat now: the knight on c7 attacks the rook on a8 and 19...♕xc7 is impossible as the rook on h6 hangs.

**19...♖g6?**

White's last move is unpleasant to face unprepared over the board and here Filippov goes astray immediately. A little later, however, with the benefit of home preparation, he found the splendid 19...♖b8!!, dealing with the threat of ♘c7 by calmly placing the rook on a square where the knight cannot attack it. Now any knight move is met by ...♕f6, attacking the unprotected white queen, when ♕xf6 ♘xf6 saves the attacked black knight on d7! 19...♖b8 also protects the loose bishop on b7, which is always useful. It may seem a little strange that Black can just play a quiet consolidating move in the middle of a tactical battle, but I think that this is mainly due to the drawbacks of 17 f3: although it performed a useful function, it did not bring any pieces into action; indeed if anything, it made the bishop on f1 more passive.

**20 ♕f5! ♘e5 21 ♘f4 ♖f6 22 ♕h3!**

22 ♕h5 would fail to the rather cruel 22...♕xd1+! 23 ♔xd1 ♗xf3+!

**22...♕xd1+ 23 ♔xd1 ♗xf3+ 24 ♔c1 ♗xh1 25 ♕h4 ♘d7 26 ♗h3 ♖d6 27 ♗xd7 ♖xd7 28 ♕h8+ ♔e7 29 ♕e5+ ♔d8 30 h4 b4 31 h5 b3 32 axb3 cxb3 33 h6?**

The crucial mistake. 33 ♕c3, pre-

venting Black's next, would have given good winning chances (Bareev).
**33...♗f3 34 ♘d5 ♖xd5 35 ♕f6+ ♔c7 36 ♕xf3 ♔c6 37 h7 ♖e8 38 ♕xb3 ♖e1+ 39 ♔c2 ♖e2+ 40 ♔b1 ♖h2 41 ♕a4+ ♔b6 42 ♕b3+ ½-½**

**1 d4 d5 2 c4 c6 3 ♘f3 ♘f6 4 ♘c3 e6 5 ♗g5 dxc4 6 e4 b5 7 e5 h6 8 ♗h4 g5 9 ♘xg5 hxg5 10 ♗xg5 ♘bd7 11 exf6 ♗b7 12 g3 c5 13 d5 ♗h6 14 ♗xh6 ♖xh6 15 ♕d2 ♕xf6 16 0-0-0 ♔f8 17 h4!?**

This interesting move aims to make use of White's kingside pawns to attack Black's exposed and hence vulnerable major pieces on f6 and h6.

**17...♘b6 18 g4**

Threatening to fork the queen on f6 and the rook on h6 with g4-g5.

**18...♘xd5!?**

18...♖xh4 19 g5 ♕f4 20 ♖xh4 ♕xh4 21 dxe6 and 18...♖h8 19 g5 ♕g7 20 ♘xb5 are both good for White according to Razuvaev.

**19 g5 ♕g6**

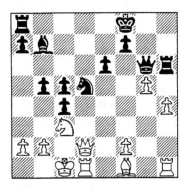

Now Black is ready to meet 20 gxh6 with 20...♘xc3 and 21...♗xh1.
**20 ♘xb5 ♘b4**

Threatening ...♘xa2 mate.
**21 ♘c3 ♗xh1 22 gxh6**

Razuvaev considers this position to be slightly better for White and I see no reason to disagree with his assessment.
**22...♗f3?**

22...♗d5 was necessary according to Razuvaev.
**23 ♖e1 ♗d5 24 a3 a5 25 ♖e5 ♕g1**

Now White elected to repeat with
**26 ♖e1? ♕g6 ½-½**

This is quite a surprising draw as in fact White has a forced win! Razuvaev realised after the game that the not so difficult 26 h7! ♕xf1+ 27 ♖e1 ♘d3+ 28 ♔b1 would have won for White.

This line with 17 h4 is definitely the most dangerous for Black to face at the moment and he needs an improvement in order to play this line with confidence.

**1 d4 d5 2 c4 c6 3 ♘f3 ♘f6 4 ♘c3 e6 5 ♗g5 dxc4 6 e4 b5 7 e5 h6 8 ♗h4 g5 9 ♘xg5 hxg5 10 ♗xg5 ♘bd7 11 exf6 ♗b7 12 g3 c5 13 d5 ♗h6 14 ♗xh6 ♖xh6 15 ♕d2 ♕xf6 16 ♘e4!?**

This is the most direct attempt to refute 15...♕xf6. White immediately attacks the queen on f6 and aims for the d6-square. Peter Wells was particularly keen on this move in *The Complete Semi-Slav*, but it has only recently had its first practical test.

**16...♕f3 17 ♘d6+ ♚e7 18 ♘xb7**

18 ♖g1 ♗xd5 and 18...♕xd5 19 ♕xh6 ♕xd6 give Black sufficient compensation according to Yusupov.

**18...♖h5!?**

This move, dealing both with the threat to the rook and the annoying idea of ♕g5+, was initially suggested by Artur Yusupov. 18...♕xh1 19 d6+! ♚e8 20 ♕xh6 ♕b7 21 ♕h4! is given as winning for White by a certain Hamovic in *ECO*.

**19 d6+ ♚e8 20 ♖g1 c3!?**

Ionov mentions 20...♖e5+ 21 ♗e2 ♕xb7 22 0-0-0 and 20...♖xh2 21 ♕f4! ♕xb7 22 0-0-0 as unclear.

**21 bxc3 ♖e5+ 22 ♗e2 ♖xe2+ 23 ♕xe2 ♕xc3+ 24 ♚f1 ♕xa1+ 25 ♚g2 ♕d4?! 26 ♖d1 ♕a4 27 ♕f3?**

27 ♕h5! would have been good for White according to Ionov.

**27...♖c8 28 ♕h5!**

White gets a second chance!

**28...♕e4+ 29 ♚g1 ♕xb7 30 ♕h8+ ♘f8 31 d7+ ♕xd7 32 ♖xd7 ♚xd7 33 ♚f1 a5 34 h4 b4 35 ♚e2 a4 36 h5 ♚e7 37 h6 ♖d8 38 ♕e5 ♖c8 39 ♕e4**

A bad mistake. 39 ♕g5+ ♚d6 40 ♕f6 would have kept White's advan-

tage according to Ionov.

**39...♘d7 40 h7 ♖h8 41 ♕h4+ f6 42 ♕h5 a3 43 ♚d2 b3 44 axb3 a2 45 ♕h1 ♚d6 46 ♕a1 ♖xh7 47 ♕xa2 ♖h5 48 ♕a6+ ♚e7 49 ♕b7 ♖d5+ 50 ♚c3 ♖d4 51 ♕c7 ♖b4 52 ♕c6 ½-½**

The next game is *the* classic Botvinnik system game. Theoretically, it is still the latest word on 13...♘b6 and aesthetically, it never ceases to amaze!

---

*Game 17*
**Polugayevsky-Torre**
*Moscow 1981*

---

**1 d4 d5 2 c4 c6 3 ♘f3 ♘f6 4 ♘c3 e6 5 ♗g5 dxc4 6 e4 b5 7 e5 h6 8 ♗h4 g5 9 ♘xg5 hxg5 10 ♗xg5 ♘bd7 11 exf6 ♗b7 12 g3 c5 13 d5 ♘b6**

**14 dxe6! ♕xd1+**

Lukacs's 14...♗xh1 15 e7! ♕d7 (15...♕xd1+ 16 ♖xd1 transposes to the main game) does not seem good after 16 ♕xd7+ (16 exf8♕+ ♚xf8 17 ♕xd7 ♘xd7 18 0-0-0 ♗c6 19 h4 ♘e5 20 ♗e3! is also good for White according to Wells) 16...♚xd7 (16...♘xd7 17 ♘xb5 ♗xe7 18 fxe7 f6 19 ♗e3 ♚xe7 20 h4 ♗f3 21 ♗xc4 ♖hc8 22 ♖c1 ♘e5 and now 23 b3, intending ♗f1 to attack c5, would have given White a clear advantage in the game Ionov-Sherbakov, Rostov on Don Open 1993, according to Ionov) 17 ♖d1+ ♔c6 18 ♖d8 is very good for White according to Wells.

**15 ♖xd1 ♗xh1 16 e7! a6 17 h4!! ♗h6 18 f4!!**

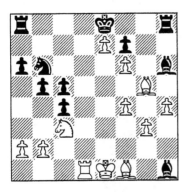

Polugayevsky comments that 'Having given up a rook, White has no intention of regaining the lost material, but contents himself with the fact that the rook on h8 is not destined to come into play for some time.'

**18...b4 19 ♖d6 ♖b8 20 ♘d1 ♗xg5 21 fxg5 ♘d5 22 ♗xc4 ♘xe7 23 fxe7 ♔xe7 24 ♖f6 ♖hf8 25 ♘e3 ♗e4 26 ♖xa6 ♖bd8 27 ♖f6 ♖d6 28 ♖f4 ♖d4 29 h5 ♗d3 30 ♘d5+ ♔d6 31 ♖xd4 cxd4 32 ♗b3 ♗c2 33 ♗xc2 ♔xd5 34 ♗b3+?**

Alas, it won't be a perfect game now! 34 h6 followed by h6-h7 would have won easily.

**34...♔e5 35 g4 ♔f4**

Black's only chance was 35...d3!

**36 g6 ♔e3 37 g7 ♖c8 38 ♔f1 d3 39 ♔g2 ♔f4 40 h6 1-0**

Finally, 13...♘e5.

**1 d4 d5 2 c4 c6 3 ♘f3 ♘f6 4 ♘c3 e6 5 ♗g5 dxc4 6 e4 b5 7 e5 h6 8 ♗h4 g5 9 ♘xg5 hxg5 10 ♗xg5 ♘bd7 11 exf6 ♗b7 12 g3 c5 13 d5 ♘e5!?**

13...b4 loses to 14 ♗xc4 bxc3 15 dxe6. The text aims for d3 but releases pressure on the f6-pawn.

**14 ♗g2 ♘d3+ 15 ♔f1 ♕d7 16 dxe6**

Natural but not the best. Vujatovic suggests 16 ♕f3 (threatening d5xe6), when 16...exd5 17 h4!! prevents queenside castling due to 17...0-0-0 18 ♗h3! Apparently this has received the Royal seal of approval from Gazza himself, so it is probably best!

**16...fxe6 17 b3!? 0-0-0 18 bxc4 ♗h6! 19 ♗h4! b4 20 ♘d5! exd5 21 ♕xd3 dxc4 22 ♗xb7+! ♕xb7 23 ♕f5+ ♔b8 24 ♖g1! ♗d2!?**

24...♖d5 25 ♕e6 c3 26 f7 ♕b5+ 27 ♔g2 ♕b7 with a draw (Illescas).

**25 f7 ♖c8 26 ♕e5+?! ♔a8 27 ♗e7? ♗c3 28 ♕d6 ♗xa1 29 f8♕ ♖hxf8 30 ♗xf8 b3 0-1**

## Summary

All these systems are worth a go on an occasional basis, but as main defences they seem a little too risky to place too much reliance on. 13...♘xf6 14 ♗g2 ♗h6!? looks interesting, while 13...♗h6 continues to survive. However, 13...♘b6 seems to be pretty much busted and 13...♘e5 devotees need an answer to 16 ♕f3.

**1 d4 d5 2 c4 c6 3 ♘f3 ♘f6 4 ♘c3 e6 5 ♗g5 dxc4 6 e4 b5 7 e5 h6 8 ♗h4 g5 9 ♘xg5 hxg5 10 ♗xg5 ♘bd7 11 exf6 ♗b7 12 g3 c5 13 d5**

**13...♘xf6**
    13...♗h6 14 ♗xh6 ♖xh6 15 ♕d2 ♕xf6 *(D)*
        16 0-0-0 ♚f8
            17 f3 – *Game 14*
            17 h4 – *Game 15*
        16 ♘e4 – *Game 16*
        13...♘b6 – *Game 17*
        13...♘e5 – *Game 18*
**14 ♗g2 ♗e7 15 0-0 *(D)* ♘xd5**
    14...♗h6 – *Game 13*
**16 ♗xe7 ♚xe7 17 ♘xb5 ♕b6 18 ♘a3 *(D)* c3**
    18...♖h4 – *Game 12*
**19 ♘c4 – *Game 11***

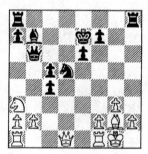

    *15...♕xf6*        *15 0-0*        *18 ♘a3*

# CHAPTER THREE

## Botvinnik Variation with 11 g3

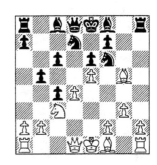

1 d4 d5 2 c4 c6 3 ♘f3 ♘f6 4 ♘c3 e6 5 ♗g5 dxc4 6 e4 b5 7 e5 h6 8 ♗h4 g5 9 ♘xg5 hxg5 10 ♗xg5 ♘bd7 11 g3

As the alert reader will have spotted, Ivanchuk and Kasparov always prefer the 'standard' move order of 11 exf6. However, Kramnik has consistently chosen to play 11 g3 and in this chapter we shall look at the differences that this move order makes. The first point to note, however, is that 11 g3 ♗b7 12 ♗g2 ♕b6 13 exf6 0-0-0 14 0-0 c5 15 d5 b4 simply takes us back to the main line position discussed in the first chapter.

With 11 g3 White delays the capture of the pinned knight in order to develop his bishop on the h1-a8 diagonal one move earlier than usual.

*Question 1:* Why is this important?

*Answer:* After 11 exf6 ♗b7 12 g3, Black can play 12...c5 opening the attack of the bishop on b7 on the rook on h1. However, after 11 g3 ♗b7 12 ♗g2, 12...c5 is impossible as the bishop is en prise on b7. By developing the bishop early to the long diagonal, White makes it harder for Black to achieve ...c6-c5.

*Question 2:* What's the downside?

*Answer:* By cutting down on some options, you give Black other possibilities. The main alternative is 11...♖g8 to break the pin by sacrificing the rook for the bishop on g5.

If Black wants to play the main line with 13...♕b6 against 11 exf6, then he can transpose back into Chapter 1 by following Timman-Tal. However, 11 g3 avoids all the main line alternatives in Chapter 2, so Black advocates of these variations will need a separate line against 11 g3.

*Game 19*
**Timman-Tal**
*Hilversum (match) 1988*

1 d4 d5 2 c4 c6 3 ♘f3 ♘f6 4 ♘c3 e6 5 ♗g5 dxc4 6 e4 b5 7 e5 h6 8 ♗h4 g5 9 ♘xg5 hxg5 10 ♗xg5 ♘bd7 11 g3 ♗b7

Threatening the typical ...c6-c5

counter-thrust.

**12 &g2 &b6 13 exf6 0-0-0 14 0-0 c5!**

After due preparation, Black has achieved the freeing ...c6-c5 break. Here 15 d5 b4 would transpose to Chapter 1. White's only independent possibility is seen in this game.

The risky 14...&e5 is considered in Game 20.

**15 dxc5**

After this move White keeps his extra pawn. However, in so doing he allows his opponent to weaken his kingside light squares by exchanging the light-squared bishops, opens the d-file for Black's rook on d8 and draws the black knight to the powerful d3-outpost via c5.

**15...&xc5! 16 &e2 &xg2 17 &xg2 &h6**

Although Black has weakened his opponent's kingside light squares, he is not set for an all-out kingside attack. Black's strength is on the queenside – the pawns on b5 and c4 give Black a queenside space advantage and a strong outpost on d3. His queenside majority is more mobile and much more potent than White's kingside

majority, although this will only really come into play in an endgame. Black must first solve the problem of his undeveloped king's bishop on f8 and win back the sacrificed f6-pawn. Then he can exchange some pieces – the queen and a pair of rooks – and utilise his long-term endgame strengths. 17...&h6 seeks to exchange the dark-squared bishops in order to weaken White's hold on the f6-pawn.

**18 h4**

Not the best. Tal's suggestion of 18 &xh6 &xh6 19 &f3 sets interesting problems: 19...a6! is the best reply, to follow up with ...&b7 to challenge for the a8-h1 diagonal.

**18...&xg5 19 hxg5 &c6+! 20 f3**

Forced.

**20...&h5!**

Now that f2-f3 has closed the d1-h5 diagonal to the white queen, Black can play this sneaky move, attacking the pawn on g5 and threatening on occasion to double on the h-file.

**21 a4**

This move, undermining the black queenside, is White's only hope for counterplay.

**21...b4 22 &b5**

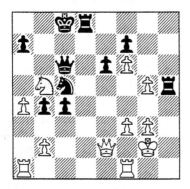

Threatening a fork on a7. Tal points out that 22...♕d5! was the strongest here, meeting 23 ♖fd1 with 23...♘d3.

Tal continues: 24 ♕e3 ♕xg5! (threatening 25...♕xg3+!! 26 ♔xg3 ♖g8+ 27 ♕g5 ♖g8+ mate!) 25 ♕e4 ♕d5! 26 ♖xd3! cxd3 27 ♕xb4 d2! (preventing ♖c1+) 28 ♘xa7+ (28 ♖a3, threatening ♖c3+, is countered by 28...d1♘!, covering the c3-square!) 28...♔c7 29 ♘b5+ ♔b8! 30 ♘c3+ ♕b7 31 ♕xb7+ ♔xb7, which is assessed as unclear by Tal, Krnic and Velickovic but looks rather nice for Black to me! It therefore seems that this line poses few problems for Black.

**22...♗b7?! 23 ♖ad1 ♘d3 24 ♕e3 ♕b6 25 ♕e4+ ♔b8?**

A critical mistake after which Timman's peerless play wraps up the game for White. 25...♕c6 26 g6 a6 27 g7 axb5 28 axb5 ♕xe4 29 fxe4 ♖g5 (Tal) would have led to great complications.

**26 g4 ♖h4 27 ♔g3!! ♖dh8 28 ♖xd3! cxd3 29 ♕e5+ ♔a8 30 ♕e4+ ♔b8 31 ♕e5+ ♔a8 32 g6 ♖h3+ 33 ♔f4 a6 34 ♕e4+ ♔b8 35 ♕e5+ ♔a8 36 ♕e4+ ♔b8 37 ♕d4! ♕xd4+ 38 ♘xd4**

fxg6 39 ♖d1 1-0

White has too many pawns for the exchange.

This game is all that the main line Black player needs to know in order to meet 11 g3 with confidence.

*Game 20*
**Yermolinsky-Kaidanov**
*USA Championship 1993*

**1 d4 d5 2 c4 e6 3 ♘f3 ♘f6 4 ♘c3 c6 5 ♗g5 dxc4 6 e4 b5 7 e5 h6 8 ♗h4 g5 9 ♘xg5 hxg5 10 ♗xg5 ♘bd7 11 exf6 ♗b7 12 g3 ♕b6 13 ♗g2 0-0-0 14 0-0 ♘e5**

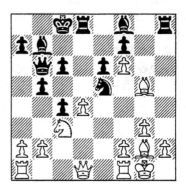

This risky move seeks to exploit the pin on the d-pawn by the rook on d8. However, White has a radical solution to the problem.

**15 dxe5! ♖xd1 16 ♖axd1**

White has a rook, knight and pawn for the queen. Black's main chances lie in his 4-2 queenside majority, but White should be able to neutalise this with accurate play.

**16...b4 17 ♘e4 ♕a5**

Attacking e5.

**18 ♗f4 c3 19 bxc3 ♗a6! 20 cxb4 ♗xb4 21 a3!**

Diverting the dark-squared bishop from b4, thus allowing the rook on f1 to move to e1.

**21...♗xa3**

21...♕xa3 22 ♖a1 ♗xf1 23 ♖xa3 ♗xg2 24 ♖xa7 ♔b8 25 ♖a4 (defending e4) wins for White according to Yermolinsky and Shabalov.

**22 ♖fe1 ♗d3 23 ♘d6+ ♗xd6 24 exd6 ♔d7 25 ♖e5 ♗b5 26 ♖c1 ♕a4 27 ♖ec5**

Our two annotators assess this position as slightly better for White.

**27...a6 28 ♗e5?!**

28 h4 allows Black the annoying 28...♖xh4 29 gxh4 ♕xf4, breaking up the white kingside, so Kaidanov suggests the interesting 28 h3, patiently giving the white king an escape hole.

**28...♖h5 29 f4 ♕a3 30 ♖5c3 ♕b4 31 h4 ♖xe5 32 fxe5 ♕d4+ 33 ♔h2 ♕xe5 34 ♗xc6+ ♗xc6 35 ♖xc6 ♕xf6 36 ♖6c2 ♔xd6 37 ♖a2 ♔e7 38 ♖c6 ♕f1 39 ♖cxa6 ♔f8 40 ♖b6 ♔g7 41 ♖bb2 ♔g6 42 ♖f2 ♕e1 43 ♖ae2 ♕d1??**

The decisive error which allows White to manoeuvre his rooks into the ideal position to attack the black pawns and defend his own king.

**44 ♖e5 ♔g7 45 ♖g5+ ♔f8 46 ♖g6!! e5 47 ♖gf6 e4 48 ♖xf7+ ♔g8 49 ♖e7 ♕d3 50 ♖f4 e3 51 ♖fe4 ♕c2+ 52 ♔h3 ♕c8+ 53 g4 ♕c1 54 ♖xe3 ♕h1+ 55 ♔g3 ♕g1+ 56 ♔f4 ♕f2+ 57 ♔g5 ♕d2 58 ♔g6 1-0**

**1 d4 d5 2 c4 c6 3 ♘c3 ♘f6 4 ♘f3** e6 5 ♗g5 dxc4 6 e4 b5 7 e5 h6 8 ♗h4 g5 9 ♘xg5 hxg5 10 ♗xg5 ♘bd7 11 g3 ♖g8

With 11...♖g8, Black seeks to exploit directly White's move order with 11 g3. Since White has deferred the 'execution' of the knight on f6, it is still alive (just!). If Black can break the pin on the knight then he can move the knight on d5 away and remain material up.

**12 h4 ♖xg5 13 hxg5 ♘d5 14 g6!**

Using the doubled g-pawn to prise open the black kingside.

**14...fxg6**

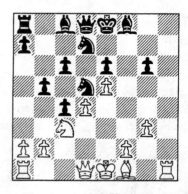

*Question 3:* Help! What's happening?

*Answer:* After the exchanges White now has unchallenged control of the h-file for his rook on h1: the rook will come to either h7, cutting across Black's seventh rank, or h8, pinning the black bishop on f8 to the king. Black also has two isolated pawns on e6 and g6 which are ideal targets for the light-squared bishop on f1 and there is also a hole on d6 that would make a perfect outpost for the white knight on c3 via the e4-square.

Black has two pieces for the rook

and possession of the bishop pair, but it is really Black's queenside which is his major strength. It may seem that Black can easily destroy White's centre with ...c6-c5, but this weakens the support of the knight on d5, which requires the support of both e6- and c6-pawns. Therefore Black often plays ...♘xc3, preventing ♘e4-d6, and creating a new pawn base on c3 which Black can then attack with ...b5-b4 before following up with ...c6-c5.

**15 ♕g4 ♕e7**

15...♕a5 has been practically refuted, as shall see in Game 25.

**16 ♗g2!**

16 ♖h8 and 16 ♕xg6+ are less precise – see Games 23 and 24.

**16...♕f7! 17 ♗e4!**

Attacking the weak g6-pawn..

**17...♘e7**

White must now activate his rooks on the h-file and invade on the seventh or eighth ranks (or both)! Black's main aim is to bring his queenside pieces – the rook on a8 and bishop on c8 – to active squares and move his king to safety there. It may seem strange to discuss positional factors when White can simply win the exchange and a pawn with 18 ♘xb5 cxb5 19 ♗xa8, but in fact they are extremely relevant here. As Julian Hodgson once remarked to me in a similar position, by taking the rook on a8, White has 'developed' this piece for Black since he no longer needs to worry about it! This manoeuvre also gives Black two tempi (...♘b6 and one other) to carry out his queenside aims. The popular 18 ♖h8 (see the next game) by contrast gives Black no

tempi towards development of his queenside, but of course it keeps the material balance in Black's favour (knight and bishop vs. rook).

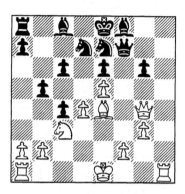

**18 ♘xb5 cxb5 19 ♗xa8 ♘b6 20 ♗e4**

Shirov prefers White here and I feel that he is right, although it must be said that this position, with its very unusual material balance, is so rich in possibilities that there is still plenty of scope for experimentation on both sides. Indeed, a little later Shirov offered this line against Khalifman – as Black!

**20...♗d7!**

Shirov praises this improvement over Kramnik's suggestion of 20...♘bd5, when Shirov proposes 21 ♖h8!, intending 22 f3, 23 ♔f2 and 24 ♖ah1, when 'White is clearly on top'.

**21 ♖h8 ♗c6 22 f3!**

Now Black will think twice about exchanging bishops with ...♗xe4 as f3xe4 will 'fill in' the hole on d5 and give White a massive centre.

**22...♘bd5?**

A serious mistake which gives White the time to carry out his ideal plan. Shirov analyses 22...♔d7 23 ♔e2 (not 23 ♔f2 ♗xe4!, when White can no longer recapture on e4 with the pawn) 23...♗g7! (evicting the rook from the eighth rank) and claims a small advantage for White after 24 ♖h7 ♘bd5.

Black's dark-squared bishop is pinned to the queen on f7 and restricted by the white pawns on d4 and e5. Moreover, the black queen is tied to its protection and thus prevented from becoming active. Black has two plans: to attack d4, probably with ...♘f5, and to expand on the queenside with ...a7-a5-a4 and ...b5-b4. Obviously, White must keep pounding the kingside since the open h-file allows him to use his big advantage: the pair of rooks. The main idea is ♖h6, attacking g6, and ♕g5-h6 is another plan.

**23 ♔f2 ♘b4**

As Shirov points out, 23...♔d7 now allows 24 ♖ah1 ♗g7 25 ♖1h7!! with great play for White.

**24 a3! ♘d3+**

24...♗xe4 25 axb4 ♗f5 26 ♕g5 ♘c8 27 ♕h6! ♔e7 28 ♕h4+! ♔d7 29 ♕f6! is even more horrible according to Shirov.

**25 ♗xd3 cxd3 26 ♖d1 ♕f5 27 ♕xf5 gxf5 28 ♖xd3**

Shirov comments here that 'two rooks and two extra pawns are too much for three minor pieces' and indeed he makes the win look easy from here.

**28...♗d5 29 ♖c3 ♘c6 30 ♔e3 ♔f7 31 ♖h7+ ♗g7 32 ♖h2 ♔g6 33 ♖hc2 ♘a5 34 ♖c7 a6 35 ♖a7 ♘c4+ 36 ♔e2 a5 37 b3 ♘xa3 38 ♖c8 ♗h6 39 ♖g8+ ♔h5 40 ♖h7 1-0**

41 g4+ will be the end.

*Game 22*
**Kalantarian-Yegiazarian**
*Armenian Championship 1994*

**1 d4 d5 2 c4 c6 3 ♘f3 ♘f6 4 ♘c3 e6 5 ♗g5 dxc4 6 e4 b5 7 e5 h6 8 ♗h4 g5 9 ♘xg5 hxg5 10 ♗xg5 ♘bd7 11 g3 ♖g8 12 h4 ♖xg5 13 hxg5 ♘d5 14 g6 fxg6 15 ♕g4 ♕e7 16 ♗g2 ♕f7 17 ♗e4 ♘e7 18 ♖h8**

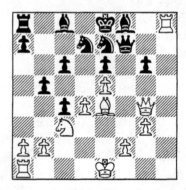

**18...♘b6! 19 ♔e2!**

Freeing the path for the queen's rook to come into the action with ♖ah1-h7.

**19...b4?**

This seems to be a mistake. Akopian suggests 19...♗d7 20 a4 b4 21 a5 ♘bd5 (21...bxc3 22 axb6 cxb2 23 ♖xa7 ♖b8 24 b7 ♔d8 25 ♕g5! is unpleasant for Black) 22 ♘a4 with an unclear position.

**20 ♖ah1 ♔d7**

Akopian suggests instead that 20...bxc3 21 ♖1h7 ♕xh7 22 ♖xh7 cxb2 23 ♕f3 ♗b7 24 ♗xg6+ ♔d7 25 ♕a3 is unclear, but the threat of ♕d6+ looks unpleasant for Black.

**21 ♖8h7! ♕g8**

21...♗g7 loses to 22 ♗xg6 ♘xg6 23 ♖1h6!, when the knight on g6 and the bishop on g7 are doomed to fall.

**22 ♘b5?**

22 d5! bxc3 23 d6! was better according to Akopian.

**22...cxb5 23 ♗xa8 ♘xa8 24 ♕f3?**

This is the fatal mistake. 24 d5! ♘c7 25 d6 ♘d5 26 ♕d4! would still have been unclear according to Akopian.

**24...♗g7 25 ♕xa8 ♘c6 26 ♔f1 ♔c7 27 d5 exd5 28 e6 c3 29 bxc3 bxc3 30 ♔g2 c2 31 e7 ♗h3+ 32 ♔xh3 ♕xh7+ 33 ♔g4 ♕xh1 34 ♕xc6+ ♔xc6 35 e8♕+ ♔c5 36 ♕e7+ ♔c4 37 ♕e2+ ♔c3 0-1**

---

## Game 23
### Khalifman-Shirov
*Pardubice 1994*

1 d4 d5 2 c4 c6 3 ♘f3 ♘f6 4 ♘c3 e6 5 ♗g5 dxc4 6 e4 b5 7 e5 h6 8 ♗h4 g5 9 ♘xg5 hxg5 10 ♗xg5 ♘bd7 11 g3 ♖g8 12 h4 ♖xg5 13 hxg5 ♘d5 14 g6 fxg6 15 ♕g4 ♕e7 16 ♖h8?!

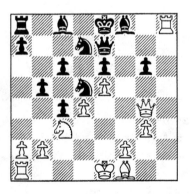

**16...♘xc3! 17 bxc3 ♕a3!! 18 ♕xg6+**

18 ♕xe6+ ♔d8 is clearly better for Black according to Khalifman.

**18...♔d8 19 ♖d1**

Very sharp. Khalifman gives 19 ♕c2 ♘b6 20 ♕c1 ♔c7 as unclear.

**19...♕xc3+ 20 ♔e2 ♕b2+! 21 ♖d2 ♕b4 22 ♕xe6 c3 23 a3!**

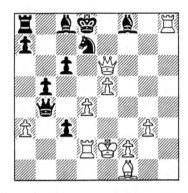

**23...♕xa3?**

The decisive mistake according to Khalifman. 23...♕b1 would have been better, when 24 ♕d6 ♕e4+ 25 ♔d1 ♕g4+!? (25...♕b1+ secures a perpetual) 26 ♖e2 ♕g7 27 ♕xc6 is unclear!

**24 ♖c2 ♔c7 25 ♖h7! b4 26 ♖a2 b3!? 27 ♖xa3 c2 28 ♖a4 c1♕ 29 ♖c4 1-0**

The threat against c6 forces Black to give up his queen (again) and 29...♕xc4+ 30 ♕xc4 b2 31 ♕a2 ♖b8 32 ♕b1 ♗a6+ 33 ♔d2 ♗xf1 34 e6 ♖b3 35 ♖xd7+ ♔b6 36 e7 ♗xe7 37 ♖xe7 ♗d3 38 ♖e3 wins (Khalifman).

I remember the next game well since I was playing on the board next to it!

---

## Game 24
### Mecking-San Segundo
*Linares Open 1995*

1 d4 d5 2 c4 c6 3 ♘f3 ♘f6 4 ♘c3

e6 5 ♗g5 dxc4 6 e4 b5 7 e5 h6 8 ♗h4 g5 9 ♘xg5 hxg5 10 ♗xg5 ♘bd7 11 g3 ♖g8 12 h4 ♖xg5 13 hxg5 ♘d5 14 g6 fxg6 15 ♕g4 ♕e7 16 ♕xg6+ ♕f7 17 ♕xf7+ ♔xf7 18 ♗g2

If White tries to avoid the exchange on c3 with 18 ♘e4, then Black has 18...♗b4+ followed by ...c4-c3 with a messy game.

**18...♘xc3 19 bxc3 ♖b8 20 f4**

20 ♗xc6 ♗b7 occurred in the game Shirov-Stisis, London (Lloyds Bank Masters) 1990, which continued 21 ♖h7+ ♔g6 22 ♖xd7 ♗xc6 23 ♖xa7, and now 23...b4 would have given Black a good game according to Wells. The text supports the white e5-pawn in anticipation of the pressure that Black is going to exert on d4 and c3.

**20...b4 21 ♔d2 c5!**

**22 d5 ♘b6! 23 dxe6+**

23 d6 is critical, when Black can try 23...♘d5 or 23...♘a4, putting pressure on the c3-pawn.

**23...♗xe6 24 ♗e4 ♖d8+ 25 ♔e3 ♘d5+ 26 ♗xd5 ♖xd5 27 ♖hd1 ♖xd1 28 ♖xd1 ♗f5 29 ♔d2 ♗e7 30 a3 bxc3+ 31 ♔xc3 ♗d3 32 ♖xd3 cxd3 33 ♔xd3**

Black should not really lose this position but he nervously ran himself into time-trouble with disastrous results.

**33...♔g6 34 g4 ♗h4 35 ♔e4 ♗g3 36 f5+ ♔g7 37 g5 ♗h4 38 g6 c4 39 ♔d4 ♗g3 40 e6 ♗d6 41 a4 ♔f6 42 ♔xc4 a5 43 ♔b5 ♗b4 44 ♔c6 1-0**

After the game, when San Segundo was discussing the game his opponent I heard him say, 'I think I was better, perhaps I could have won somehow.' Mecking, an extremely devout Christian who credits God's intercession for his recovery from a usually terminal disease abruptly replied that 'God would not have let it happen!'

> **Game 25**
> **Knaak-Van der Wiel**
> *Lugano 1989*

**1 d4 d5 2 c4 c6 3 ♘f3 ♘f6 4 ♘c3 e6 5 ♗g5 dxc4 6 e4 b5 7 e5 h6 8 ♗h4 g5 9 ♘xg5 hxg5 10 ♗xg5 ♘bd7 11 g3 ♖g8 12 h4 ♖xg5 13 hxg5 ♘d5 14 g6 fxg6 15 ♕g4 ♕a5?**

This aggressive counterattack against the knight on c3 seems to lose by force after White's splendid reply.

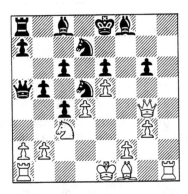

**16 ♕xe6+ ♔d8 17 ♗g2!! ♘xc3 18 ♔f1!! ♘d5 19 ♕xc6 ♘5b6**

19...♘c7 20 e6 is also very painful according to Knaak.

**20 ♖h8**

Threatening ♕d6.

**20...♕b4 21 e6 ♖b8 22 exd7 ♘xd7 23 a3! ♕e7**

23...♕xb2 24 ♖xf8+! ♘xf8 (24...♔e7 25 ♖e1+) 25 ♕f6+ ♔c7 26 ♕f4+! is no better according to Knaak.

**24 ♕xg6 ♖b6 25 ♕h5 ♖f6 26 ♖e1 ♕d6 27 ♖e8+ ♔c7 28 ♕h4 ♘b6 29 ♕e4 ♘d7 30 ♖h7**

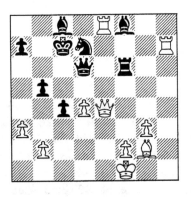

**30...b4 31 axb4 ♕a6 32 ♕e5+ ♕d6 33 ♗h3 1-0**

A very impressive game by the German grandmaster.

We shall now examine the popular sideline with 11...♕a5. This line can arise after either 11 g3 ♕a5 12 g3 or 11 exf6 ♕a5, when 12 g3 is the automatic choice. Even if you prefer the 11 exf6 move order, this section will therefore still be important for you.

11...♕a5 removes the queen from the h4-d8 diagonal and thus forces the immediate capture on f6. As with ...♕b6, it also prepares queenside castling. However, unlike ...♕b6, ...♕a5 does not protect the bishop on b7 and thus the chances of a quick ...c6-c5 are very small. This move aims not at White's weakness on d4, but to make the most of Black's queenside strength, supporting ...b5-b4. This would not only attack the knight on c3, but also open the fifth rank for the queen to attack the unprotected bishop on g5 and support ...c4-c3. If Black can play both ...b5-b4 and ...c4-c3 he will open the a6-f1 diagonal to which the black bishop on c8 can move in one go.

> ## Game 26
> ### Oll-Kaidanov
> *Kuibysev 1986*

**1 d4 ♘f6 2 ♘f3 d5 3 c4 e6 4 ♘c3 c6 5 ♗g5 dxc4 6 e4 b5 7 e5 h6 8 ♗h4 g5 9 ♘xg5 hxg5 10 ♗xg5 ♘bd7 11 g3 ♕a5 12 exf6 b4 13 ♘e4 ♗a6 14 ♕f3**

By transposition, we would reach the same position after 12...♗a6 13 ♕f3 b4! 14 ♘e4. This position is critical for the evaluation of the 11...♕a5 variation. 14 b3 is seen in the next game.

**14...0-0-0 15 b3**

Rather risky; this gives Black an extra means of opening up the queenside while White's king is in the centre.

15 ♗e3 is the most dangerous move, when Hertneck-Mueller, German Bundesliga 1989, continued 15...♕d5 16 ♗e2 ♗b7 17 ♘g5! c5 18 ♕xd5 ♗xd5, and now 19 0-0 e5 20 dxc5 would have given White the advantage, according to Hertneck.

**15...♘b6!**

The text hits the d4-pawn, by unmasking the attack of the rook on d8.

**16 ♘c5?**

16 ♗e3 ♗b7 17 ♗g2 (17 bxc4 b3+!) 17...cxb3 18 ♕e2 (18 0-0 bxa2) looks very dodgy for White.

**16...♗b5!**

Protecting the pawn on c6.

**17 ♗e3 ♖d5! 18 a4 bxa3+! 19 ♗d2 ♕xd2+!! 20 ♔xd2 ♗xc5 21 bxc4 ♖xd4+**

The rest must have been very painful for White.

**22 ♔c3 ♘xc4 23 ♗xc4 ♖xc4+ 24 ♔b3 ♖b4+ 25 ♔c3 ♖b2 26 ♖ab1 ♗b4+ 27 ♔d4 c5+ 28 ♔e5 ♖e2+ 0-1**

29 ♔d6 ♖d2+ 30 ♔e5 ♖d5+ 31 ♔e4 ♗c6 wins according to Kaidanov.

*Game 27*
**Mecking-Matsuura**
*Sao Paulo Zonal 1995*

**1 d4 d5 2 c4 c6 3 ♘f3 ♘f6 4 ♘c3 e6 5 ♗g5 dxc4 6 e4 b5 7 e5 h6 8 ♗h4 g5 9 ♘xg5 hxg5 10 ♗xg5 ♘bd7 11 g3 ♕a5 12 exf6 b4 13 ♘e4 ♗a6 14 b3**

**14...♘b6**

14...0-0-0 is considered stronger, as 15 ♕c2 ♘b6 16 ♗e3 e5! 17 dxe5 ♕xe5 gave Black good play in Khenkin-Feher, Cappelle la Grande 1992.

**15 bxc4 ♘xc4 16 ♕b3 ♕d5 17 f3 ♗b5 18 ♖c1 ♘a3 19 ♕xd5 cxd5 20 ♘d2 ♗d6 21 ♔f2**

White is slightly better.

**21...♗xf1 22 ♘xf1 ♘b5 23 ♔e3 ♔d7 24 h4 ♖ac8 25 ♖xc8 ♖xc8 26 h5 ♖c3+ 27 ♔f2 ♘xd4 28 h6 ♖c8 29 ♘e3 a5 30 ♗f4 a4 31 ♗xd6 ♔xd6 32 f4 b3 33 axb3 axb3 34 g4 b2 35 ♖b1 ♖b8 36 ♘d1 e5 37 ♖xb2 ♖h8 38 g5 exf4 39 ♘c3 ♘e6 40 ♖b5 d4 41 ♘e4+ ♔c6 42 ♖e5 d3 43 ♖xe6+ fxe6 44 g6 ♖xh6 45 g7 1-0**

We shall now consider less precise

move orders for Black: 12...b4 13 ♘e4 c3 and 12...♗a6 13 ♕f3 ♖c8.

**1 d4 d5 2 c4 c6 3 ♘c3 ♘f6 4 ♘f3 e6 5 ♗g5 dxc4 6 e4 b5 7 e5 h6 8 ♗h4 g5 9 ♘xg5 hxg5 10 ♗xg5 ♘bd7 11 g3 ♕a5 12 exf6 b4 13 ♘e4 c3 14 bxc3 bxc3 15 ♕d3! ♗b7 16 ♗e2 c5 17 0-0! c4 18 ♕e3 ♘b6?**

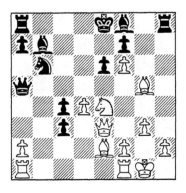

Piket suggests that 18...♕f5 19 f3 ♘b6 is worthy of attention.

**19 ♘c5! ♗xc5 20 dxc5 ♘d5 21 ♕d4 ♖c8 22 ♖ab1 ♗a6 23 ♖fc1 ♕xc5 24 ♕xc5 ♖xc5 25 ♖b8+ ♗c8 26 ♗e3 ♘xe3 27 fxe3 0-0 28 ♖xc3 ♗a6 29 ♖xf8+ ♔xf8 30 g4 ♔g8 31 ♔f2 ♔h7 32 h4 ♔g6 33 g5 ♔f5 34 ♔g3 ♗b5 35 ♗d3+ ♔e5 36 ♗c2 ♔d6 37 ♔g4 ♖d5 38 h5 ♖d3 39 ♖xd3+ cxd3 40 ♗d1 1-0**

**1 ♘f3 d5 2 d4 ♘f6 3 c4 c6 4 ♘c3**

**e6 5 ♗g5 dxc4 6 e4 b5 7 e5 h6 8 ♗h4 g5 9 ♘xg5 hxg5 10 ♗xg5 ♘bd7 11 g3 ♕a5 12 exf6 ♗a6**

**13 ♕f3**

This move attacks the point most weakened by the light-squared bishop's unusual development on a6 rather than b7 – the pawn on c6 – and also prevents Black from castling queenside immediately. By moving the queen off the d-file White also prevents his opponent from using a pin on the d-file to transfer the knight to d3 via e5 or c5. Moreover, the queen supports the knight if it goes to e4, protecting the bishop on g5 after ...b5-b4.

The alternative 13 a3 is sometimes seen, but Black can then use the pin on the d-file with 13...0-0-0 14 ♗g2 ♘c5 15 0-0 ♘b3 with an acceptable game.

**13...♖c8**

Black's only reasonable choice here is to transpose the line 12...b4 13 ♘e4 ♗a6 14 ♕f3 (Game 26) with 13...b4 14 ♘e4. White cannot play 14 ♕xc6 as both 14...♖c8 15 ♕a4 ♕xa4 16 ♘xa4 ♗b7 17 ♖g1 ♖xh2 and 14...♗b7!? 15 ♕xb7 ♖b8! 16 ♕xb8+ (the only move:

16 ♕e4 loses to 16...bxc3) 16...♘xb8 17 ♘e4 (protecting the bishop on g5) 17...b3+! 18 ♗d2 ♕xa2!! are good for Black.

**14 ♗e2 b4 15 ♘e4 c5 16 d5! exd5 17 ♕f5!!**

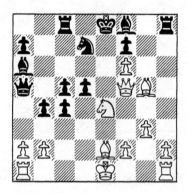

The text indicates that White is willing to sacrifice the knight on e4 in order to exploit the main drawback of 13...♖c8: the uncastled black king.

**17...dxe4**

17...d4 loses to 18 ♗g4 and 17...c3 18 ♗g4 ♕b5 (18...♗b5 19 ♕xd5 cxb2 20 ♖d1) 19 ♕xd5 cxb2 20 ♖d1 is also good for White according to Kramnik.

**18 0-0-0 ♖c7 19 ♗g4 ♗b5 20 ♕xe4+ ♔d8 21 ♗xd7 ♗xd7 22 ♖he1**

Threatening 23 ♕e8 checkmate.

**22...♗h6 23 ♕a8+ ♖c8 24 ♖xd7+ ♔xd7 25 ♕d5+ 1-0**

25...♔c7 26 ♖e7+ ♔b6 27 ♕b7+ mate (Kramnik).

**1 d4 ♘f6 2 c4 c6 3 ♘c3 d5 4 ♘f3 e6 5 ♗g5 dxc4 6 e4 b5 7 e5 h6 8 ♗h4 g5 9 ♘xg5 hxg5 10 ♗xg5**

♘bd7 11 g3 b4

Euwe's analysis of 11...♘xe5 seems convincing: 12 dxe5 ♕xd1+ 13 ♖xd1 ♘d5 14 ♘e4 ♗b4+ 15 ♔e2 when Black suffers from severe weaknesses on the dark squares. The text gains three pieces for the queen, but the looseness of Black's structure and the weakness of his king conspire against Black.

**12 ♘e4 ♘xe4 13 ♗xd8 ♔xd8 14 ♗xc4 ♘b6 15 ♗d3 f5 16 ♗xe4 fxe4 17 ♕g4**

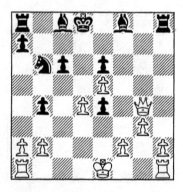

**17...♗d7 18 ♕xe4 ♔c7 19 0-0 ♗e7**

Ivanchuk suggests that 19...♔b7 20 a3 ♘d5 would have been a better defensive plan.

**20 ♖ac1 ♔b7 21 f4 ♖af8 22 ♖f3 ♘d5 23 a3 ♖hg8 24 axb4 ♗xb4 25 ♕h7 ♔c7 26 ♖f2 ♔d8**

26...♗e7 was no better according to Ivanchuk due to 27 ♖a1 ♔b7 28 b4 ♖b8 29 ♕d3 ♘b4 30 ♖b2 winning.

**27 ♔h1 ♖h8 28 ♕d3 a5 29 ♖fc2 ♖h3 30 ♖xc6 ♖xf4 31 ♕c2 ♖f5 32 ♖c8+ ♔e7 33 ♖g8 ♖h7 34 ♔g1 a4 35 ♖b8 ♖hf7 36 ♖xb4 ♖f1+ 37 ♖xf1 ♖xf1+ 38 ♔xf1 ♘e3+ 39 ♔f2 ♘xc2 40 ♖c4 ♘a1 41 h4 ♗e8 42 g4 ♘b3 43 h5 ♘a5 44 ♖c7+ 1-0**

## Summary

11 g3 is my recommended move order for White players, when 11...♗b7 12 ♗g2 ♕b6 13 exf6 0-0-0 14 0-0 c5! is the best reply, leading to the main lines after 15 d5 b4 since Timman's 15 dxc5 does not seem to be dangerous. The lines with 11...♕a5 are still quite unexplored, but 12 exf6 b4 13 ♘e4, to meet 13...♗a6 with 14 ♕f3, and Kramnik's 12 exf6 ♗a6 13 ♕f3 seem very good ways to counter it.

**1 d4 d5 2 c4 c6 3 ♘f3 ♘f6 4 ♘c3 e6 5 ♗g5 dxc4 6 e4 b5 7 e5 h6 8 ♗h4 g5 9 ♘xg5 hxg5 10 ♗xg5 ♘bd7 11 g3**

**11...♗b7**
    11...♖g8 12 h4 ♖xg5 13 hxg5 ♘d5 14 g6 fxg6 15 ♕g4 *(D)*
        15...♕e7
            16 ♗g2 ♕f7 17 ♗e4 ♘e7
                18 ♘xb5 – *Game 21*
                18 ♖h8 – *Game 22*
            16 ♖h8 – *Game 23*
            16 ♕xg6+ – *Game 24*
        15...♕a5 – *Game 25*
    11...♕a5 12 exf6 *(D)*
        12...b4 13 ♘e4
            13...♗a6
                14 ♕f3 – *Game 26*
                14 b3 – *Game 27*
            13...c3 – *Game 28*
        12...♗a6 – *Game 29*
    11...b4 – *Game 30*
**12 ♗g2 ♕b6 13 exf6 0-0-0 14 0-0 *(D)* c5**
    14...♘e5 – *Game 20*
**15 dxc5 – *Game 19***

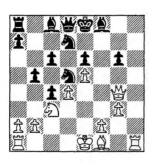

*15 ♕g4*

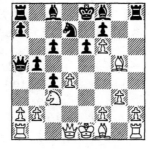

*12 exf6*

*14 0-0*

# CHAPTER FOUR

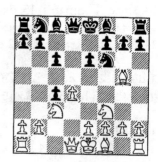

## Botvinnik Variation: Early Deviations after 5 ♗g5 dxc4

1 d4 d5 2 c4 c6 3 ♘f3 ♘f6 4 ♘c3 e6 5 ♗g5 dxc4

In this chapter we consider various offshots in the Botvinnik variation for White and Black.

The first two games deal with two attempts by Black to deviate from the main lines, neither of which is considered to be completely sound by opening theory. In Game 33 we then take a look a dubious double gambit by White: 9 exf6 gxh4 10 ♘e5 ♕xf6.

The rest of this chapter is devoted to games in which White plays an early a2-a4, with either 6 e4 b5 7 a4 (Games 34-37) or 6 a4 (Games 38-41).

First we consider 10...♗e7 in the main line Botvinnik system, which has been practically put out of business by the following variation.

1 d4 d5 2 c4 c6 3 ♘f3 ♘f6 4 ♘c3 e6 5 ♗g5 dxc4 6 e4 b5 7 e5 h6 8 ♗h4 g5 9 ♘xg5 hxg5 10 ♗xg5 ♗e7 11 exf6 ♗xf6 12 ♗e3!

It may seem strange to avoid the exchange of dark-squared bishops when Black has so many dark-squared weaknesses, but White wants to gain a tempo in the future with ♘e4!

**12...♗b7**

12...♘a6 13 a4 ♘c7 is the latest attempt to resurrect this line. However, 14 ♕f3 (14 g3 c5!? 15 dxc5 ♗b7 16 ♖g1 b4 17 ♘b5 was unclear in Levitt-Landero, Seville 1989) 14...♗d7 15 axb5 cxb5 16 ♗f4 ♖c8 17 ♘e4 ♘d5 18 ♘d6+ ♔e7 19 ♘xc8+ followed by ♗e2 and 0-0 was good for White in Schoen-Polajzer, Biel 1990.

**13 ♕f3! ♗xd4**

13...♗e7!? 14 g3 ♘a6 15 ♗g2 ♖b8 16 0-0 c5 enabled Black to unravel in Schmidt-Hracek, Poznan 1987, and seems to be Black's only hope in this line.

**14 0-0-0 ♗xe3+ 15 fxe3 ♕e7 16 ♘e4 ♔f8 17 ♘c5!**

Threatening 18 ♖d8+ ♕xd8 19 ♘xe6+!, forking the king and queen.

17...♕xc5 18 ♖d8+ ♔e7 19 ♖xh8 ♘d7 20 ♖xa8 ♗xa8 21 ♗e2 ♘e5 22 ♕e4 ♘d3+ 23 ♔b1 f5 24 ♕h4+ ♔d7 25 ♕h7+ ♕e7 26 ♕h8 ♕e8 27 ♕d4+ ♔c8 28 ♗xd3 cxd3 29 ♖d1 c5 30 ♕xc5+ ♕c6 31 ♕xc6+ ♗xc6 32 ♖d2 e5 33 ♔c1 e4 34 ♖f2 ♗d7 35 b4 ♔c7 36 h4 ♔d6 37 g4 fxg4 38 h5 ♔d5 39 h6 g3 40 ♖g2 ♗f5 41 ♖xg3 ♔e6 42 ♖g7 ♔f6 43 ♖xa7 1-0

Though always fascinating, the line with 9...♘d5 never quite manages to look totally convincing.

*Game 32*
**Stefansson-Inkiov**
*Gausdal 1990*

1 d4 ♘f6 2 c4 e6 3 ♘f3 d5 4 ♘c3 c6 5 ♗g5 dxc4 6 e4 b5 7 e5 h6 8 ♗h4 g5 9 ♘xg5 ♘d5

*see following diagram*

10 ♘xf7! ♕xh4 11 ♘xh8 ♗b4 12 a3!?

On the evidence of this game, this looks almost like a forced win! Ionov-Korneev, El Vendrell 1996, continued 12 ♖c1 c5 13 dxc5 ♕g5 14 ♗e2 ♗b7

15 ♗h5+ ♔f8 16 ♕f3+ ♔g8 17 0-0 ♔xh8 18 ♕f8+ ♔g8 19 ♕xh6+ ♕h7, and now 20 ♕xh7+ ♔xh7 23 ♘xb5 would have been clearly better for White according to Ionov. White has a pleasant choice!

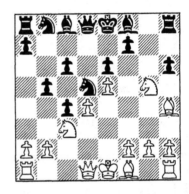

12...♘xc3 13 ♕f3! ♕xd4

13...♗a5 14 bxc3 ♕xd4 15 ♕f7+ ♔d8 16 ♖d1 wins for White according to Tangborn.

14 ♕h5+ ♔d8 15 axb4 ♕e4+ 16 ♗e2 ♘xe2 17 ♕xe2 ♕h7 18 ♕d2+ ♔c7 19 ♕d6+ ♔b7 20 ♖d1 ♕xh8 21 ♕e7+ ♗d7 22 f4 ♕e8 23 ♕g7 ♔c7 24 0-0 a5 25 f5 axb4 26 fxe6 ♕xe6 27 ♖d6 ♕e8 28 ♖xh6 c3 29 bxc3 b3 30 e6 b2 31 c4 ♖a2 32 cxb5 cxb5 33 ♕e5+ 1-0

We shall now consider the strange line 6 e4 b5 7 e5 h6 8 ♗h4 g5 9 exf6 gxh4 10 ♘e5 ♕xf6 11 a4.

*Game 33*
**Alvarez-Antunes**
*Mondariz Balneario 1996*

1 ♘f3 d5 2 d4 ♘f6 3 c4 c6 4 ♘c3 e6 5 ♗g5 dxc4 6 e4 b5 7 e5 h6 8 ♗h4 g5 9 exf6 gxh4 10 ♘e5 ♕xf6

**11 a4**

Instinctively, I have always found White's position repulsive here: he has given up two pawns and the bishop pair for seemingly only a negligible lead in development. However, this intuitive judgement completely overlooks the most important positional factor in White's favour: the extremely powerful knight on e5 which exerts great influence on both sides of the board. White's main field of influence is on the queenside, where his pieces show excellent coordination. The trio of black pawns on b5, c4 and c6 are under intense pressure: the knight on e5 attacks the pawn on c6, preventing the knight on b8 from moving; the knight on c3 and pawn on a4 combine against the b5-pawn; and the knight on e5 and the bishop on f1 eye the c4-pawn. White's general plan is to place his light-squared bishop on to the h1-a8 diagonal via ♗e2-f3 or g2-g3 and ♗g2 to attack c6 and the rook on a8 beyond it. As a little bonus, the knight on e5 attacks f7 and when White plays ♗e2, he also threatens ♗h5, attacking f7.

Black's problems are entirely due to the knight on e5. Therefore, by exchanging this piece, Black should logically be able to greatly reduce White's activity. The natural carry out an exchange is to play ...♘d7, but this is impossible immediately due to 11...♘d7 12 ♘xc6 ♗b7 13 axb5 (This incidentally is the point behind playing a2-a4 on move 11. The old 11 ♗e2 allows 11...♘d7 12 ♘xc6 ♗b7 13 ♗f3 a6 14 0-0 ♗g7 15 a4 b4 16 ♘e4 ♕f4 17 ♕c1 ♕c7 18 ♕xc4 ♗xc6 19 ♖ac1 0-0 with equality, as in Barlov-Karaklaic, Yugoslavia 1987). In order to play ...♘d7 in the game Antunes first protects the c6-pawn with 11...♗b7 and then after 12 ♗e2 plays 12...♘d7.

**11...♗b7 12 ♗e2 ♘d7! 13 ♘xd7**

Perhaps 13 f4!? ♕xf4 14 ♘xf7!?, intending either 14...♕xf7 15 ♗h5! or 14...♔xf7 15 ♖f1 winning the queen in both cases. Antunes mentions that 13 ♘e4 is met by 13...♕f5.

**13...♔xd7**

Although the black king has had to move, it is in no real danger. I think that Black is already better here.

**14 ♗f3 a6 15 axb5?! axb5 16 ♖xa8 ♗xa8 17 ♕a1 ♗b7 18 ♕a7 ♔c8 19 0-0**

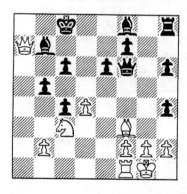

19 ♘xb5 ♗b4+ is clearly better for Black according to Antunes.

**19...♖g8 20 ♔h1 ♕f4 21 ♘e4 h3! 22 ♘c5 ♗xc5 23 dxc5 hxg2+ 24 ♗xg2 ♖g5 25 ♕b6 ♕c7 26 ♕a7 ♕e7 27 b4 cxb3 28 ♕a3 ♕xc5 29 ♕xb3 ♕c4 30 ♕a3 b4 31 ♕f3 ♕xf1+??**

Oh no!! Virtually anything would win here, but not this!

**32 ♗xf1 c5 33 ♗a6!**

Ouch!

**33...♗xa6 34 ♕a8+ ♔d7 35 ♕xa6 ♔e7 36 ♕c8 ♔f6 37 ♕h8+ ♔g6 38 ♕g8+ ♔f6 39 ♕h8+ ♔g6 40 ♕g8+ ½-½**

Black's position was so good that even after blundering his queen, he could still hold the draw! In this line he has a fortress position that White cannot break down. In my opinion, this idea marks the end of the road for this interesting variation.

---

### Game 34
### D.Garcia-Kramnik
*Pamplona 1992*

---

**1 d4 d5 2 ♘f3 c6 3 c4 ♘f6 4 ♘c3 e6 5 ♗g5 dxc4 6 e4 b5 7 a4**

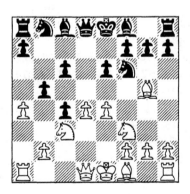

Instead of the immediate 7 e5 White

keeps e4-e5 in reserve and attacks b5 instead. Black cannot protect the b-pawn with 7...a6 due to 8 axb5 cxb5 9 ♘xb5!

**7...♗b7**

By protecting the rook on a8, Black threatens ...a7-a6, supporting the b5-pawn. Note that the seemingly natural 7...♗b4 can be met by 8 e5 h6 9 exf6 hxg5 10 fxg7 ♖g8 (the g-pawn isn't defended any more!) 11 h4! with a promising position for White. Black's other alternatives here are discussed in Games 36 and 37.

**8 axb5**

8 e5 is considered in the next game.

**8...cxb5 9 ♘xb5 ♗xe4**

The alternative 9...♕b6 10 ♕a4 was played in P.Cramling-Galliamova, Tilburg Women's Candidates 1994, and now 10...♗c6 11 ♕xc4 ♘xe4 is the critcial continuation. The immediate 9...♗b4+ 10 ♘c3 will most likely transpose to the game after 10...♗xe4 11 ♗xc4.

**10 ♗xc4**

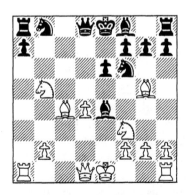

White has re-established material equality at the cost of the dismantling of his pawn centre. The resulting iso-lated queen's pawn (IQP) structure with Black's b-pawn exchanged for White's a-pawn favours Black in the long run for two reasons: he has gained the valuable b4-square for his knight (since White cannot play a2-a3); and has additional counterplay along the b-file. However, in the short term White has extra tactical chances (for example along the a4-e8 diagonal).

**10...♗b4+ 11 ♘c3 0-0 12 0-0 ♗b7**

12...♗xc3 13 bxc3 resembles the Karpov variation of the Nimzo-Indian (1 d4 ♘f6 2 c4 e6 3 ♘c3 ♗b4 4 e3 0-0 5 ♗d3 d5 6 ♘f3 c5 7 0-0 dxc4 8 ♗xc4 cxd4 9 exd4 b6 10 ♗g5 ♗b7), but without the pawns on b6 and a2. In that variation Black often plays ...♗xc3, but here this is less effective since the c-pawn is not restricted by a pawn on b6 and can thus easily move forwards to c5. Moreover, the pawn on a7 is isolated.

**13 ♕e2**

The queen should move to b3, making use of the exposed position of the bishop on b7 and combining with a knight on e5 and a rook on e1 in a typical IQP formation: 13 ♖e1 ♘bd7 14 ♕b3 a5 15 ♘e5! and now 15...♘b6 16 ♘xf7 ♖xf7 17 ♗xe6 ♕e8 18 ♖e5 ♔f8 19 ♗xf7 ♕xf7 20 ♕xf7+ ♔xf7 21 ♖b5 ♘fd7 22 ♘a4 ♘xa4 23 ♖xb7 ♘ab6 24 d5 gave White good chances in the endgame in Lutz-Zso.Polgar, Rimaska Sobota 1994.

**13...♗e7 14 ♖fd1 ♘bd7 15 d5**

White simply plays for a draw against his illustrious opponent...

**15...exd5 16 ♘xd5 ♗xd5 17 ♗xd5 ♘xd5 18 ♖xd5 ♗xg5 19 ♘xg5 h6 20 ♕d2 hxg5 21 ♖xd7 ♕f6 ½-½**

...and gets it!

**1 ♘f3 d5 2 d4 ♘f6 3 c4 e6 4 ♘c3 c6 5 ♗g5 dxc4 6 e4 b5 7 a4 ♗b7 8 e5 h6**

Now 9 ♗h4 g5 10 exf6 gxh4 is even better for Black than in the main line, but White has an interesting alternative.

**9 ♗d2!?**

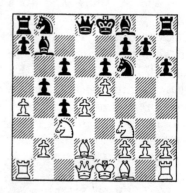

This interesting idea is reminiscent of the Slav Gambit (1 d4 d5 2 c4 c6 3 ♘f3 ♘f6 4 ♘c3 dxc4 5 e4!? b5 6 e5 ♘d5 7 a4). White's knight will come to e4 and eye the huge hole on c5, while ...h7-h6 has weakened Black's kingside.

**9...♘d5 10 ♘e4 a6 11 b3! cxb3 12 ♕xb3 ♘d7 13 ♗d3 ♗e7 14 0-0 0-0 15 ♗b1!**

15 ♖fe1 allows Black the time to play 15...♕b6 and ...♖fc8.

**15...♖e8 16 ♕c2 ♘f8 17 ♘c5**

Maksimenko suggests 17 ♖e1 f5 18 exf6 ♘xf6 (18...♗xf6!?) 19 ♘c5 with compensation.

**17...♗xc5 18 dxc5 a5!?**

18...f5 19 exf6 ♕xf6 20 ♗a2 ♖ad8 21 ♖fe1 e5 22 ♗a5 ♖d7 23 ♘d2 ♔h8 24 ♗b1 ♘f4 25 ♖a3 gave White a slight edge in Maksimenko-Pinter, Copenhagen 1995.

**19 axb5 cxb5 20 c6 ♗c8 21 ♗xa5 ♖xa5 22 c7 ♖xa1 23 cxd8♕ ♖xd8 24 ♕b2 ♖a8 25 ♖e1 b4 26 ♗e4 ♗b7 27 h3 ♖ab8 ½-½**

Black is actually better here: White has few targets, while Black can try to push his b-pawn.

> ### Game 36
> **Kallai-Lukacs**
> *Budapest 1995*

**1 d4 ♘f6 2 c4 e6 3 ♘f3 d5 4 ♘c3 c6 5 ♗g5 dxc4 6 e4 b5 7 a4 b4!?**

Although Black can drive the white knight away with this move, this move loosens his defence of the c-pawn.

**8 ♘b1 ♗e7 9 e5 ♘d5 10 ♗xe7 ♕xe7 11 ♗xc4 0-0 12 ♘bd2 c5! 13 dxc5?!**

13 ♗xd5 exd5 14 dxc5 ♗a6! prevents White from castling and 13 ♘b3 ♘d7 14 0-0 ♗b7 is fine for Black. 13 ♘e4 is therefore best, but after

13...cxd4 14 ♕xd4 ♗b7 Black has reasonable chances according to Lukacs.

**13...♗b7 14 ♘b3?**

This is too risky. 14 0-0 ♘d7 (14...♘f4!?) 15 ♘b3 ♘xc5 16 ♘a5 ♖fd8 is fine for Black according to Lukacs.

**14...♘f4 15 ♕d6**

15 0-0 ♘xg2 16 ♔xg2 ♕g5+ 17 ♔h1 ♖d8! 18 ♕e2 ♕g4! wins according to Lukacs.

**15...♘xg2+ 16 ♔e2 ♗xf3+ 17 ♔xf3 ♕g5 18 ♖hg1 ♖d8 19 ♖xg2**

A sad necessity. Lukacs shows that 19 ♕c7 ♘d7! 20 ♖xg2 ♘xe5+ 21 ♔e2 ♕xg2 22 ♕xe5 ♕g4+ wins for Black, picking up the bishop on c4.

**19...♕f5+ 20 ♔e3 ♖xd6 21 exd6 ♘d7 22 ♖ag1 ♕e5+ 23 ♔d3 ♕xb2 24 ♖xg7+ ♔h8 25 ♔e3 ♘e5 0-1**

An attractive and theoretically important game.

> ### Game 37
> **Bellon-Antunes**
> *Platja d'Aro Barcino 1994*

**1 d4 d5 2 c4 c6 3 ♘c3 ♘f6 4 ♘f3 e6 5 ♗g5 dxc4 6 e4 b5 7 a4 ♕b6!?**

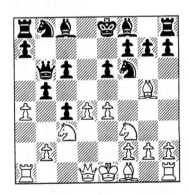

Black protects the pawn on b5, sacrificing a move in development to keep hold of the gambit pawn. He also unpins the knight on f6, drawing the teeth from e4-e5.

**8 &xf6 gxf6**

8 &xf6 doubled Black's f-pawns and weaken his kingside. Although Black's control of the central dark squares is enhanced (the doubled f-pawn controls e5 effectively), he has less control of the central light squares since there is no longer a knight on f6 attacking d5 or e4. White's general plan therefore is to play d4-d5, which will combine with the pawn on a4 and the knight on c3 to attack the black queenside.

**9 &e2 &b7 10 0-0 a6 11 d5?!**

This produces a quite stunning game, but my experience of such positions from both sides is that White should not rush this move. 11 b3!, opening the queenside, was played in Lerner-Kaidanov, USSR 1985, and gave White good play after 11...cxb3 (or 11...b4 12 a5 &c7 13 &a4 c3 14 &b6 &a7 15 &c4 with compensation) 12 &xb3 &d7 13 d5! cxd5 14 exd5.

**11...&d7 12 &d4 c5?**

Two years later Antunes improved significantly with 12...cxd5 13 exd5 &c5! 14 dxe6 fxe6, when 15 &f3 &xd4 16 &xb7 &d8! 17 &c6 0-0! 18 &xd7 &xd7 19 &e2 &h8 gave Black a large advantage in Campos-Antunes, Mondariz Balneario 1996.

**13 &c6 &g8 14 &h5 &xc6 15 dxe6!! &e5 16 axb5 &xb5 17 &d5! &a7 18 &xb5 &xb5 19 &fd1 &b6 20 &xa6 &xg2+**

20...&xa6 allows 21 &d8+ mate, while 20...&xa6 allows a supremely

artistic touch: 21 exf7+ &e7 22 g8&!! mate (Bellon).

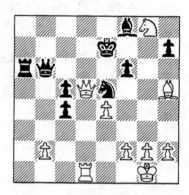

**21 &xg2 &xa6 22 &xf7+ &e7 23 &d7+ 1-0**

23...&xd7 24 &xd7+ is mate.

The immediate 6 a4 has developed a small following in recent years.

**1 c4 c6 2 d4 d5 3 &c3 &f6 4 &f3 e6 5 &g5 dxc4 6 a4 &b4**

The immediate 6...c5!? 7 e3 cxd4 8 exd4 &e7 9 &xc4 0-0 10 0-0 &c6, as in Ilundain-Korneev, Zaragoza 1995, is not stupid either, as Black has a standard IQP position in which White has helpfully conceded the b4-square for his queen's knight.

**7 e4 c5**

Here 7...b5 transposes to the note to Black's seventh move in Game 34. 7....&xc3+ is somewhat greedy – see Game 41.

**8 &xc4 cxd4 9 &b5+**

For 9 &xd4!? see Game 40.

**9...&c6**

9...♘bd7 is met by 10 ♕xd4! according to Makarov.

**10 ♘xd4 0-0!?**

A very interesting pawn sacrifice. The restrained 10...♗d7 is seen in the next game.

**11 ♘xc6**

11 ♗xc6 bxc6 12 ♘xc6 ♗xc3+ 13 bxc3 ♕c7 is fine for Black (Tisdall).

**11...♕xd1+ 12 ♖xd1 bxc6 13 ♗xc6 ♖b8 14 e5?!**

This move is dubious according to Tisdall.

**14...♘g4 15 ♗f4 ♗a5! 16 0-0 ♖xb2 17 ♘b5 ♗b6 18 ♗g3 ♗a6 19 ♖b1 ♖a2 20 ♖a1 ♖b2 21 ♖ab1 ½-½**

*Game 39*
**Cu.Hansen-Tisdall**
*Reykjavik Zonal 1995*

**1 c4 c6 2 ♘c3 d5 3 d4 ♘f6 4 ♘f3 e6 5 ♗g5 dxc4 6 a4 ♗b4 7 e4 c5 8 ♗xc4 cxd4 9 ♗b5+ ♘c6 10 ♘xd4 ♗d7**

In this game Tisdall studiously avoids a repitition of his 10...0-0 from the previous game, perhaps fearing a prepared improvement.

**11 0-0**

11 ♘xc6 bxc6 12 ♗d3 h6 (12...♕a5!?) 13 ♗e3 e5 14 f3 ♕a5 15 ♕c1 ♗c5 16 ♗c4 ♗xe3 17 ♕xe3 ♖b8 (17...♕b6!?) 18 b3 was a tiny bit better for White in Makarov-Bagirov, Podolsk 1992.

**11...h6 12 ♗e3 0-0**

The pawn grab is a little dangerous: 12...♗xc3 13 bxc3 ♘xe4 14 ♕g4 ♘g5 15 h4 or 15 ♖ad1 is good for White according to Tisdall.

**13 f3 ♘e5 14 ♘c2 ♗xc3 15 bxc3 ♕c7 16 ♗d4 ♖fd8 17 ♘e3 a6?!**

Tisdall criticises this move, which weakens the queenside dark squares. 17...♗c6 immediately would have been better.

**18 ♗e2 ♗c6 19 ♕b3 ♘g6 20 ♗b6 ♕f4 21 g3 ♕g5 22 f4 ♘xf4 23 ♖xf4 ♘xe4 24 ♘f1 ♕e5 25 ♗f3 ♘xc3 26 ♗xd8 ♖xd8 27 ♖c1 ♖d3 28 ♕c4 ♖xf3 29 ♖xf3 ♘e2+ 30 ♔f2 ♘xc1 31 ♕xc1 ½-½**

*Game 40*
**Yermolinsky-Atalik**
*Hastings 1995*

**1 d4 d5 2 ♘f3 ♘f6 3 c4 c6 4 ♘c3 e6 5 ♗g5 dxc4 6 a4 ♗b4 7 e4 c5 8 ♗xc4 cxd4 9 ♘xd4!? h6 10 ♗e3!?**

10 ♗b5+ ♘bd7 11 ♗xf6 ♕xf6 12 ♘de2 a6 13 bxd7+ ♗xd7 14 0-0 ♗c6 15 ♕b3 ♗d6 was poor for White in Kiselev-Dreev, Helsinki 1992.

**10...0-0**

The safe option. 10...♘xe4 11 0-0 ♘d6 12 ♗a2 0-0 13 ♕f3 ♕e7 14 ♖fd1 ♔h8 15 ♘c2 ♗xc3 16 bxc3 ♘f5 17 ♗c1 ♖e8 18 ♗a3 ♕f6 19 ♘d4 ♘xd4 20 ♕xf6 ♘e2+ 21 ♔f1 gxf6 22 ♔xe2 led to an unclear ending in Sergeev-

Savchenko, St Petersburg Open 1993.
**11 f3 ♕e7 12 0-0 ♘c6 13 ♘xc6 bxc6 14 ♕e2 a5!**

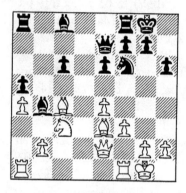

Black's weak c-pawn is not too significant because White has weakened his queenside with a2-a4.
**15 e5 ♘d5 16 ♘e4 ♘xe3 17 ♕xe3 ♖d8 18 ♖ad1 ♗a6 19 ♖xd8+ ♕xd8 20 b3 ♗xc4 21 bxc4 ♕c7 22 f4 ♖d8 23 ♘f2 ♗d2 24 ♕f3 ♕b6 25 ♖d1 ♖d4 26 g3 ♕c5 27 ♕e2 ♗c3 28 ♔f1 ♕b4 29 ♖xd4 ♗xd4 30 ♕c2 ♕a3 31 ♔g2 ♕e3 32 h4 ♔f8 33 h5 ♔e7 34 ♘h3 ♔d7 35 g4 ♔c7 36 ♕h7 ♕e2+ 37 ♔g3 ♕d2 ½-½**

---

### Game 41
### Cebalo-Palac
*Croatian Ch., Slavonski Brod 1995*

---

**1 d4 d5 2 c4 c6 3 ♘f3 ♘f6 4 ♘c3 e6 5 ♗g5 dxc4 6 a4 ♗b4 7 e4 ♗xc3+ 8 bxc3 ♕a5 9 e5 ♘e4 10 ♗d2 ♕d5**

Defending the extra c4-pawn, but after 10...c5 11 ♗xc4 cxd4 (11...♘c6 12 d5 ♘xd2 13 ♕xd2 exd5 14 ♗xd5 0-0 15 0-0 ♗f5 16 ♕f4 ♗g6 17 c4 was better for White in McCambridge-Kaidanov, Las Vegas 1993) 12 cxd4

♘xd2 13 ♘xd2 ♘c6 14 ♗b5 0-0 15 ♗xc6 bxc6 16 0-0 ♕d5 17 ♕c2 ♗a6 18 ♖fd1 the Donaldson suggestion of 18...♕xd4 would have equalised in Lputian-Kaidanov, Lucern 1993.
**11 a5!**

Making it much harder for Black to achieve ...b7-b5.
**11...♘d7 12 ♗e2 0-0**

Here the immediate 12...b5 13 axb6 ♘xb6 14 0-0 also leaves Black's pawns on the queenside rather exposed.
**13 0-0 c5 14 ♕c2 ♘xd2 15 ♕xd2 cxd4 16 cxd4 b5 17 axb6 ♘xb6**

Black's dark squares are vulnerable but he does still have his extra pawn.
**18 ♘g5 ♗b7 19 ♗f3 ♕d7 20 ♕c2 g6 21 ♗xb7 ♕xb7 22 ♘e4 ♖fd8 23 ♖fd1 ♖ac8 24 ♘d6 ♖xd6 25 exd6 ♕d7 26 ♕e4 ♕xd6 27 ♖xa7 ♘d5!**

The passed c-pawn is now extremely dangerous.
**28 g3 c3 29 ♕f3 ♖c7 30 ♖a8+ ♔g7 31 ♕e4 ♘b4 32 ♖a3 ♖c4 33 ♔g2 c2 34 ♖c1 ♖xd4 35 ♕e3 ♖d1 36 ♖aa1 ♕c6+ 37 ♔h3 ♖xc1 38 ♖xc1 ♘a2 39 ♕d4+ ♔g8 40 ♕d8+ ♔g7 41 ♕d4+ e5 42 ♕xe5+ f6 43 ♕e7+ ♔g8 44 ♕d8+ ♔g7 45 ♕e7+ ♔g8 46 ♕e8+ ♔g7 47 ♕e7+ ½-½**

## Summary

6 a4 and 6 e4 b5 7 a4 are quite worth a try in the odd game, as they are quite tricky in places. However, none of the other lines here really inspire much confidence.

**1 d4 d5 2 c4 c6 3 ♘f3 ♘f6 4 ♘c3 e6 5 ♗g5 dxc4**

**6 e4**

> 6 a4 ♗b4 7 e4
>> 7...c5 8 ♗xc4 cxd4 *(D)*
>>> 9 ♗b5+ ♘c6 10 ♘xd4
>>>> 10...0-0 – *Game 38*
>>>> 10...♗d7 – *Game 39*
>>> 9 ♘xd4 – *Game 40*
>> 7...♗xc3+ – *Game 41*

**6...b5 7 e5**

> 7 a4
>> 7...♗b7 *(D)*
>>> 8 axb5 – *Game 34*
>>> 8 e5 – *Game 35*
>> 7...b4 – *Game 36*
>> 7...♕b6 – *Game 37*

**7...h6 8 ♗h4 g5 9 ♘xg5** *(D)*

> 9 exf6 – *Game 33*

**9...hxg5**

> 9...♘d5 – *Game 32*

**10 ♗xg5 ♗e7** – *Game 31*

*8...cxd4*

*7...♗b7*

*9 ♘xg5*

# CHAPTER FIVE

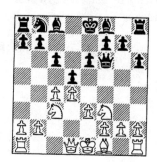

## Moscow Variation with 7 e3

**1 d4 d5 2 c4 c6 3 ♘f3 ♘f6 4 ♘c3 e6 5 ♗g5 h6 6 ♗xf6 ♕xf6 7 e3**

The Botvinnik system is fascinating, but sometimes you may feel you need a break from all that dangerous living! In recent years the Moscow variation has become the most popular way to try and defuse 5 ♗g5. By playing 5...h6, Black seeks an improved Botvinnik: if now 6 ♗h4, then after 6...dxc4 7 e4, Black can break the pin one move earlier with 7...g5! and after 8 ♗g3 b5 Black has retained his extra pawn on c4 without allowing White an early e4-e5. Therefore, White players usually capture the knight on f6.

*Question 1:* But 6 ♗xf6 ♕xf6 gives up the bishop pair. What is White's compensation?

*Answer:* First, White buys himself a tempo for development. Second, by removing the knight on f6, White weakens Black's control of e4; this allows White to achieve the e2-e4 break which shows up the exposed position of the black queen, as after e2-e4 d5xe4, ♘xe4 White gains a

tempo on the queen on f6. Finally, by removing the knight and diverting the queen from d8, White weakens Black's support of his d5-pawn. If Black wishes to play his freeing breaks ...c6-c5 or ...e6-e5, he must first release the central tension with...d5xc4.

In this chapter we look at the most common move 7 e3, preparing to develop the bishop on f1 and thus allowing kingside castling, to which Black invariably replies 7...♘d7 supporting both the ...c6-c5 and the ...e6-e5 breaks.

The fashionable way for Black to handle this position is a kingside fianchetto with 7...♘d7 8 ♗d3 dxc4 (Black releases the central tension to facilitate his two breaks, but only after White has played his bishop to d3, so that it takes two moves to reach c4 instead of one) 9 ♗xc4 g6.

*see following diagram*

It may seem strange to play another pawn move to develop Black's dark-squared bishop when it has three posts available on the a3-f8 diagonal. However, on b4 it is vulnerable to attack, while on e7 it blocks the retreat of the queen and on d6 it is vulnerable to e3-e4 or perhaps ♘e4 (if Black plays ...d5xc4). On g7, the bishop is out of range of White's knight on c3, supports ...e6-e5, while it does not block the retreat of the black queen. However, apart from the time involved, the placement of the bishop on the a1-h8 diagonal further weakens the d6-square and slightly weakens the black kingside. Furthermore, after h2-h4-h5, Black will have to play ...g6-g5 as h5xg6 is an unpleasant threat.

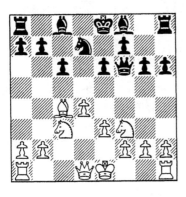

Having seen this position many times in tournament games, I have accepted it as normal play. However, looking at it afresh, I am struck by how strange and amateurish Black's position looks. If you were to just see this position without any knowledge of the opening, you might think that a beginner was handling the black pieces – why has Black made all these pawn moves instead of developing his pieces and why is the black queen on f6?

In fact, despite his seemingly eccentric opening, Black's position is fully

playable. White has no concrete targets to aim at since Black is developing only on his first three ranks, out of the range of White's pieces and pawns. Black reasons that if White opens up the position, then although it may cause him some danger, it will also be to the advantage of Black's two bishops. If White decides to build up carefully before opening the position, then this gives Black extra time to develop his pieces and prepare his position both to carry out his own breaks and to anticipate White's actions.

White has three basic approaches in this variation:

1) Central systems
2) Manoeuvring systems
3) Queenside systems

## Central systems

First we shall examine White's plans involving the natural central push e3-e4, starting with the immediate 10 0-0 ♗g7 11 e4.

> *Game 42*
> ### Khalifman-Akopian
> *Yerevan 1996*

**1 d4 d5 2 c4 c6 3 ♘c3 ♘f6 4 ♘f3 e6 5 ♗g5 h6 6 ♗xf6 ♕xf6 7 e3 ♘d7 8 ♗d3 dxc4**

Black usually elects to capture on c4 either here or on the next move, since after 8...g6 9 0-0 ♗g7?! he has to reckon with 10 e4 dxc4 11 e5! ♕e7 12 ♗xc4, when White has achieved his desired advance in the centre and Black is somewhat passively placed.

**9 ♗xc4 g6 10 0-0 ♗g7 11 e4 e5**

This is almost a reflex response to

e3-e4 in this variation.

**12 d5 ♘b6 13 ♗b3 ♗g4!**

Taking advantage of the fact that his queen stands on f6, Black creates a weakness in White's position to compensate for his own future weakness on c6. The careless 13...0-0 allows White to play 14 h3, preventing the awkward ...♗g4.

**14 h3 ♗xf3 15 ♕xf3 ♕xf3 16 gxf3 ♔e7 17 dxc6 bxc6**

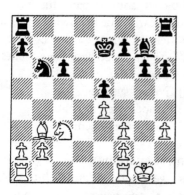

This ending is a touch better for White, since Black's weakness on c6 is more vulnerable than White's on f3, but it is eminently defensible for Black.

**18 ♖fc1 ♖hd8 19 ♘d1 ♖d6 20 ♖c3 a5 21 ♘e3 h5 22 ♖ac1 a4 23 ♗d1 ♔d7 24 ♔f1 ♗h6 25 ♔e1 ♔c7 26 ♗e2 ♔b7 27 ♖1c2 ♖a5 28 a3 ♗xe3 29 fxe3 f5 30 ♖c5 ♖xc5 31 ♖xc5 fxe4 32 fxe4 ♖e6 33 ♖a5 ♔c7 34 ♔d2 ♔d6 35 ♖a6 ♔c5 36 ♖a5+ ♔d6 37 ♖a6 ♔c5 38 ♖a5+ ½-½**

White's lack of success after 13 ♗b3 ♗g4! has led to various experiments with other moves. In the next game White meets 12...♘b6 with 13 ♘d2!? and in Game 44 with 13 dxc6 bxc6 14 ♗e2.

*Game 43*
**Piket-Kramnik**
*Linares 1997*

**1 d4 d5 2 c4 c6 3 ♘f3 ♘f6 4 ♘c3 e6 5 ♗g5 h6 6 ♗xf6 ♕xf6 7 e3 ♘d7 8 ♗d3 dxc4 9 ♗xc4 g6 10 0-0 ♗g7 11 e4 e5 12 d5 ♘b6 13 ♘d2!?**

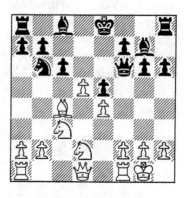

This offers an unusual position with two knights against two bishops. In general these positions are not very active for White: once he gets his desired set-up it is not easy to continue to make progress.

**13...0-0!?**

The immediate 13...♘xc4!? was also possible.

**14 a4!?**

14 ♗b3!?, preserving the bishop, might have been more prudent.

**14...♖d8 15 a5 ♘xc4 16 ♘xc4 ♕g5 17 ♕b3 ♗h3 18 ♘e3 ♖ab8 19 ♖ac1 ♗f8 20 ♔h1 ♗d7 21 ♘e2 cxd5 22 ♘xd5 ♗e6 23 ♖c7 ♖dc8 24 ♖xc8 ♖xc8 25 ♘ec3 ♖c7 26 h3 ♔g7 27 ♕b5 ♖d7 28 a6 bxa6 29 ♕xa6 ♗c5 30 ♕c6 ♗d4 31 ♘b5 ♕d8 32 ♘xd4 ♗xd5 33 ♕c5 ♕b6 34 ♕xb6 axb6 35 ♘f3 ♗xe4 36 ♘xe5 ♖d5 37 ♘c4**

b5 38 ♘b6 ♖d2 39 b4 ♗d3 40 ♖e1 ♖xf2 41 ♖e3 ♗b1 42 ♘c8 ♖b2 43 ♘d6 ♖xb4 44 ♖e7 ♗a2 45 ♖b7 ♖b1+ 46 ♔h2 b4 47 ♘e8+ ♔f8 48 ♘f6 h5 49 g4 h4 50 ♔g2 ♗e6 0-1

---

**Game 44**
**Lalic-Arduman**
*European Team Ch., Pula 1997*

---

1 d4 d5 2 c4 c6 3 ♘f3 ♘f6 4 ♘c3 e6 5 ♗g5 h6 6 ♗xf6 ♕xf6 7 e3 ♘d7 8 ♖c1 g6 9 ♗d3 dxc4 10 ♗xc4 ♗g7 11 e4

Although in this game White has played ♖c1 instead of 0-0, this makes no intrinsic difference to the position: the strategies for both sides are identical to the two previous games.
**11...e5 12 d5 ♘b6 13 dxc6 bxc6 14 ♗e2 0-0 15 0-0 ♖b8 16 ♕c2 ♗e6 17 b3 ♕e7 18 ♘b1**

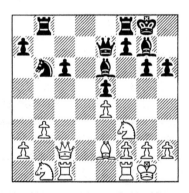

Freeing the c-file for White's major pieces and supporting the e4-pawn from d2.
**18...f5 19 ♘bd2 fxe4 20 ♘xe4 ♗d5 21 ♘fd2 h5 22 ♖cd1 ♖be8 23 ♗d3 h4 24 h3 ♖f4 25 ♖fe1 ♖ef8 26 f3 ♘d7 27 ♘f2 ♘c5 28 ♗c4 ♔h7 29 ♘de4 ♘xe4 30 ♘xe4 ♗xe4 31 ♖xe4**

♕c5+ 32 ♔h1 ♕e7 33 ♗d3 ♖8f6 34 ♖de1 ♖xe4 35 ♖xe4 ♖d6 36 ♖g4 1-0

In the next four games White prefaces e3-e4 with both 10 0-0 and 11 ♖c1. As we shall see, this should not be too dangerous for Black; usually he will meet still e3-e4 with ...e6-e5.

---

**Game 45**
**Ivanchuk-Kramnik**
*Novgorod 1996*

---

1 d4 d5 2 c4 c6 3 ♘c3 ♘f6 4 ♘f3 e6 5 ♗g5 h6 6 ♗xf6 ♕xf6 7 e3 ♘d7 8 ♗d3 dxc4 9 ♗xc4 g6 10 0-0 ♗g7

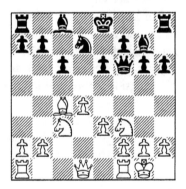

**11 ♖c1**
This is White's most non-committal move. After 11...0-0 he retains the option of playing in the centre (Games 45-48), manoeuvring with ♘e4 and ♗b3 (Game 50) or playing b2-b4 (Games 53-54).
**11...0-0 12 ♖e1 ♕e7**
A typical move, pulling the queen back to a 'holding position' on e7 where it supports either ...c6-c5 or ...e6-e5. However, as we shall see in Game 47, 12...♖d8 is more accurate.
**13 e4 ♖d8**
13...e5 is seen in the next game.

**14 e5!**

This accomplishes three tasks: it blocks the h8-a1 diagonal and thus reduces the activity of Black's dark-squared bishop on g7; it establishes an outpost on d6 for a white knight; and it deprives Black's knight of the defensive square f6 and therefore makes Black's kingside more vulnerable to h2-h4-h5.

The most important factor here is that White has protected e5 with the e1-rook, so that the undermining ...c6-c5 can be powerfully met by d4-d5!

**14...b6**

14...b5 frees b7 for the light-squared bishop with gain of tempo, but after 15 ♗d3 ♗b7 16 ♘e4! the rook on c1 combines with the knight on e4 to prevent ...c6-c5.

**15 ♕e2!**

White aims to meet 15...♗b7 with 16 ♗a6!, exchanging the light-squared bishops.

*Question 2:* Why is this good for White?

*Answer:* A future ...c6-c5 will open the a8-h1 diagonal and threaten ...♗xf3, destroying the major defender of White's centre and leaving it close

to collapse. By exchanging light-squared bishops, White reinforces his centre and maintains the advantages that this gives him.

**15...♖b8!?**

A clever move, intending to play ...♗b7 and meet ♗a6 with ...♗a8.

**16 ♗d3!**

White transfers the bishop to the long diagonal to make sure that he will exchange Black's light-squared bishop once the a8-h1 diagonal is opened.

**16...♗b7**

16...♕f8!? 17 h4 c5 18 d5 ♗b7!? 19 h5 exd5 20 hxg6 occurred in Dautov-Fridman, European Team Championship, Pula 1997, and now 20...f6!? 21 e6 (21 exf6 ♕xf6) 21...♘e5!? would have been interesting.

**17 ♗e4 ♘f8 18 g3 ♖bc8 19 a3 ♖c7 20 ♖ed1 c5 21 ♗xb7 ♖xb7 22 ♘e4 ♖c7**

22...♘d7 23 ♘d6 ♖bb8 24 ♕e4 cxd4 25 ♕xd4 ♘c5 26 ♕f4 was Black's best try according to Ivanchuk.

**23 dxc5 ♖xd1+ 24 ♖xd1 bxc5 25 h4 ♘d7 26 ♘d6 ♘b6 27 ♘d2 ♖d7 28 f4 ♖xd6 29 exd6 ♕xd6 30 ♘e4 ♕c6 31 ♖d8+ ♔h7 32 h5 ♕c7 33 hxg6+ fxg6 34 ♖d6 ♗d4+ 35 ♔h2 ♘d5 36 ♖xe6 ♕b7 37 ♕g4 ♘e7 38 ♘d6 ♕d7 39 ♕e2 ♘g8 40 ♕e4 ♗f6 1-0**

*Game 46*
**Piket-Novikov**
*Antwerp Open 1996*

**1 d4 d5 2 c4 e6 3 ♘f3 ♘f6 4 ♘c3 c6 5 ♗g5 h6 6 ♗xf6 ♕xf6 7 e3 ♘d7 8 ♗d3 g6 9 0-0 dxc4 10 ♗xc4 ♗g7**

Here we see a slightly different

move order to the previous game, but the resulting position is the same.

**11 ♖c1 0-0 12 ♖e1 ♕e7 13 e4 e5**

Preventing White from playing his desired e4-e5.

**14 d5 ♘b6 15 dxc6!?**

Piket suggests that 15 ♗b3! would have been slightly better for White here.

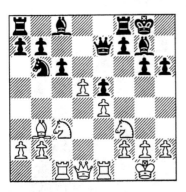

The insertion of the extra moves 11 ♖c1 0-0 12 ♖e1 ♕e7 has drawn the strength from ....♗g4 since White does not end up with doubled pawns after h2-h3. In this quiet position, Black's bishops are fairly ineffective since there are no raking diagonals on which they can be activated. The d5-pawn pressures Black's queenside and cramps his pieces, but Black does not want to capture on d5 since 15...cxd5 16 ♘xd5 ♘xd5 17 ♗xd5 ♗e6 18 ♗xe6 ♕xe6 19 ♕a4 gives White a nice pull due to his superior minor piece, while 16 exd5, threatening d5-d6, may also be dangerous.

**15...bxc6**

Piket shows that 15...♕c5 16 b3 bxc6 17 ♖xc4 ♕d6 18 ♖xc6 wins, as 18...♕xc6 loses to 19 ♘e7+!

**16 ♗b3 ♖d8 17 ♕c2 ♗d7?!**

17...♗g4! 18 ♘d2 h5!, to activate the dark-squared bishop with ....♗h6, would have been stronger according to Piket.

**18 h3!**

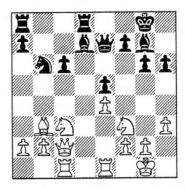

Piket assesses this position as slightly better for White. The cramping d5-pawn has gone, but Black has a weakness on c6 and his bishops don't seem to have any good squares.

*Question 3:* Is this position very bad for Black?

*Answer:* It isn't disastrous – Black is just slightly worse – but since Black cannot create active play that easily, it is much more fun for White to play.

**18...♗e8**

This is a typical plan. On e8 the bishop defends two weaknesses: f7 and c6.

**19 ♘a4! ♘xa4 20 ♗xa4 ♖ab8 21 ♖e3 ♕b4 22 b3 ♖bc8 23 ♖c3 ♖d6 24 ♕e2**

Piket suggests that the more dynamic 24 ♖c5 ♖e6 25 ♕c4! ♕xc4 26 ♖1xc4 f6 27 ♖a5 would have been better than the quiet text.

**24...♕b6 25 ♖c5 ♖e6 26 a3!? ♗f8?**

Black is tempted! Piket prefers 26...a5! 27 ♕d2 ♖a8, intending ....♗f8 at a later stage.

27 ♖xe5 ♗xa3 28 ♖xe6 fxe6 29 ♖c2 ♗f8 30 e5 ♖d8 31 ♕c4 ♖d5 32 ♕g4 ♗f7 33 ♖xc6 ♖d1+ 34 ♔h2 ♕xf2 35 ♖c8 ♕b6 36 ♕h4 ♕b7 37 ♖xf8+ ♔xf8 38 ♕xh6+ ♔e7 39 ♕h4+ ♔f8 40 ♘g5 ♗g8 41 ♕f4+ ♔g7 42 ♕f6+ ♔h6 43 ♗e8 ♕g7 44 ♘f7+ 1-0

How should Black counter the plan of ♖c1, ♖e1 and e3-e4 in this variation? The answer is to keep the black queen on f6 for as long as possible.

Game 47
**Timman-Gelfand**
*Yerevan Olympiad 1996*

1 d4 d5 2 c4 c6 3 ♘f3 ♘f6 4 ♘c3 e6 5 ♗g5 h6 6 ♗xf6 ♕xf6 7 e3 ♘d7 8 ♗d3 dxc4 9 ♗xc4 g6 10 0-0 ♗g7 11 ♖c1 0-0 12 ♖e1 ♖d8!

Black plays a useful move, pressuring d4 rather than retreating his queen. Now 13 e4 e5 14 d5 is met by the typical 14...♘b6 15 ♗b3 ♗g4! White could now try 16 ♖e3!?, preparing to play h2-h3 to drive the bishop back. Timman didn't fancy the risk and played:

13 ♕e2 ♕e7 14 ♘e4 a5 15 ♗b3 b6

16 ♘c3 ♗b7 ½-½

Game 48
**Van Wely-Dreev**
*Wijk aan Zee 1996*

1 d4 d5 2 c4 c6 3 ♘c3 ♘f6 4 ♘f3 e6 5 ♗g5 h6 6 ♗xf6 ♕xf6 7 e3 ♘d7 8 ♗d3 dxc4 9 ♗xc4 g6 10 0-0 ♗g7 11 ♖c1 0-0 12 ♕e2

This is rather slow.

**12...♕e7 13 ♖fd1 a6 14 a3 b6 15 e4 ♗b7**

Here Black doesn't need to play ...e6-e5 as he has everything ready for ...c6-c5 instead.

**16 e5 c5 17 d5**

Superficially this looks attractive, but it is difficult for White to find a follow-up. He cannot play d5-d6 as after ...♕d8, it is hard to meet ...♗xf3.

**17...b5 18 ♗a2 c4 19 ♗b1 exd5 20 ♘xd5 ♗xd5 21 ♖xd5 ♖fe8 22 ♖e1 ♖ad8 23 ♕d2 ♘xe5 24 ♘xe5 ♖xd5 25 ♕xd5 ♗xe5 26 ♔f1 ♕f6 27 a4 ♔g7 28 f3 bxa4 29 ♗a2 a3 30 bxa3 c3 31 ♗b3 ♖b8 32 ♖e3 ♗xh2 33 ♕c4 ♗e5 34 g3 ♗xg3 35 ♕xc3 ♕xc3 36 ♖xc3 ♗d6 37 ♗c4 ♖c8 38 a4 a5 39 ♖c2 ♔f6 40 ♗d3 ♖d8 41**

♖c6 ♔g5 42 ♗c4 f6 43 ♖a6 ♗b4 44 f4+ ♔xf4 45 ♖xf6+ ♔g5 46 ♖a6 h5 47 ♔e2 ♖e8+ 48 ♔d3 ♖e7 49 ♔d4 h4 50 ♗d3 ♖d7+ 51 ♔e3 ♖xd3+ 52 ♔xd3 h3 53 ♖a8 ♔g4 54 ♔e2 h2 55 ♖h8 ♔g3 56 ♔f1 ♗e7 0-1

### Game 49
### Ehlvest-Kharlov
*Novosibirsk 1995*

1 c4 c6 2 ♘f3 d5 3 d4 ♘f6 4 ♘c3 e6 5 ♗g5 h6 6 ♗xf6 ♕xf6 7 e3 ♘d7 8 ♗d3 dxc4 9 ♗xc4 g6 10 0-0 ♗g7 11 h3!?

I am surprised that this has not been tried more often. White calmly prepares to play e3-e4, but with the g4-square under control. In the game Black played along standard lines and did not enjoy himself, so perhaps he should adopt a different treatment.

**11...0-0 12 e4 e5**

Here 12...♕e7 makes sense, as 13 e5 is much less dangerous now that White has spent a tempo on h2-h3.

**13 d5 ♘b6 14 ♗b3!**

White reaches the desired formation.

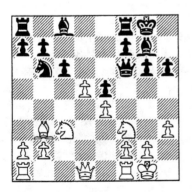

**14...♖d8 15 ♕e2 ♗f8 16 ♖ac1 ♗d7**

17 ♖fd1 ♗e8 18 a3 ♔g7 19 ♗a2 ♖ac8 20 ♕e3 c5 21 ♕e2 c4? 22 ♘d2 ♗c5 23 ♖f1 ♖c7 24 ♘xc4 ♘xc4 25 ♗xc4 ♖dc8 26 ♗b5 ♗xb5 27 ♕xb5 ♕f4 28 ♕e2 ♗d4 29 ♖c2 ♖c5 30 ♖d1 a6 31 ♖d3 h5 32 g3 ♕f6 33 h4 ♕d6 34 ♕f3 ♖8c7 35 ♔g2 ♖c4 36 ♕d1 b5 37 ♕f3 ♕c5 38 ♕d1 ♕d6 39 ♕f3 ♕c5 40 g4 hxg4 41 ♕xg4 ♕d6 42 ♕g3 b4 43 axb4 ♖xb4 44 ♖e2 ♖cc4 45 ♔f1 ♕b8 46 h5 ♖xb2 47 hxg6 fxg6 48 ♖xb2 ♕xb2 49 ♘e2 ♗xf2 50 ♔xf2 ♖xe4 51 ♖e3 ♕b6 52 ♘c3 ♖f4+ 53 ♔g2 ♕b4 54 ♕e1 ♖g4+ 55 ♔h3 ♕f4 56 ♘e4 ♕f5 57 ♔h2 g5 58 ♘g3 ♖h4+ 59 ♔g1 ♕c2 60 ♖e2 ♕c5+ 61 ♖f2 ♖f4 62 ♘h5+ 1-0

### Manoeuvring systems

The next three games deal with White trying to play solidly in the centre, avoiding any weakening pawn moves.

### Game 50
### Dautov-Dreev
*Reggio Emilia 1995*

1 d4 d5 2 c4 c6 3 ♘f3 ♘f6 4 ♘c3 e6 5 ♗g5 h6 6 ♗xf6 ♕xf6 7 e3 ♘d7 8 ♗d3 dxc4 9 ♗xc4 g6 10 0-0 ♗g7 11 ♖c1

In Games 51 and 52 White preferred to preface ♘e4 with 11 ♕c2 rather than 11 ♖c1.

**11...0-0 12 ♘e4 ♕e7 13 ♗b3!**

White aims to prevent Black both from developing his queenside with ...b7-b6 and ...♗b7, and from breaking out with ...c6-c5.

**13...♖d8 14 ♕c2 ♘f6 15 ♘c5 b6?**

This is a little careless.

16 ♘e5! ♖d6 17 ♘cd3 ♗b7 18 ♗a4 ♖c8 19 b4!

This is something close to the ideal for White as both Black's breaks have been prevented and he is attacking a black weakness on c6. However, Dreev defends well and manages to turn the game around.

19...♘d7 20 f4 ♘f6 21 ♗b3 ♖dd8 22 a3 ♘d5 23 ♕e2 ♗a6 24 ♗c4 ♗b7 25 e4 ♘f6 26 f5 ♖xd4 27 fxg6 fxg6 28 ♘xg6 ♕e8 29 ♘df4 ♖xe4 30 ♕a2 ♘d5 31 ♖ce1 ♖xe1 32 ♖xe1 ♕f7 33 ♖xe6 ♖e8 34 ♕e2 ♖xe6 35 ♕xe6 ♗d4+ 36 ♔h1 ♕xe6 37 ♘xe6 ♗f6 38 ♘gf4 ♘xf4 39 ♘xf4+ ♔f8 40 a4 ♔e7 41 ♔g1 ♗c3 42 ♘d3 c5 43 bxc5 bxc5 44 ♘f4 ♔d6 45 ♔f2 ♗c6 46 ♗b3 ♔e5 47 g3 ♔e4 48 ♘e6 ♗b4 49 ♔e2 ♗d7 50 h4 a5 51 ♗c2+ ♔e5 52 ♘f8 ♗g4+ 53 ♔e3 ♗e1 54 ♘g6+ ♔f6 55 ♘f4 ♗xg3 56 ♘d5+ ♔e6 57 ♗b3 ♗xh4 58 ♔f4 ♗h3 59 ♘e3+ ♔d7 60 ♘c4 ♗e1 0-1

1 d4 d5 2 c4 c6 3 ♘f3 ♘f6 4 ♘c3 e6 5 ♗g5 h6 6 ♗xf6 ♕xf6 7 e3 ♘d7 8 ♗d3 dxc4 9 ♗xc4 g6 10 0-0 ♗g7 11 ♘e4 ♕e7 12 ♕c2 0-0 13 ♗b3

White must be careful in these systems that he is ready to meet ...e6-e5 by d4-d5. Here this is not so and Black gets a comfortable game.

**13...e5!**

The somewhat passive 13...♖d8 is considered in the next game

**14 ♖fe1 ♔h8 15 ♘ed2 ♖e8 16 ♘c4 e4 17 ♘fe5 ♘xe5 18 dxe5?**

This is just bad, 18 ♘xe5 ♗xe5 19 dxe5 ♗f5 20 e6 ♗xe6 21 ♕xe4 would just have held the balance (Dreev).

**18...♗f5 19 ♖ad1 ♖f8 20 ♘d6 ♗xe5 21 ♘xf5 gxf5 22 ♖d2 ♖ad8 23 ♖ed1 ♔g7 24 ♕c4 ♖xd2 25 ♖xd2 ♖c8 26 a4 ♖c7 27 g3 a6 28 ♗d1 b5 29 ♕b3 ♕e6 30 ♕c2 c5 31 axb5 axb5 32 b3 c4 33 bxc4 bxc4 34 ♕a2 ♔f6 35 ♕a8 ♖c8 36 ♕a5 c3 37 ♖a2 h5 38 h4 ♕d6 39 ♕a6 ♖b8 40 ♕xd6+ ♗xd6 41 ♗c2 ♔e5 42 ♔f1 ♔d5 43 ♔e1 ♔c4 44 ♖a7 f6 45 ♖a6 ♖d8 46 ♖a1 ♗b4 47 ♖d1 ♖a8 48 ♖b1 ♖a3 49 ♔e2 ♖a6 50 ♔e1 ♖a3 51 ♔e2 ♖a7 52 ♔e1 ♔c5 53 ♔e2 ♖a2 54 ♔d1 ♔c4 55 ♔c1 ♗a3+ 56 ♔d1 ♗b4 57 ♔c1 ♖a5 58 ♗b3+ ♔d3 59

♗c2+ ♔c4 60 ♗b3+ ♔d3 61 ♗c2+ ♔e2 62 ♖xb4 ♔xf2 63 ♗d1 ♔xe3 64 ♔c2 ♔f2 65 ♗xh5 ♔xg3 66 ♗d1 e3 67 ♔xc3 f4 68 ♖b6 ♖d5 69 ♗e2 f3 70 ♗xf3 ♔xf3 71 ♖xf6+ ♔g2 72 ♖e6 ♔f2 73 ♖f6+ ♔e1 74 ♔c2 0-1

## Game 52
### Bareev-Dreev
*Wijk aan Zee (match) 1995*

1 d4 d5 2 c4 c6 3 ♘f3 ♘f6 4 ♘c3 e6 5 ♗g5 h6 6 ♗xf6 ♕xf6 7 e3 ♘d7 8 ♗d3 dxc4 9 ♗xc4 g6 10 0-0 ♗g7 11 ♕c2 0-0 12 ♘e4 ♕e7 13 ♗b3 ♖d8 14 ♖ad1

14 ♖ac1 would have transposed to Game 50.

14...a5 15 a3 ♖a6 16 ♖d2 ♘f6 17 ♘c5 ♖a7 18 ♘e5

Finally, Black can also consider the very solid option of developing his bishop to the solid square e8, and avoid weakening the queenside with ...b7-b6.

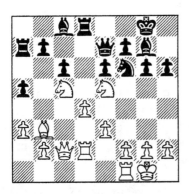

18...♗d7! 19 ♖fd1 ♗e8 20 ♘a4 ♖aa8 21 e4 ♕c7 22 ♘f3 ♖ac8 23 e5 ♘d7 24 ♖c1 c5 25 ♕e4 b6 26 g3 ♕b8 27 d5 ♘xe5 28 ♘xe5 ♕xe5 29 ♕xe5 ♗xe5 30 ♘xb6 ♖b8 31 ♘c4

♗d4 32 ♘xa5 exd5 33 ♗a2 ♖xb2 34 ♖xb2 ♗xb2 35 ♖xc5 d4 36 ♘c4 ♗c1 37 ♘e5 ♗xa3 38 ♖c7 ♔f8 39 ♘xf7 ♖a8 40 ♘xh6 ♗d6 41 ♖c2 d3 42 ♖d2 ♗b4 43 ♖xd3 ♖xa2 44 ♘g4 ♗c6 45 ♘e3 ♖e2 46 ♖d1 ♗c5 47 ♔f1 ♗f3 48 ♖e1 ♖a2 49 h4 ♔g7 50 ♖c1 ♗b6 51 ♖b1 ♗d4 52 ♖c1 ♔h6 53 ♖b1 ♗xe3 54 fxe3 ♖g2 0-1

### Queenside systems

In the next four games we consider ideas for White involving b2-b4. This move stops Black from playing ...c6-c5 and gives White the opportunity later to open up the queenside with b4-b5.

## Game 53
### Beliavsky-Dreev
*Novosibirsk 1995*

1 d4 d5 2 c4 c6 3 ♘f3 ♘f6 4 ♘c3 e6 5 ♗g5 h6 6 ♗xf6 ♕xf6 7 e3 ♘d7 8 ♗d3 dxc4 9 ♗xc4 g6 10 0-0 ♗g7 11 b4

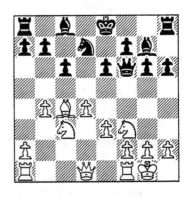

11...0-0 12 ♖c1 ♖d8

The immediate 12...e5 can be met by 13 ♗b3! exd4 14 exd4, when White enjoys better cental control.

13 ♕b3 ♕e7 14 a4

Perhaps this is premature. White can also consider 14 ♖fd1!?, reserving his options.

**14...a5!**

As soon as White plays a2-a4, Black strikes back with ...a7-a5 to grab some dark squares on the queenside.

**15 bxa5 ♖xa5 16 ♖fd1 b6!**

Black then develops his queenside by playing ...b7-b6 and ...♗b7 to prepare ...c6-c5.

**17 ♗e2**

The immediate 17 ♘d2 is considered in the next game.

**17...♗b7 18 ♘d2 c5 19 ♘c4 ♖aa8 20 d5 ♗xc3!**

This is a common idea: Black does not want White to recapture with a knight on d5 and so gives up his dark-squared bishop for the knight on c3.

**21 dxe6 ♕xe6 22 ♖d6 ♕e7 23 ♕xc3 ♗a6 24 ♖d2 ♗xc4 25 ♗xc4 ♘e5 26 ♖xd8+ ♖xd8 27 ♗f1 ♘g4 28 h3 ♘f6 29 ♕b2 ♘d5 30 ♕b5 ♕g5 31 a5 ♘xe3 32 axb6 ♘xf1 33 ♖xf1 ♖b8 34 ♖b1 ♕d5 35 b7 ♕d6 36 ♖e1 ♔f8 37 ♕b2 ♔g8 38 ♕b5 ♔f8 39 ♖b1 ♕c7 40 ♕b2 ♔g8 41 ♕b6 ♕xb6 42 ♖xb6 ♔f8 43 ♔f1 ♔e7 44 ♔e2 ♔d7 45 ♔d3 ♔c7 46 ♖f6 ♖f8 ½-½**

**Game 54**
**Nikolic-Kramnik**
*Yerevan Olympiad 1996*

1 d4 d5 2 c4 c6 3 ♘c3 ♘f6 4 ♘f3 e6 5 ♗g5 h6 6 ♗xf6 ♕xf6 7 e3 ♘d7 8 ♗d3 dxc4 9 ♗xc4 g6 10 0-0 ♗g7 11 ♖c1 0-0 12 b4 ♕e7 13 ♕b3 ♖d8 14 a4 a5! 15 bxa5 ♖xa5 16 ♖fd1 b6 17 ♘d2 c5 18 d5 ♗xc3!

The other advantage of removing the knight on c3 is that it makes it harder for White to maintain his pawn on d5.

**19 ♖xc3 ♘f6 20 dxe6 ♗xe6 21 ♖cc1 ♖a7 22 ♗xe6 ♕xe6 ½-½**

White has sought to improve upon these positions by playing a2-a3 and b2-b4 before ♗d3, reasoning that if Black plays ...d5xc4, then White will be able to recapture on c4 in one move, gaining a tempo.

**Game 55**
**Piket-Dreev**
*Wijk aan Zee 1996*

1 d4 d5 2 c4 c6 3 ♘c3 ♘f6 4 ♘f3 e6 5 ♗g5 h6 6 ♗xf6 ♕xf6 7 e3 ♘d7

**8 a3 g6 9 b4 ♗g7**

Black waits for White to commit his bishop before taking on c4.

**10 cxd5 exd5**

White's aim is to provoke this recapture. Although the c8-h3 diagonal is now opened for the light-squared bishop, Black's ...e6-e5 recapture is taken away and this makes it harder for Black to activate his bishop on g7. White has the simple plan of the minority attack whereby White will isolate Black's c-pawn and leave it backward on the half-open c-file by playing b4-b5xc6. These positions are not objectively in White's favour, but since they restrict Black's activity, they are perhaps easier for White to play.

Now we can understand why White doesn't play c4xd5 earlier: 9 cxd5 exd5 10 b4 is met by 10...♗d6!, as in Van Wely-M.Gurevich, Germany 1996, when 11 ♗d3 ♕e7 12 0-0 ♘f6 allowed Black his ideal set-up in these positions.

For 10...cxd5! see the next game.

**11 ♗d3 0-0 12 0-0 ♘b6! 13 ♕b3 ♕d6! 14 ♖fc1 ♗e6 15 ♘d2 ♖fb8 16 ♖ab1 a5!**

This strike opens up the white queenside a little and gives Black active play on the dark squares.

**17 bxa5 ♘d7 18 a4 ♖xa5 19 ♕c2 ♖a7 20 ♘e2 ♘f8 21 h3 ♗c8 22 ♘c3 ♘e6 23 ♔h1 ♗d7 24 ♖b6 ♕c7 25 ♖cb1 ♖a5 26 f4 ♘c5!! 27 dxc5 ♖xc5 28 ♖6b3 b5 29 axb5 cxb5 30 ♘xd5 ♖xc2 31 ♘xc7 ♖xd2 32 ♗xb5 ♗f5 33 ♗c6 ♖xb3 34 ♖xb3 ♖c2 35 ♘d5 ♔h7 36 ♘b4 ♖c1+ 37 ♔h2 ♗f8 38 ♗d5 ♖c5 39 ♗xf7 ♔g7 40 ♗e8 ♖c2??**

A terrible blunder: 40...♖c8 would have held the draw.

**41 ♘xc2 1-0**

> ### Game 56
> ### Van Wely-Gelfand
> *Tilburg 1996*

**1 d4 d5 2 c4 c6 3 ♘c3 ♘f6 4 ♘f3 e6 5 ♗g5 h6 6 ♗xf6 ♕xf6 7 e3 ♘d7 8 a3 g6 9 b4 ♗g7 10 cxd5 cxd5!**

This is an even safer way for Black to play. By keeping the pawn structure fairly symmetrical, Black restricts his opponent's active chances.

**11 ♗d3 0-0 12 0-0 ♕e7 13 ♕b3**

White's only superiority is a tempo advantage on the queenside: he has advanced his pawns to a3 and b4, while Black's pawns are on a7 and b7.

**13...♘b6 14 a4 ♗d7 15 ♘d2 ♘c8 16 ♖fc1 ♘d6!**

The knight is well-placed on d6, eyeing c4 while defending b7.

**17 b5 ♖fc8 18 a5 ♕d8 19 ♕b2 e5 20 ♘b3 exd4 21 ♘xd4 ♘c4 22 ♗xc4 dxc4 23 ♕e2 a6 24 b6 ♗c6 25 ♖d1 ♕e7 26 ♕d2 ♗e4 27 ♖ac1 ♖c5 28 ♘a4 ♗xd4 29 exd4 ♖g5 30 g3 ♗f3 31 ♖e1 ♕d7 ½-½**

## Summary

The central lines considered in Games 41-49 offer White quite good chances of a small structural edge in positions where e3-e4 ...e6-e5, d4-d5 and then d5xc6 occurs. White can also play in manoeuvring style (Games 50-52) but he must be careful that he does not allow a quick ...e6-e5 by Black; 11 ♖c1 0-0 12 ♘e4 ♕e7 13 ♗b3 (Game 50) seems the best try. If White plays on the queenside with 11 ♖c1 0-0 12 b4, then Black should be fine as long as he adopts the ...a7-a5 plan of Games 53-54. 8 a3 (Games 55-56) does not seem dangerous with careful play.

**1 d4 d5 2 c4 c6 3 ♘f3 ♘f6 4 ♘c3 e6 5 ♗g5 h6 6 ♗xf6 ♕xf6 7 e3 7...♘d7 8 ♗d3**

> 8 a3 g6 9 b4 ♗g7 10 cxd5
>> 10...exd5 – *Game 55*; 10...cxd5 – *Game 56*

**8...dxc4 9 ♗xc4 g6 10 0-0**

> 10 ♖c1 – *Game 44*

**10...♗g7 11 e4**

> 11 ♖c1 0-0 *(D)*
>> 12 ♖c1
>>> 12...♕e7 (12...♖d8 – *Game 47*) 13 e4
>>>> 13...♖d8 – *Game 45*; 13...e5 – *Game 46*
>>> 12 ♕e2 – *Game 48*; 12 ♘e4 – *Game 50*
>> 11 h3 – *Game 49*
> 11 ♘e4 ♕e7 12 ♕c2 0-0 13 ♗b3 *(D)*
>> 13...♖d8 (13...e5 – *Game 51*)
>>> 14 ♖ad1 – *Game 52*; 14 ♖c1 – *Game 50* (by transposition)
> 11 b4 0-0 12 ♖c1 ♖d8 13 ♕b3 ♕e7 14 a4 a5! 15 bxa5 ♖xa5 16 ♖fd1 b6
>> 17 ♗e2 – *Game 53*; 17 ♘d2 – *Game 54*

**11...e5 12 d5 ♘b6 *(D)* 13 ♗b3**

> 13 ♘d2 – *Game 43*

**13...♗g4 – *Game 42***

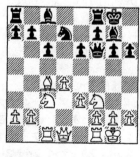

*11...0-0*

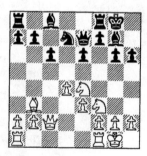

*13 ♗b3*

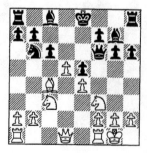

*12...♘b6*

# CHAPTER SIX

## Moscow Variation: White's 6th and 7th Move Alternatives

1 d4 d5 2 c4 c6 3 ♘f3 ♘f6 4 ♘c3 e6 5 ♗g5 h6

In this chapter we consider ways in which White can avoid the main line of the Moscow variation, either by playing for an early e2-e4 after 6 ♗xf6 ♕xf6 (Games 57 and 58), fianchettoing (Game 59) or by gambitting the c-pawn with 6 ♗h4 (Game 60).

### Game 57
### Timman-Gelfand
### Belgrade 1995

1 d4 d5 2 c4 c6 3 ♘c3 ♘f6 4 ♘f3 e6 5 ♗g5 h6 6 ♗xf6 ♕xf6 7 ♕b3

With this move White protects c4 and covers the b4-square in order to allow a quick e2-e4 without a disruptive check on b4.

The immediate 7 e4 dxe4 8 ♘xe4 does not pose any problems due to 8...♗b4+ 9 ♔e2 ♕f4 10 ♕c2 ♗e7. In Lautier-Kramnik, Paris (rapidplay) 1995, White now suffered from an attack of misguided inspiration with 11 ♘e5?!, a pawn sacrifice which pro-

vided little compensation after 11...f5! 12 ♘d2 (12 ♘g6 ♕g4+!) 12...♕xd4 13 ♘df3 ♕xc5 14 ♘g6 ♖g8 15 ♘xe7 ♕xe7 16 g3 e5!

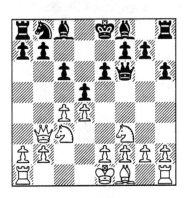

7...dxc4!? 8 ♕xc4 ♘d7 9 g3

9 e4 is also met by simply 9...e5!

9...e5! 10 0-0-0 ♗e7 11 ♘e4 ♕f5 12 ♕c2 0-0 13 h4

13 ♔b1 was seen in Korchnoi-Dreev, Yalta 1995, when 13...♘f6! equalises at once (Timman).

13...exd4 14 ♘xd4 ♕a5 15 ♔b1 ♘f6 16 e3 ♘d5 17 a3 ♗g4!

This equalises and now Black builds up a slight initiative.

18 ♗e2 ♗xe2 19 ♘xe2 ♘f6 20 ♘d2 ♖fd8 21 ♘d4 ♗f8 22 ♖hg1 ♘g4 23 ♘c4 ♕c5 24 ♘b3 ♕e7 25 e4 ♕e6 26 f3 ♖xd1+ 27 ♖xd1 b5 28 ♘d4 ♕xc4 29 ♕xc4 bxc4 30 fxg4 c3 31 bxc3 ♗xa3 32 ♘xc6 ♖c8 33 ♘e5 f6 34 ♘g6 ♖xc3 35 h5 ♖xg3 36 ♖d8+ ♔f7 37 ♖d7+ ♔g8 38 ♖xa7 ♗c5 39 ♖c7 ♗d6 40 ♖d7 ♗b4 41 ♖b7 ½-½

## Game 58
### Atalik-Bacrot
### *Wijk aan Zee B 1997*

1 d4 d5 2 c4 c6 3 ♘f3 ♘f6 4 ♘c3 e6 5 ♗g5 h6 6 ♗xf6 ♕xf6 7 ♕c2!?

White again supports a quick e2-e4. Now 7...dxc4 8 e3 b5 9 a4!? is quite risky for Black.

7...♘d7 8 e4 dxe4 9 ♕xe4 g6 10 ♗d3 ♗g7 11 0-0 0-0 12 ♖fe1 c5 13 d5 ♘b6 14 d6 ♕d8!

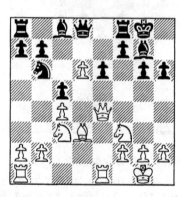

15 ♕f4 ♗d7! 16 ♖ad1 ♗c6!

This plan really hits the spot! Black intends ...♘d7, solidly blocking the white d-pawn and preventing ♘e5.

17 ♗e4? ♘xc4 18 ♗xc6 ♘xb2 19 ♗xb7 ♖b8

It is always a horrid moment when you realise that too many of your pieces are hanging!

20 ♘e5 ♘xd1 21 ♘c6 ♕b6 22 ♖xd1 ♖xb7 23 ♘e7+ ♔h7 24 ♘e4 f5 25 ♘g5+ hxg5 26 ♕xg5 ♖xe7 27 dxe7 ♖e8 28 h4 ♕c7 29 h5 ♕xe7 30 ♕xg6+ ♔h8 31 ♖d3 0-1

## Game 59
### Petursson-Dreev
### *Yerevan Olympiad 1996*

1 c4 c6 2 ♘f3 d5 3 d4 ♘f6 4 ♘c3 e6 5 ♗g5 h6 6 ♗xf6 ♕xf6 7 g3

7...♘d7 8 ♗g2 dxc4 9 0-0 ♗e7 10 ♘e4 ♕f5! 11 ♘ed2 e5!

This plan of taking on c4 and playing ...e6-e5 seems very effective here.
12 ♘xc4

12 e4 was played in Komarov-Renet, France 1996, but after 12...♕e6 13 ♕e2 b5 14 a4 and now 14...0-0 15 d5 ♕d6 16 dxc6 ♕xc6 17 axb5 ♕xb5 18 ♘xc4 Black would have equalised quite easily according to Komarov.
12...exd4 13 ♘xd4 ♕f6 14 e3

Komarov suggests the more aggressive 14 e4, intending f2-f4 and e4-e5.
14...0-0 15 ♕h5 ♘b6 16 ♘d2 ♕g5 17 ♕d1 ♗g4 18 ♕c2 ♖ad8 19 ♖ac1 ♖fe8 20 a3 ♕h5 21 ♘e4 ♗h3 22

♗f3 ♗g4 23 ♗g2 ♗h3 24 ♗f3 ½-½

**1 d4 d5 2 c4 c6 3 ♘f3 ♘f6 4 ♘c3 e6 5 ♗g5 h6 6 ♗h4 dxc4 7 e4 g5 8 ♗g3 b5**

Frustrated by the Black's solidity in the 6 ♗xf6 lines, White players have recently turned back to this venerable gambit, the only way for him to obtain sharp play against 5...h6.

As compensation for the pawn, White has a strong pawn centre and chances against the enemy king (Black's ...g7-g5 has weakened f6 and makes kingside castling a fraught affair). If Black develops his dark-squared bishop to g7, then the d6-square is extremely weak.

**9 ♗e2 ♗b7**

9...b4 is rather loosening but breaks up the white centre: 10 ♘a4 ♘xe4 11 ♗xc4!? (11 ♗e5 ♘f6 12 ♗xc4 ♘bd7 13 0-0 ♗g7 14 ♕e2 ♘b6 15 ♗b3 0-0 16 ♘c5 gave White good compensation in Relange-Giorgadze, Ubeda Open 1997) 11...♘xg3 12 hxg3 ♘d7 13 0-0 ♗g7 14 ♖e1 0-0 15 ♖c1, and now Korchnoi's 15...♘b6! would have equalised in Korchnoi-Timman, Wijk aan Zee 1997.

**10 0-0 ♘bd7 11 a4!?**

Also possible is 11 d5 cxd5 12 exd5 ♘xd5 13 ♘xb5, opening the centre.

**11...b4**

Mikhail Gurevich preferred 11...a6, keeping the queenside solid, and asking White to make further efforts to find some compensation, against Sher-

bakov in Niksic 1996. Sherbakov suggests 12 axb5 cxb5 13 d5 ♘c5 14 ♘d4.

**12 e5! ♘h5**

12...bxc3 13 exf6 cxb2 14 ♖b1 c3 15 ♕b3 with an edge (Gelfand).

**13 ♘e4 c5 14 ♘fd2 ♘xg3 15 fxg3 ♗e7!**

15...cxd4 16 ♗h5! ♘xe5 17 ♘xc4! ♘xc4 18 ♖xf7 wins for White! This shows how White can strike seemingly from nowhere in this line.

**16 ♘d6+ ♗xd6 17 exd6 c3 18 bxc3 bxc3 19 ♘c4 0-0 20 ♖c1 f5 21 dxc5 ♖c8 22 ♗f3?**

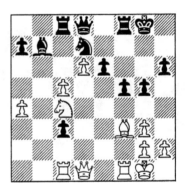

Missing Black's next. 22 ♖xc3 ♖xc5 was unclear according to Gelfand.

**22...♗a6 23 c6 ♗xc4 24 c7 ♕f6 25 ♖e1 ♘c5 26 ♖e3 ♘e4 27 h3 ♗d5 28 ♗xe4 fxe4 29 ♖exc3 ♖f7 30 ♔h2 ♕e5 31 ♖c6 e3 32 ♕e2 ♗xc6 33 ♖xc6 ♕d5 34 ♕a6 ♖ff8 35 ♖c3 ♔g7 36 ♖d3 ♕e4 37 ♕xc8 ♖xc8 38 d7 ♖xc7 39 d8♕ ♖f7 40 ♕d4+ ♕xd4 41 ♖xd4 ♖b7 42 ♖e4 ♔f6 43 ♖xe3 ♖b4 44 ♖f3+ ♔e7 45 ♖c3 ♖xa4 46 ♖c7+ ♔d6 47 ♖h7 a5 48 ♖xh6 ♖c4 49 ♖h8 a4 50 h4 g4 51 h5 ♔e7 52 h6 ♔f7 53 ♖e8 ♖c5 54 ♖a8 ♖h5+ 55 ♔g1 ♖xh6 56 ♖xa4 ♖g6 57 ♔f2 ♔g7 58 ♔f1 ½-½**

## Summary

It seems that Black has few problems in the offbeat lines after 6 ♗xf6. Only Yermolinsky's 7 ♕c2 looks like it is worth further analysis. However, if you like gambits and fancy having a go at Black's position, then the 6 ♗h4 line may be for you, as it drags Black out of the solidity of the main line Moscow lines.

**1 d4 d5 2 c4 c6 3 ♘f3 ♘f6 4 ♘c3 e6 5 ♗g5 h6** *(D)*

**6 ♗xf6**
   6 ♗h4 – *Game 60*
**6...♕xf6** *(D)* **7 ♕b3** *(D)*
      7 ♕c2 – *Game 58*
      7 g3 – *Game 59*
**7...dxc4** – *Game 57*

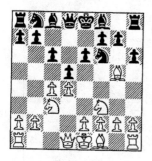
5...h6

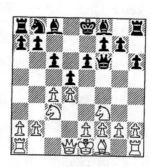
6...♕xf6

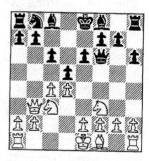
7 ♕b3

# CHAPTER SEVEN

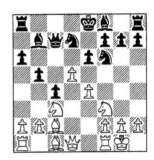

## Meran Variation: Main Line

1 d4 d5 2 c4 c6 3 ♘f3 ♘f6 4 ♘c3 e6 5 e3 ♘bd7 6 ♗d3 dxc4 7 ♗xc4 b5 8 ♗d3 ♗b7 9 0-0 a6 10 e4 c5 11 d5 c4 12 ♗c2 ♕c7

In recent times this has become the crucial position in the Meran system and a major battleground in the Semi-Slav as a whole. First we need to get our bearings – a lot of things have happened in just 12 moves!

With

**5 e3**

White takes a more relaxed approach to Black's fourth move than with 5 ♗g5. 5 e3 neutralises Black's threat of ...d5xc4 by protecting c4 with his light-squared bishop. In so doing, he prepares to complete his kingside development with ♗d3 and castle his king to safety on the kingside. Furthermore, White will soon be in a position to play e3-e4.

*Question 1:* Sounds great! What's the catch?

*Answer:* Unfortunately it also blocks White's dark-squared bishop inside the pawn chain which obvi-ously reduces the activity of his own position (although Black's own light-squared bishop has the same problem).

After 5 e3 Black usually plays

**5...♘bd7**

Now White's main move is

**6 ♗d3**

threatening the e3-e4 push. This will gain space in the centre and open the c1-h6 diagonal for the dark-squared bishop, thus solving the only drawback to the white set-up: the bishop on c1.

This is a crucial situation for Black. White has developed his pieces smoothly and is on the verge of playing e3-e4. Invariably Black now plays

**6...dxc4 7 ♗xc4 b5**

*Question 2:* What's the point?

*Answer:* This marks the beginning of Black's plan to deal with his blocked-in bishop on c8. With ...d5xc4, Black removes one of his pawns from the a8-h1 diagonal, and allows Black to follow up with ...b7-b5, freeing the b7-square for the light-squared bishop. All Black has to do after ...♗b7 is play ...c6-c5 and the bishop will be free!

Now after

**8 ♗d3**

returning to support the push e3-e4, Black usually puts his bishop to its best square with

**8...♗b7**

and after

**9 0-0**

Black can protect the pawn on b5 with

**9...a6**

Black is now ready to break against the white centre with ...c6-c5, attacking the d4-pawn and opening the a8-h1 diagonal for the light-squared bishop. White must therefore take the centre with

**10 e4 c5 11 d5**

This move has a nice logic to it: now that Black's light-squared bishop has finally found a good post on b7, White sets up a central pawn wedge on e4 and d5 to block the diagonal!

*Question 3:* Doesn't White just lose a pawn after 11...exd5?

*Answer:* By taking on d5, Black opens the e-file. With his king on e8 and no immediate chance of castling,

11...exd5 is a huge risk. After 12 exd5 ♘xd5 13 ♖e1+ ♗e7 14 ♕e2! Black cannot castle due to 15 ♘xd5 ♗xd5 16 ♕xe7 winning a piece.

Since 11...exd5 is too dangerous, Black usually plays

**11...c4 12 ♗c2 ♕c7**

reaching the starting position of this chapter.

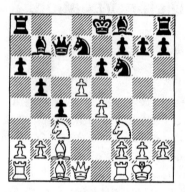

*Question 4:* Why does Black need to play 12...♕c7 here?

*Answer:* White's attacking plan is to play d5xe6 ...f7xe6, and then e4-e5! 12...♕c7 anticipates this thrust by protecting the e5-square.

The critical position after 12...♕c7 has developed very logically from the plan that Black selected on his sixth move. By exchanging his d-pawn for White's c-pawn, Black simultaneously obtained a queenside pawn majority and removed the barrier to its expansion – the white pawn on c4. However, the price of this queenside initiative was a loss of central influence. By relinquishing his pawn attack on e4, Black freed White to play e3-e4. A similar conflict was evident after 10...c5: although this move gained queenside space, it also loosened

Black's grip on the d5-square, allowing White to increase his central territory with 11 d5.

After 12...♛c7 Black's queenside pawns on a6, b5 and c4 restrict White's light-squared bishop on c2, which is White's problem piece in this line. These queenside pawns are also extremely hard to dislodge – for example, 13 b3 loses a piece to 13...cxb3, while 13 a4 b4 does not help White's cause either. Once Black has completed his development and put his king to safety, he will use his queenside initiative to cripple White's centre, chasing the white knight from c3 with ...b5-b4 and thus weakening White's support of e4 and d5. White must act in the centre while Black's king is uncastled and his lead in development can make a difference.

The first two of White's major plans in this position are introduced by playing 13 dxe6 fxe6.

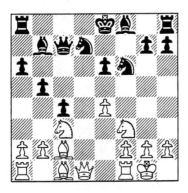

The exchange on e6 is a double-edged decision, as it increases the potential activity of Black's pieces. Black's light-squared bishop has one less pawn to bite against on the a8-h1 diagonal and the d- and f-files are opened for Black's rooks. The d-file is particularly valuable, since with the help of a rook on d8 Black can establish a knight on the strong d3-outpost provided by the pawn on c4.

The strength of d5xe6 is that by creating an isolated pawn on e6, White loosens the protection afforded to the black king. This gives him the chance to cause Black some discomfort by attacking e6 with ♘g5 or ♘d4, and also furnishes him with the dangerous idea of e4-e5, attacking the knight on f6. If Black captures this pawn on e5, this will allow the white major pieces to directly attack the e6-pawn in front of the black king. On the other hand, if Black moves his knight, then Black's kingside becomes vulnerable. The white bishop on c2 attacks g6 and h7 along the newly-opened b1-h7 diagonal, while the white queen can now check the black king from h5.

Incidentally, 11 d5 does rather 'wrong foot' Black, since an irony of these lines is that Black would almost rather have his bishop back on c8, defending the weak pawn on e6!

We shall now (finally!) examine the specific ways in which White has sought to attack the black position.

The first four games in this chapter deal with 13 dxe6 fxe6 14 ♘d4, while 13 dxe6 fxe6 14 ♘g5 is considered in Games 65-69. Finally, the immediate 13 ♘d4 is seen in Games 70-73.

*Game 61*
**Lautier-Gelfand**
*Amsterdam 1996*

**1 d4 d5 2 c4 c6 3 ♘f3 ♘f6 4 ♘c3**

e6 5 e3 ♘bd7 6 ♗d3 dxc4 7 ♗xc4
b5 8 ♗d3 ♗b7 9 0-0 a6 10 e4 c5 11
d5 c4 12 ♗c2 ♕c7 13 dxe6 fxe6 14
♘d4

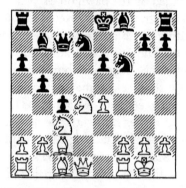

It took White players a long time to realise the full strength of the knight on d4. Obviously, it inconveniences Black by attacking e6 and frees the white f-pawn to move to f4, supporting e4-e5, but that is also true of 14 ♘g5, the old main line. But 14 ♘d4 has two advantages over 14 ♘g5. First, the white knight on d4 combines with the knight on c3 against Black's b5-pawn, offering the possibility of a knight sacrifice on b5 if Black ever castles queenside. Second, after 14 ♘g5, White's knight is easily removed by ...h7-h6; but this is not so easy after 14 ♘d4.

Note that after 14 ♕e2 Black can play 14...♗d6, preparing to castle kingside and ready to meet either 15 ♘g5 or 15 ♘d4 with 15...♘c5.

**14...♘c5**

The best way to defend the e6-pawn. 14...♘c5 brings the knight in contact with the outpost on d3 and frees the d-file so that Black can bring a rook to d8 to bear on the d4-knight.

**15 ♗e3!**

This move completes White's set-up by supporting the knight on d4. After Black brings a rook to d8, White can move his queen to e2 or f3, sidestepping the pin along the d-file. Black will then be vulnerable to b2-b4, attacking the knight on c5, the sole protector of the e6-pawn. Sooner or later, Black will have to force the knight from d4 and the only way to do so is via the committal ...e6-e5.

*Question 5:* But ...e6-e5 just looks good to me.

*Answer:* This move does indeed have many positive points: Black chases the white knight from d4 and prevents the push e4-e5 by occupying the e5-square with a pawn himself; removes the barrier on the d-file, thereby making it possible to support a knight on the d3-outpost with a rook on d8; and creates a strong outpost on d4 which the black knight on c5 can reach via e6. The negative side to ...e6-e5 is that it weakens the light squares, particularly f5 and d5. After ...e6-e5, White can also envisage a2-a4 (softening up the black queenside) ...b5-b4, ♘d5 – even as a pawn sacrifice. After Black captures on d5, White can recapture with e4xd5, activating White's light-squared bishop by opening the b1-h7 diagonal and opening up the e-file for his major pieces.

**15...0-0-0**

Black gets his king out of the centre and his rook to the d-file in one move, and threatens to win a piece with ...e6-e5 due to the pin on the d4-knight. The drawback is that the black king is not safe on the queenside. As we shall see, Black can be a pawn up with no immediate threats against him, but because his king is exposed, White always seems to have good chances. The immediate 15...e5 is dealt with in Game 64.

**16 ♕e2 e5 17 ♘f3!**

This is the key to White's whole concept. The first strength of 17 ♘f3 is its calmness: White shows that he understands that the black king on c8 is a long-term problem and will not run away. Second, the knight is well-placed on f3, where it ties the black queen on c7 to the defence of the e5-pawn, combines well with White's idea of ♘d5 – since it leaves the b1-h7 diagonal free for the bishop on c2 – and is free to jump to g5, attacking the e6-square.

**17...♘cxe4?**

A bad decision. Although Black wins a pawn, he does nothing to contribute to his own activity. 15...0-0-0 was an active move and Black needs to continue in the same vein. With 17...♘cxe4, Black is accepting a very meagre price for his gamble of placing the king in a vulnerable position. The improvement 17...♘e6 is considered in Games 62 and 63.

**18 ♘xe4 ♘xe4 19 a4! ♘c5 20 axb5 axb5 21 b3!**

Very simple and very effective – White just opens lines on the queenside and lets Black do the worrying!

**21...cxb3 22 ♗f5+ ♔b8 23 ♕xb5 g6 24 ♗h3 ♖d5 25 ♖fb1! ♕c6 26 ♕c4 ♗e7 27 ♘d2! ♖hd8 28 ♘xb3 ♕a4?!?**

A fantastic saving attempt that Gelfand found with only a couple of minutes left on his clock, but unfor-

tunately it is insufficient.

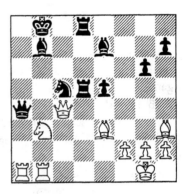

**29 ♘xc5! ♖d1+ 30 ♖xd1 ♖xd1+**

30...♕xc4 loses to 31 ♖xd8+ ♗xd8 32 ♘d7+ ♔c7 33 ♖c1 picking up the queen, according to Lautier.

**31 ♖xd1 ♕xc4 32 ♘d7+ 1-0**

32...♔c7 33 ♖c1 wins.

---

## Game 62
### Gelfand-Akopian
*Yerevan Olympiad 1996*

---

**1 d4 d5 2 c4 c6 3 ♘c3 ♘f6 4 e3 e6 5 ♘f3 ♘bd7 6 ♗d3 dxc4 7 ♗xc4 b5 8 ♗d3 ♗b7 9 0-0 a6 10 e4 c5 11 d5 c4 12 ♗c2 ♕c7 13 dxe6 fxe6 14 ♘d4 ♘c5 15 ♗e3! 0-0-0 16 ♕e2 e5 17 ♘f3! ♘e6**

Gelfand was obviously impressed with the previous game since he soon decided to give it an outing from the other side of the board! Black's 17th move is a definite improvement, as White must react to the threat of ...♘d4.

**18 ♖ad1!?**

Since White is planning to attack on the queenside, it would seem more natural to keep the rook on a1 and play the rook on f1 to the d-file.

However, Gelfand intends to first soften up the queenside with a2-a4 ...b5-b4, and then play ♘d5. In this case, the a-file will remain closed, so there is no point in keeping a rook on a1. The sacrificial 18 ♘d5 is the subject of the next game.

**18...♗d6 19 a4! ♘d4**

19...b4 20 ♘d5 ♘xd5 21 exd5 is clearly better for White, according to Gelfand.

**20 ♗xd4! exd4 21 ♘xd4**

This unstereotyped capture on d4 has given Black enormous problems: the b5-pawn is attacked and the fork ♘e6 is threatened.

**21...♗xh2+ 22 ♔h1 ♕f4 23 g3 ♗xg3 24 fxg3 ♕xg3 25 ♘f5 ♕e5 26 ♕h2 ♕xh2+ 27 ♔xh2 ♔b8 28 axb5**

White has a clear advantage, but from here onwards he begins to let things slip and this, together with a sterling defensive performance from Akopian, contributes towards a drawn result.

**28...axb5 29 ♘xb5 ♘xe4 30 ♖xd8+ ♖xd8 31 ♘fd4 ♘d6 32 ♘c3 ♖e8 33 ♖f2 h5 34 ♖e2 ♖xe2+ 35 ♘dxe2 g5 36 ♘d4 h4 37 ♗d1 ♘f7 38 ♘f5 ♘e5 39 ♘e3 ♗c8 40 ♗e2 ♗e6 41 ♘e4**

g4 42 ♘c5 g3+ 43 ♔g1 ♗g8 44 ♘f5 ♔c7 45 ♘xh4 ♔b6 46 ♘a4+ ♔a5 47 ♘c3 ♔b4 48 ♘f5 ♔b3 49 ♘d1 ♘c6 50 ♔g2 ♗e6 51 ♘fe3 ♘d4 52 ♗h5 c3 53 bxc3 ♘b5 54 c4 ♗xc4 55 ♔xg3 ♘c3 56 ♘f2 ♘d5 57 ♘f5 ♘f6 58 ♗d1+ ♔b4 59 ♘e3 ♔c5 60 ♗c2 ♔d4 61 ♔f3 ♗d5+ 62 ♔e2 ♗c4+ 63 ♔d2 ♗e6 64 ♗g6 ♘d5 65 ♘c2+ ♔e5 66 ♘d3+ ♔f6 67 ♗e4 ♘e7 ½-½

The next game shows a crazy alternative path for White. I really don't feel that it is necessary to play like this, but it made for a great game!

1 d4 d5 2 c4 c6 3 ♘c3 ♘f6 4 e3 e6 5 ♘f3 ♘bd7 6 ♗d3 dxc4 7 ♗xc4 b5 8 ♗d3 ♗b7 9 0-0 a6 10 e4 c5 11 d5 c4 12 ♗c2 ♕c7 13 dxe6 fxe6 14 ♘d4 ♘c5 15 ♗e3 0-0-0 16 ♕e2 e5 17 ♘f3 ♘e6 18 ♘d5!?

Thematic.

**18...♘xd5 19 exd5 ♗xd5 20 a4! b4 21 ♖ad1 g6**

Stopping the bishop on c2 from activating itself via f5.

**22 ♖xd5!?**

A typical exchange sacrifice, freeing a myriad of light squares for White's own light-squared bishop and depriving Black of a crucial defensive piece.

**22...♖xd5 23 ♗e4 ♖d8 24 ♖c1 ♔b8 25 g3 ♗c5?**

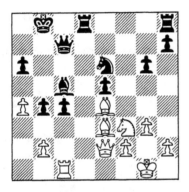

A mistake according to Krasenkov who prefers 25...♖c8 26 ♗d5 ♕d6 27 ♗xc4 with compensation for the sacrificed material.

**26 ♖xc4 ♕d6 27 ♗xc5 ♘xc5 28 ♖xc5?!**

An exchange sacrifice too far! 28 ♖xb4+ ♔c8 (28...♔a7 29 ♕e3 wins) 29 ♕e3! ♖d7 30 ♘xe5! ♖e7 (30...♕xe5 31 ♗b7+ wins) 31 f4 would have given Black terrible problems according to Krasenkov.

**28...♕xc5 29 ♕xa6 ♔c7 30 ♘g5 ♔d7 31 ♕e6+ ♔c7 32 ♕a6 ♔d7 33 ♕b7+ ♔d6 34 ♘f7+ ♔e6 35 ♘xd8+ ♖xd8 36 ♕xh7 ♖f8 37 ♕xg6+ ♔e7 38 ♕g5+ ♖f6 39 ♕g7+ ♖f7 40 ♕g5+ ♖f6 41 ♕d2 ♖d6 42 ♕e2 ♕c1+ 43 ♔g2 ♖d2 44 ♕h5 ♕xb2 45 ♕g5+ ♔e6 46 ♕f5+ ♔e7 47 ♕g5+ ♔e6 48 ♕f5+ ♔e7 49 h4 ♕d4 50 a5 b3 51 a6 b2 52 ♕h7+ ♔d6 53 a7 b1♕ 54**

♗xb1 ♕xf2+ 55 ♔h3 ♕g2+ 56 ♔g4 ♖d4+ 57 ♔h5 ♕f3+ 58 ♔h6 ♕xg3 59 h5 ♕e3+ 60 ♔g7 ♕g5+ 61 ♕g6+ ♕xg6+ 62 hxg6 ♖a4 63 ♗e4 ♖xa7+ 64 ♔f6 ♖c7 65 g7 ½-½!

Recently, Black players have preferred to expend a little more time in order to put the king to the relative safety of the kingside.

*Game 64*
**Krasenkov-Oll**
*Polanica Zdroj 1996*

**1 d4 d5 2 c4 c6 3 ♘c3 ♘f6 4 e3 e6 5 ♘f3 ♘bd7 6 ♗d3 dxc4 7 ♗xc4 b5 8 ♗d3 ♗b7 9 0-0 a6 10 e4 c5 11 d5 c4 12 dxe6 fxe6 13 ♗c2 ♕c7 14 ♘d4 ♘c5 15 ♗e3 e5**

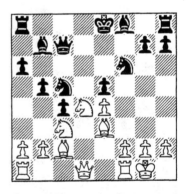

Black chases the knight from d4 immediately.

**16 ♘f5**

Black wants to develop his dark-squared bishop and then put his king to safety. However, 16...♗e7 leaves g7 hanging, while 16...g6 is met by 17 ♘h6, stopping the black king from castling kingside. Although the knight would then be precariously placed on h6, it does have a strong move backwards to g4, removing the knight on f6 and thus increasing the strength of ♘d5.

**16...♖d8!**

16...♘cxe4 17 ♘xe4 ♘xe4 18 a4 ♛c6 19 axb5 axb5 20 ♖xa8+ ♗xa8 21 ♛g4 gave White good attacking chances in Lautier-Kramnik, Monaco (rapidplay) 1996.

**17 ♛f3 ♗d6 18 ♖ad1 ♗c8?**

This rather timorous move leads directly to disaster. The only consistent move in this position is 18...0-0, when Krasenkov suggests 19 ♛g3, putting extra pressure on g7 and threatening 20 ♖xd6! ♖xd6 21 ♗xc5 winning everything, as 21...♛xc5 loses to 22 ♛xg7+ mate. However, as Krasenkov points out, Black can play 19...♘fxe4! here.

20 ♘xe4 is met not by 20...♘xe4, when 21 ♗xe4 ♗xe4 22 ♘xd6 ♖xd6 23 ♛xe5 ♗d3 24 ♗c5! ♖d7 25 ♛xc7 ♖xc7 26 ♗xf8 ♗xf1 27 ♖d8 wins for White due to the double threat of 28 ♗d6+ and 28 ♔xf1, but by 20...♗xe4! (Krasenkov), when 21 ♗xc5 (not 21 ♘xd6 ♗xc2; while 21 ♖xd6 ♖xd6 22 ♗xc5 ♗xf5! 23 ♛xe5 ♖d7 24 ♛xc7

♖xc7 25 ♗xf8 ♗xc2 draws and 21 ♘h6+ ♔h8 22 ♗xc5 ♗xc5 23 ♗xe4 gxh6 is nice for Black) 21...♗xf5 22 ♗xd6 ♖xd6 23 ♛xe5 ♖d7! holds for Black. 20 ♗xe4 by contrast is met by 20...♘xe4 21 ♘xe4 ♖xf5! with a good position for Black.

So it seems that 18...0-0 is sufficient (just!) for Black.

**19 ♘d5! ♘xd5 20 ♘xd6+ ♖xd6 21 ♛h5+!**

A very uncomfortable move to face. 21...g6 loses to 22 ♛xe5+.

**21...♖g6 22 exd5 ♘d3**

Forced, to block the bishop's attack on the rook on g6.

**23 ♗xd3 cxd3 24 ♖c1 ♛b8 25 ♗a7! 1-0**

A nice finish! Krasenkov shows that 25...♛a8 loses to 26 ♛xe5+ ♗e6 27 ♖c6! (White must be careful; 27 dxe6 loses to 27...♛xg2+ mate!) 27...0-0 28 ♖xe6.

We now move on to a line that became popular after some Karpov magic.

---

### Game 65
### Karpov-Kramnik
*Linares 1994*

**1 d4 d5 2 c4 c6 3 ♘f3 ♘f6 4 ♘c3 e6 5 e3 ♘bd7 6 ♗d3 dxc4 7 ♗xc4 b5 8 ♗d3 a6 9 e4 c5 10 d5 c4 11 dxe6 fxe6 12 ♗c2 ♗b7 13 0-0 ♛c7 14 ♘g5 ♘c5 15 e5!**

The plan with 14 ♘g5 demands much more urgency from White than 14 ♘d4, since after 14...♘c5, Black is already threatening to neutralise White's pressure on e6 by chasing away the knight with ...h7-h6. Karpov's idea forces the game into a complicated endgame.

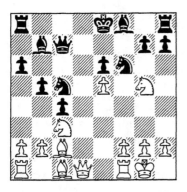

**15...♕xe5 16 ♖e1 ♕d6 17 ♕xd6! ♗xd6 18 ♗e3**

18 ♘xe6 ♘xe6 19 ♖xe6+ ♔d7 is harmless for Black, who is ready to take advantage of his queenside pawn majority

**18...0-0**

Karpov dismisses 18...♘d3 due to 19 ♗xd3 cxd3 20 ♖ad1, but in Kramnik-Kuczynski, German Bundesliga 1994, Black held the position quite easily after 20...0-0 21 ♖xd3 ♗d5 22 ♘xe6 ♗xh2+ 23 ♔xh2 ♗xe6 24 ♖d6 ♖fe8. I have not seen this idea repeated since.

**19 ♖ad1!**

Gaining a tempo on the bishop on d6.

**19...♗e7 20 ♗xc5 ♗xc5 21 ♘xe6 ♖fc8 22 h3!!**

At first sight, White's play seems unimpressive. Although he has some activity – his two rooks occupy the open central files, and the e6-knight attacks the bishop on c5 and the pawn on g7, while covering the d8-square – Black has the two bishops and a menacing queenside majority. However, a

closer analysis reveals that Black's pieces lack coordination; it is hard for Black to generate any activity. For example, the bishop on c5 attacks f2, but Black is unable to utilise this: ...♘g4 was prevented by 22 h3!! and Black is unable to bring a rook to the f-file. Moreover, by removing the e6-pawn, White has Black's outpost on d5, leaving the black knight stuck on f6.

*Question 6:* Why does this matter?

*Answer:* This is the genius of Karpov's concept. 22 h3 prepares g2-g4-g5 to drive the black knight away from f6. If the knight can be forced to a passive or wayward square, then White will be able invade the seventh rank with ♖d7 or play ♘d5, bringing Black's position to breaking point.

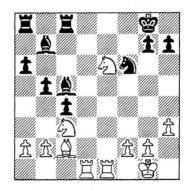

**22...♗f8?!**

Although the text is solid, it does nothing to interfere with White's plan. 22...♖ab8 is considered in Games 66-68.

**23 g4! h6 24 f4!**

Reinforcing the threat of g4-g5.

**24...♗f3 25 ♖d2 ♗c6**

To give the knight a square on d7 after White attacks it with g4-g5.

26 g5 hxg5 27 fxg5 ♘d7 28 ♘xf8
♘xf8 29 ♖d6 b4 30 ♘e4

30 ♘d5 was possibly even stronger
according to Karpov.

30...♖e8 31 ♘g3 ♖d8 32 ♘f5 ♖xd6
33 ♘xd6 ♗g6 34 ♗xg6 ♘xg6 35
♘xc4 ♖d8 36 ♖e4 b3 37 axb3 ♖d3
38 ♔g2 ♖xb3 39 h4 ♘f8 40 ♖e8 1-0

In this very difficult position,
Kramnik lost on time.

## Game 66
### Gelfand-Shirov
*Biel 1995*

1 d4 d5 2 c4 c6 3 ♘f3 ♘f6 4 ♘c3
e6 5 e3 ♘bd7 6 ♗d3 dxc4 7 ♗xc4
b5 8 ♗d3 a6 9 e4 c5 10 d5 c4 11
♗c2 ♕c7 12 dxe6 fxe6 13 0-0 ♗b7
14 ♘g5 ♘c5 15 e5 ♕xe5 16 ♖e1
♕d6 17 ♕xd6 ♗xd6 18 ♗e3 0-0 19
♖ad1 ♗e7 20 ♗xc5 ♗xc5 21 ♘xe6
♖fc8 22 h3!! ♖ab8!

A superb defensive concept! Black
fully understands the value of keeping
his dark-squared bishop on the a7-g1
diagonal. By pinning the f2-pawn to
White's king on g1, he prevents White
from advancing this and fully activating his kingside majority. Moreover,
the bishop restricts the movement of
White's rooks by covering the d4- and
e3-squares. Since 22...♗b6 and
22...♗a7 are both met by 23 ♘xg7!
♔xg7 (23...♗xg2 24 ♔xg2 [24 ♘f5
♗xh3 25 ♘e7+ ♔f7 is more risky for
White] 24...♔xg7 25 ♖e7+ is also difficult for Black) 24 ♖e7+ winning the
loose bishop on b7, Black defends this
piece, preparing to retreat the dark-
squared bishop along its best diagonal
without incurring material loss. The
rook is also well-placed on b8 to support the advance of the b-pawn.

**23 ♘xc5**

23 g4 (Game 67) is more critical,
while 23 a3 is seen in Game 68.

**23...♖xc5 24 ♖d6**

With 23 ♘xc5 ♖xc5, White aims
just for a safe, stable endgame edge.
The removal of the troublesome
bishop on c5 costs Black the bishop
pair and frees several important dark
squares for the white rooks to exploit.
24 ♖d6 floats the threat of ♖b6, pinning the b7-bishop, and thereby hopes
to slow Black's counterplay on the
queenside. Of course, 24 a3 is just met
by 24...a5, renewing the threat.

**24...b4**

Although this move loosens Black's
position a little, it gains space on the
queenside and by chasing the knight
away from c3, allows Black to challenge White's control of the d-file by
...♖d5.

**25 ♘a4 ♖d5! 26 ♖b6 ♖b5**

Yagupov criticises this move, claim-
ing an edge for White after 28 ♘c5,
and I agree with this assessment.
Black's counterplay is based on an attack on the backward pawn on a2

with a rook on a8, but before he can do this, he must move his bishop from b7. Unfortunately, the natural and desirable 28...♗d5 loses a pawn to 29 ♘a6! ♖a8 30 ♘xb4!

Black should therefore have played Yagupov's 26...a5, protecting the b4-pawn and intending to drive the rook from b6 with ...♘d7. Yagupov gives 27 ♖e7 ♘d7 28 ♖be6 ♘f8 29 ♖b6 ♘d7 with a draw by repetition.

**27 ♖xb5 axb5 ½-½**

Now we turn our attention to the most aggressive and consistent idea for White, 23 g4.

*Game 67*
**Greenfeld-Av.Bykhovsky**
*Beersheva 1996*

1 d4 d5 2 c4 c6 3 ♘c3 ♘f6 4 e3 e6 5 ♘f3 ♘bd7 6 ♗d3 dxc4 7 ♗xc4 b5 8 ♗d3 ♗b7 9 0-0 a6 10 e4 c5 11 d5 c4 12 dxe6 fxe6 13 ♗c2 ♕c7 14 ♘g5 ♘c5 15 e5 ♕xe5 16 ♖e1 ♕d6 17 ♕xd6 ♗xd6 18 ♗e3 0-0 19 ♖ad1 ♗e7 20 ♗xc5 ♗xc5 21 ♘xe6 ♖fc8 22 h3!! ♖ab8! 23 g4

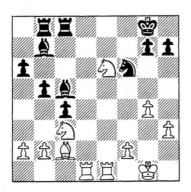

**23...♗f3**

This annoying intermediate move

disrupts the coordination of White's rooks.

**24 ♖d2 ♖e8!?**

A new idea. Black accepts that his knight will be driven to the side after g4-g5. However, by pinning the knight on e6, he hopes to be able to activate the knight with ...♘f4.

The alternative 24...b4!? 25 ♘a4 ♗a7 26 g5 ♘d5 has been the subject of intensive high-level testing. After 27 g6! h6 (27...hxg5 28 ♘g5!) 28 ♘d4 c3! 29 bxc3 bxc3 30 ♖d3 ♘b4! 31 ♖xf3 ♗xd4 32 ♗f5 ♖c7 33 a3 ♘c6 34 ♔g2 (and not 34 ♖f4?? ♗e5 when Black was winning in Nikolic-Shirov, Horgen 1994) 34...♘e7 35 ♗c2 ♗f6, as in Alterman-Akopian, Haifa 1995, 36 ♖d1 ♔f8 37 ♖e3 would have kept a small edge according to Alterman.

**25 ♗d1**

The calmest approach. 25 ♔f1 ♗b4! 26 a3 (26 g5 ♘d5! is good for Black) 26...♗xc3 27 bxc3 ♖b6! 28 ♘f4 (28 ♘g5+ ♗g2+! wins the exchange) 28...♖xe1+ 29 ♔xe1 g5! presented Black with no problems in Filgueira-Sorokin, Villa Balester 1996.

**25...♗xd1 26 ♖dxd1 ♖bc8 27 g5 ♘h5 28 ♘d5 ♗d6 29 ♖d4 ♖c6 30 ♖de4 ♖b8 31 h4 b4**

White has an impressive looking position, but it is not easy to do much with it whereas Black has the simple plan of creating a passed c-pawn.

**32 ♖c1 ♖e8 33 ♔f1 ♗f8 34 ♖ce1 c3 35 bxc3 bxc3 36 ♘d4 ♖xe4 37 ♘xc6 ♖xh4 38 ♔e2 ♖e4+ 39 ♘e3 ♘f4+ 40 ♔f3 ♘d3 41 ♔xe4 ♘xe1 42 ♘d4 ♗c5 43 ♘b3 ♗a7 44 f4 c2 45 f5 ♗b6 46 ♘d5 ♗c5 47 ♘f4 ♗a3 48 ♘e2 ♗e7 49 f6 gxf6 50 gxf6**

♗xf6 51 ♘c5 a5 52 ♘d3 ♘g2 53 ♔f3 ♘h4+ 54 ♔g4 h5+ 55 ♔xh5 ♘f3 56 ♘dc1 ♗b2 57 ♘d3 ♘d4 58 ♘ec1 ♗c3 59 ♔g5 ♗d2+ 60 ♔f6 ♔f8 61 a3 a4 62 ♘a2 ♘e2 63 ♔e5 ♘c3 64 ♘xc3 ♗xc3+ 65 ♔d5 ♔e7 66 ♔c4 ♗d2 67 ♔b5 ½-½

1 d4 d5 2 c4 c6 3 ♘c3 ♘f6 4 e3 e6 5 ♘f3 ♘bd7 6 ♗d3 dxc4 7 ♗xc4 b5 8 ♗d3 ♗b7 9 0-0 a6 10 e4 c5 11 d5 c4 12 ♗c2 ♕c7 13 dxe6 fxe6 14 ♘g5 ♘c5 15 e5 ♕xe5 16 ♖e1 ♕d6 17 ♕xd6 ♗xd6 18 ♗e3 0-0 19 ♖ad1 ♗e7 20 ♗xc5 ♗xc5 21 ♘xe6 ♖fc8 22 h3!! ♖ab8! 23 a3

This prevents ...b5-b4 and hopes to stop any queenside counterplay.

23...♗b6! 24 ♖d6 ♗a5 25 ♖e3 b4! 26 axb4 ♗xb4 27 ♖d4 ♖e8 28 ♖xc4?

A mistake according to Azmaiparashvili who recommends instead 28 ♘c7 ♖xe3 29 fxe3 ♗c5 30 ♖xc4 ♗xe3+ 31 ♔h1, assessing it as unclear.

28...♗xc3 29 ♖cxc3 ♘d5 30 ♗b3

♘xe3 31 ♘c7+ ♘d5 32 ♘xe8 ♖xe8 33 ♖c7 ♗a8 34 ♖d7 ♖b8

This leads to an easy draw and yet, as pointed out by Ivanchuk, 34...♔f8!! 35 ♗xd5 ♖e1+ 36 ♔h2 ♔e8! 37 ♖xg7 ♗xd5 38 ♖xh7 ♖e2! would have given Black the advantage.

35 ♗xd5+ ♗xd5 36 ♖xd5 ♖xb2 37 ♖d8+ ♔f7 38 ♖d7+ ♔g8 39 ♖a7 ♖b6 40 ♔h2 ♖c6 41 f3 h6 42 ♔g3 ♔h7 43 f4 ♔g6 44 ♔f3 ♖b6 45 g3 ½-½

This is not the whole story of this variation because, in typically inventive fashion, Shirov has devised another risky idea. To quote him, '15...♕c6 has not been refuted yet, but it looks dangerous!'

1 d4 d5 2 c4 c6 3 ♘c3 ♘f6 4 ♘f3 e6 5 e3 ♘bd7 6 ♗d3 dxc4 7 ♗xc4 b5 8 ♗d3 a6 9 e4 c5 10 d5 ♕c7 11 0-0 ♗b7 12 dxe6 fxe6 13 ♗c2 c4 14 ♘g5 ♘c5 15 e5 ♕c6!?

Threatening mate on g2, and thus forcing White to block the queen's path to the h5-square.

**16 f3 ♘fd7 17 ♘xh7**

17 ♕e2 was played in I.Sokolov-Shirov, Leon 1995. White claims that achieving e4-e5 is more than enough for an advantage and avoids risk with ♘xh7. However, 17...♘d3!? (17...♗e7 18 ♔h1 ♘d3 19 ♗xd3 cxd3 20 ♕xd3 ♘xe5 21 ♕d4 ♕c4 22 ♕xc4 ♘xc4 23 ♘xe6 ♔f7 gave Black good compensation for the pawn in Krasenkov-Luther, Tilburg 1994) 18 ♗xd3 cxd3 19 ♕xd3 ♘xe5 20 ♕e2 h6! 21 ♕xe5 ♕c5+ 22 ♕xc5 ♗xc5+ 23 ♔h1 hxg5 24 ♗xg5 ♗d4! was only minutely better for White.

**17...♘xe5 18 ♘xf8 ♖xf8 19 ♕d4 ♘cd3!**

Black is now threatening 20...♖xf3! 21 gxf3 ♘xf3+ 22 ♖xf3 ♕xf3 followed by mate!

**20 ♗xd3 ♘xd3 21 ♘e4 e5?!**

A slight inaccuracy. In a later round of the same tournament against Illescas, Shirov played 21...♖d8! 22 ♕xg7 ♕b6+! 23 ♘f2 ♘xf2 24 ♕g6+ ♖f7 25 ♕g8+ ♖f8 26 ♕g6+ ♖f7 with a draw, as 27 ♖xf2 allows 27...♖d1+ mate.

**22 ♕e3 0-0-0 23 b3 c3 24 ♗a3 b4 25 ♖fd1 ♕b5 26 ♘xc3 ♖xf3 27 gxf3 bxc3 28 ♖ac1 ♘xc1 29 ♕xc3+ ♕c6 30 ♕xc6+ ♗xc6 31 ♖xd8+ ♔xd8 ½-½**

And now the last of our 'big three' main lines: 13 ♘d4

*Game 70*
**Gelfand-Dreev**
*Tilburg 1993*

**1 d4 d5 2 c4 c6 3 ♘c3 ♘f6 4 ♘f3 e6 5 e3 ♘bd7 6 ♗d3 dxc4 7 ♗xc4 b5 8 ♗d3 ♗b7 9 0-0 a6 10 e4 c5 11** **d5 c4 12 ♗c2 ♕c7 13 ♘d4**

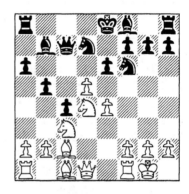

By avoiding the preliminary d5xe6, White forgoes two benefits: the loosening of the pawn cover around the black king; and the possibility of e4-e5 (which is now met by ...♘xd5). However, by maintaining the d5-pawn, White aims to hold the knight on d4 – and thus his pressure on e6 – indefinitely. First, the d-pawn shields the knight from attack along the d-file. Second, ...e6-e5 is met by ♘f5, after which Black cannot develop his bishop from f8 as g7 will hang (unlike after 13 dxe6 fxe6, when the queen on c7 protects the g7-pawn), so he will find it hard to put his king to safety on the kingside.

**13...e5**

13...exd5 14 ♘xd5! ♘xd5 15 exd5 0-0-0 16 a4 b4 17 ♘c6 gives White a powerful attack, while 13...♘c5 is the subject of the next game.

**14 ♘f5 g6 15 ♘h6 ♘h5**

I don't like Black's position here. 16 g3 would now have kept the knight out of f4 and given White a definite advantage.

**16 ♕f3 ♘f4 17 ♘xf7!?**

Dreev suggests 17 ♘g4!? here.

17...♔xf7 18 g3 g5 19 gxf4 gxf4 20 ♕h5+ ♔e7 21 ♕h4+ ♔f7 22 ♗d1?!

White would have done better to repeat moves with 22 ♕h5+. The rest of the game is simply stunning!

22...♖g8+ 23 ♔h1 ♘f6 24 ♗h5+ ♖g6!! 25 ♗xg6+ hxg6 26 ♖g1 ♗e7 27 ♕h6 ♖g8 28 f3 b4 29 ♘e2 ♘xd5!! 30 exd5 ♗xd5 31 ♖f1 ♗f6 32 ♕h7+ ♖g7 33 ♕h3 ♗e6 34 ♕g2 g5 35 a3 g4 36 axb4 ♗d5 37 ♘c3 gxf3 38 ♕f2 ♗b7 39 ♖a5 ♕d7 40 ♘d5 ♗xd5 41 ♕d2 ♗c6 42 ♕xd7+ ♗xd7 43 ♖xa6 ♗h3 44 ♖f2 ♗h4 0-1

---

### Game 71
### Sadler-Madwekwe
*London (Lloyds Bank) 1994*

---

1 d4 d5 2 c4 c6 3 e3 ♘f6 4 ♘c3 e6 5 ♘f3 ♘bd7 6 ♗d3 dxc4 7 ♗xc4 b5 8 ♗b3 ♗b7 9 0-0 a6 10 e4 c5 11 d5 c4 12 ♗c2 ♕c7 13 ♘d4 ♘c5!

This is Black's best choice.

**14 b4**

For 14 ♕f3 see Game 73.

**14...cxb3 15 axb3 b4!**

Preventing White from chasing away the black knight from c5 with b3-b4 and weakening the white centre by forcing the knight offside to a4.

**16 ♘a4 ♘xa4?**

This is definitely wrong, although the refutation is far from obvious. The correct 16...♘cxe4! is seen in the next game.

**17 ♖xa4 exd5 18 e5! ♘e4**

18...♕xe5 fails to 19 ♖e1 ♘e4 20 f3 (20 ♖a5!? ♕c7 21 ♖xd5 ♗xd5 22 ♗xe4 0-0-0 23 ♕g4+ is also very dangerous for Black) 20...♗c5 21 ♗e3, when 21...♘c3 22 ♗f2 wins.

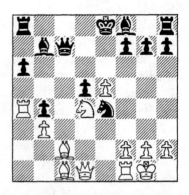

**19 ♗f4!! ♗c5**

A desperate attempt to get his pieces out. Instead 19...♘c3 20 ♕f3 ♘xa4 21 e6 ♕b6 22 bxa4 gives White a huge attack, as 22...♕xd4 loses to 23 ♗e5.

**20 ♗xe4 dxe4 21 ♘f5 f6?**

Losing. 21...0-0 22 ♕g4 g6 23 e6! is also pretty horrible, however.

**22 e6! ♕c6 23 ♗d6 1-0**

---

### Game 72
### Kasparov-Kramnik
*Dos Hermanas 1996*

---

1 d4 d5 2 c4 c6 3 ♘c3 ♘f6 4 ♘f3 e6 5 e3 ♘bd7 6 ♗d3 dxc4 7 ♗xc4 b5 8 ♗d3 ♗b7 9 0-0 a6 10 e4 c5 11 d5 c4 12 ♗c2 ♕c7 13 ♘d4 ♘c5 14 b4 cxb3 15 axb3 b4 16 ♘a4 ♘cxe4! 17 ♗xe4!?

An earlier game Yakovich-Sorokin, Calcutta 1991, continued 17 dxe6 ♖d8 18 exf7+ ♔xf7 19 ♗e3 ♗d6 20 h3 ♖he8 21 ♖c1, and now 21...♘c3 22 ♘xc3 bxc3 would have been unclear according to Yakovich.

**17...♘xe4 18 dxe6 ♗d6 19 exf7+!?**

The most forcing move. White players could also consider the tricky 19 ♕h5 0-0 20 ♗b2.

**19...♕xf7!**

This is best and almost forced, as 19...♔xf7 is unpleasantly met by 20 ♕h5+ g6 21 ♕h3!

**20 f3! ♕h5! 21 g3**

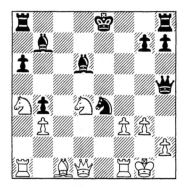

**21...0-0!**

Kramnik states that 21...♘xg3!! 22 hxg3 (22 ♕e1+ ♘e4 23 ♖a2 0-0 gives a virulent attack) 22...0-0! 23 ♖a2 ♗xg3 24 ♖g2 ♗e5 25 ♘c5 ♖ad8 26 ♗e3 ♗c8 was Black's best chance, when White can only save himself with 27 f4! ♕xd1 28 ♖xd1 ♗xf4 29 ♗xf4 ♖xf4 30 ♖gd2 with reasonable drawing chances. The rest of the game is thus not theoretically important, but play through it – it has to be enjoyed!

**22 fxe4 ♕h3! 23 ♘f3? ♗xg3 24 ♘c5 ♖xf3 25 ♖xf3 ♕xh2+ 26 ♔f1 ♗c6!**

This is what Kasparov had missed when calculating his 23rd move.

**27 ♗g5 ♗b5+ 28 ♘d3 ♖e8 29 ♖a2 ♕h1+**

Winning, but as Kramnik shows, 29...♗xd3+ 30 ♖xd3 ♕h1+ 31 ♔e2 ♕xg2+ 32 ♔e3 ♖xe4 was checkmate!

**30 ♔e2 ♖xe4+ 31 ♔d2 ♕g2+ 32 ♔c1 ♕xa2 33 ♖xg3 ♕a1+ 34 ♔c2 ♕c3+ 35 ♔b1 ♖d4 0-1**

A magical game!

*Game 73*
**Tkachiev-Handoko**
*Jakarta (match) 1996*

**1 d4 d5 2 c4 c6 3 ♘c3 e6 4 e3 ♘f6 5 ♘f3 ♘bd7 6 ♗d3 dxc4 7 ♗xc4 b5 8 ♗d3 ♗b7 9 0-0 a6 10 e4 c5 11 d5 c4 12 ♗c2 ♕c7 13 ♘d4 ♘c5 14 ♕f3!?**

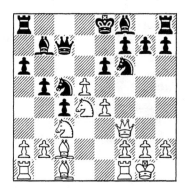

White supports d5 and prepares to put extra pressure on e6 by ♕h3.

**14...♗d6**

14...0-0-0 is interesting, looking to win the d5-pawn without giving up the light-squared bishop.

**15 ♕h3 b4 16 ♘a4 ♘cxe4 17 dxe6 0-0 18 f3 ♗e5 19 ♗e3 ♘g5 20 exf7+ ♖xf7 21 ♕h4 ♖d8 22 ♘f5 ♘e6 23 ♗b6!**

Winning the exchange and essentially the game.

**23...♕b8 24 ♗xd8 ♘xd8 25 ♖ad1 ♗d5 26 ♘e3 ♕a7 27 ♕f2 b3 28 axb3 cxb3 29 ♘xd5 bxc2 30 ♘xf6+ ♗xf6 31 ♕xa7 ♖xa7 32 ♖d2 ♖c7 33 ♖c1 ♖c4 34 b3 ♖b4 35 ♖d3 ♘e6 36 ♖xc2 ♘f4 37 ♖c8+ ♔f7 38 ♖d7+ ♔g6 39 ♖c4 1-0**

## Summary

I would recommend the 13 dxe6 fxe6 14 ♘d4 line to White players since it combines solidity and aggression and does not require the refined endgame skills demanded by Karpov's 14 ♘g5 ♕xe5 15 e5. Tkachiev's 13 ♘d4 ♘c5 14 ♕f3 is also worth a try. For Black players, I would suggest that 13 dxe6 fxe6 14 ♘d4 is best met by 14...♘c5 15 ♗e3 e5.

**1 d4 d5 2 c4 c6 3 ♘f3 ♘f6 4 ♘c3 e6 5 e3 ♘bd7 6 ♗d3 dxc4 7 ♗xc4 b5 8 ♗d3 ♗b7 9 0-0 a6 10 e4 c5 11 d5 c4 12 ♗c2 ♕c7**

**13 dxe6**

      13 ♘d4

            13...e5 – *Game 70*

            13...♘c5 *(D)*

                  14 b4 cxb3 15 axb3 b4 16 ♘a4

                        16...♘xa4 – *Game 71*; 16...♘cxe4 – *Game 72*

                  14 ♕f3 – *Game 73*

**13...fxe6 14 ♘d4**

      14 ♘g5 ♘c5 15 e5

            15...♕xe5 16 ♖e1 ♕d6 17 ♕xd6 ♗xd6 18 ♗e3 0-0

            19 ♖ad1 ♗e7 20 ♗xc5 ♗xc5 21 ♘xe6 ♖fc8 22 h3 *(D)*

                22...♗f8 – *Game 65*

                22...♖ab8

                    23 ♘xc5 – *Game 66*; 23 g4 – *Game 67*; 23 a3 – *Game 68*

            15...♕c6 – *Game 69*

**14...♘c5 15 ♗e3 0-0-0**

      15...e5 – *Game 64*

**16 ♕e2 e5 17 ♘f3 *(D)* ♘cxe4**

      17...♘e6

            18 ♖ad1 – *Game 62*; 18 ♘d5 – *Game 63*

**18 ♘xe4 – *Game 61***

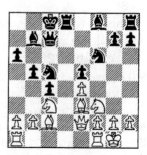

    *13...♘c5*             *22 h3*             *17 ♘f3*

# CHAPTER EIGHT

## Meran Variation:
## Move Orders and Sidelines

**1 d4 d5 2 c4 c6 3 ♘f3 ♘f6 4 ♘c3 e6 5 e3 ♘bd7 6 ♗d3 dxc4 7 ♗xc4 b5 8 ♗d3**

This chapter will be of particular value for players who like to confuse their opponents! Since we only reach the critical main line position that arose in the previous chapter after 12 moves, there is plenty of scope for trickery and treachery along the way!

There is no definitive path which Black should adopt to reach the main line position. Kramnik prefers 8...♗b7 9 0-0 a6 (threatening ...c6-c5) 10 e4 c5 11 d5 c4 12 ♗c2 ♕c7; Shirov's favourite, however, is 8...a6 (threatening ...c6-c5 immediately) 9 e4 c5 10 d5 c4 11 ♗c2 ♗b7 12 0-0 ♕c7.

*Question 1:* What is the difference?

*Answer:* After 8...♗b7, Black must also be prepared against 9 e4 and 9 a3, whereas after 8...a6, Black must be prepared for 9 e4 c5 10 e5!?

8...♗b7 is more solid than 8...a6 since 8...a6 9 e4 c5 10 e5 leads to wild positions with random pawn structures and is more difficult to

'understand' than the lines arising after 8...♗b7 9 e4 or 9 a3.

*Question 2:* Is that all?

*Answer:* I'm afraid not! Black has great scope for inverting moves in the lead up to the main line position. For example, when does Black play his queen to c7? After 8...♗b7 9 0-0 a6 10 e4 c5 11 d5

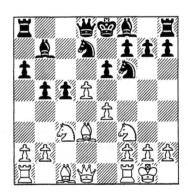

is 11...♕c7 possible instead of 11...c4 here? And after 8...a6 9 e4 c5 10 d5 c4 11 ♗c2, can Black play 11...♕c7 before he develops his bishop to b7 ?

In fact there are really only two important issues for move orders: Black can delay or avoid ...c5-c4 or, via the 8...a6 move order (Games 74-78), Black can delay or avoid ...♗b7 (Game 79).

The rest of this chapter is devoted to systems in which Black plays an early ...e6-e5 (Games 80-81) or takes the white bishop on d3 in response to d5xe6 (Games 82-83).

### Black delays or avoids ...c5-c4

The most important position in this section arises from either 8...♗b7 9 0-0 a6 10 e4 c5 11 d5 ♕c7 or 8...a6 9 e4 c5 10 d5 ♗b7 (or 10...♕c7 11 0-0 ♗b7) 11 0-0 ♕c7.

Usually instead of 11...♕c7 Black plays 11...c4 to gain space on the queenside and to increase the activity of Black's minor pieces. The ....c5-c4 advance frees c5 for the black knight and also allows Black to play his king's bishop to d6. Without it, 12...♗d6 for example would fail to 13 dxe6 fxe6 14 ♗xb5 axb5 15 ♘xb5 forking the queen and bishop.

*Question 3:* So why avoid playing 11...c4 in that case?

*Answer:* Delaying ...c5-c4 has two advantages. Although it deprives Black of ...♘c5 to defend e6, it prevents White from attacking e6 with ♘d4. Moreover, in the event of d5xe6, the white bishop on d3 will be a useful target for a black rook on d8.

---

### Game 74
### Bareev-Dreev
*Russian Ch., Elista 1996*

1 d4 d5 2 c4 c6 3 ♘f3 ♘f6 4 ♘c3 e6 5 e3 ♘bd7 6 ♗d3 dxc4 7 ♗xc4

b5 8 ♗d3 ♗b7 9 0-0 a6 10 e4 c5 11 d5 ♕c7 12 dxe6!?

A committal decision. The prophylactic 12 ♗c2 is considered in Games 75-77 and 12 b3, preventing ...c5-c4, in Game 78.

12...fxe6 13 ♗c2

White retreats the bishop from its exposed position on d3 and thus draws the sting from Black's d-file ambitions. Despite abandoning the attack on b5, White does not give Black the chance to play 13...♗d6 due to 14 ♘g5!, as Black has neither ...♘c5 nor ...♕c6 to defend e6.

*Question 4:* Can't Black just transpose into the main line with 13...c4?

*Answer:* Yes, that is the normal move.

13...0-0-0!?

The maximum activity and maximum risk approach. Black gets his king out of the centre and brings a rook to the d-file in one move, but hides his king behind his queenside pawns, which are better placed for attack than defence.

14 ♘g5 ♘e5! 15 ♕e1!?

The 'normal' 15 ♕e2 would allow Black's knight on e5 to transfer to d4 via c6 with tempo.

**15...♛b6 16 f4 ♞d3 17 ♕g3 c4+ 18 ♗e3 ♗c5 19 ♗xc5 ♞xc5!**

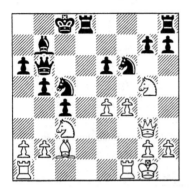

A very nice move, keeping the queen on b6, where it defends the e6-pawn, and supporting ...b5-b4 by covering the a4-square.

**20 ♔h1 b4 21 ♞a4 ♞xa4 22 ♗xa4 h6 23 ♞f7 ♞xe4 ½-½**

This was a strange place to offer a draw, as Black seems to have very good compensation for the exchange.

*Question 5:* So what about 12 ♗c2 without exchanging on e6 first?

*Answer:* This is the most flexible move; in all the games I have seen, Black has either transposed to the main line with 12...c4 or played 12...♗e7. However, Black could also try 12...0-0-0!? to meet 13 ♞g5 with 13...♞b6 (but not 13...♞e5 14 f4! ♞c6 15 dxc6! ♜xd1 16 cxb7+ and 17 ♜xd1), ganging up on the d-pawn.

---

**1 d4 d5 2 c4 c6 3 ♞c3 ♞f6 4 e3 e6 5 ♞f3 ♞bd7 6 ♗d3 dxc4 7 ♗xc4 b5**

**8 ♗d3 ♗b7 9 0-0 a6 10 e4 c5 11 d5 ♕c7 12 ♗c2 ♗e7**

Black makes the most of White's unforced retreat with 12 ♗c2 by opting for a developing move rather than playing the routine 12...c4, transposing to the previous chapter.

**13 dxe6 fxe6 14 ♞g5 ♕c6**

The queen is well placed here, defending e6 and preventing a e4-e5 due to ...♕xg2 checkmate!

**15 ♕f3!?**

White reasons that without ...c5-c4, Black cannot deal comfortably with two attacks on e6. 15 ♕f3 aims for the h3-square, where it will combine with the knight against the e6-pawn. From h3, the white queen also protects g2 and allows White to consider the e4-e5 push; for example 15...c4 16 ♕h3 ♞c5 is met by 17 e5! However, Black's idea is much more daring! (See Game 77 for 15 f4.)

**15...h6!? 16 ♕h3 hxg5 17 ♕xh8+ ♔f7 18 ♕h3 g4**

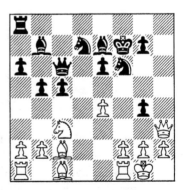

I find this exchange sacrifice hard to believe for Black, but it has caused White serious problems. Although White's material advantage should pay in the end, by winning the rook on h8

for his king's knight, he has given up a very valuable piece for attacking the black position. In the short term he now has no real way of creating play against the black position, and thus he will have to take on the chin whatever Black can throw at him. Black will have to make the most of a mixture of factors: the half-open h-file; pressure against the e4-pawn; and the vulnerable white queen.

**19 ♕h4**

To stop the black rook from coming immediately to the h-file.

**19...♘e5 20 f4**

20 ♖d1 is considered in the next game.

**20...gxf3 21 gxf3 ♘g6! 22 ♕g5**

22 ♕g3 is met by 22...♗d6 according to Dreev.

**22...♖h8! 23 e5 ♘h4!**

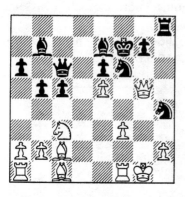

A very nice way of countering White's attack. Now 24 exf6 gxf6 25 ♕e3 (to play ♗e4) 25...f5! gives Black huge play for the rook according to Dreev.

**24 ♗e4 ♘d5 25 ♕g4 b4 26 ♘e2 ♕c7!**

Dreev now assesses the position as clearly better for Black.

**27 ♕g3 ♖h5 28 ♗f4 ♘f5 29 ♕e1 c4 30 ♔h1 ♗h4 31 ♕d2 ♕e7 32 ♖g1 g5 33 ♗g3 ♘xg3+?**

A blunder according to Dreev who claims a win with 33...♘de3, with the idea of 34...♗xe4 35 fxe4 ♕b7!

**34 ♘xg3 ♖h8 35 ♘f5 exf5 36 ♗xd5+ ♔g6 37 ♗xb7 ♕xb7 38 ♕d6+ ♔h5 39 ♖af1 g4 40 ♕e6 ♖f8 41 ♖xg4 ♗g5 42 ♖g3 1-0**

> *Game 76*
> **L.B.Hansen-Illescas**
> *Moscow Olympiad 1994*

**1 d4 d5 2 c4 c6 3 ♘f3 ♘f6 4 ♘c3 e6 5 e3 ♘bd7 6 ♗d3 dxc4 7 ♗xc4 b5 8 ♗d3 a6 9 e4 c5 10 d5 ♕c7 11 0-0 ♗b7 12 dxe6 fxe6 13 ♗c2 ♗e7 14 ♘g5 ♕c6 15 ♕f3!? h6!? 16 ♕h3 hxg5 17 ♕xh8+ ♔f7 18 ♕h3 g4 19 ♕h4 ♘e5 20 ♖d1!?**

**20...♗d6 21 ♗e3?!**

Illescas recommends instead 21 ♗f4 ♘g6 22 ♖xd6 ♘xh4 23 ♖xc6 ♗xc6, giving back the material for a slight endgame edge. This seems a reasonable enough strategy, although in Jelen-Pavasovic, Vienna 1996, the game ended in a draw after 24 ♖e1 ♖d8 25

♗g5 ♘g6 26 e5 b4 27 ♘e4 ♗xe4 28 ♖xe4 ♖d5 29 exf6 ♖xg5 30 fxg7 ♘e5 31 ♗b3 ♔f6 32 ♔f1 ♖xg7 33 f4 gxf3 34 gxf3.

**21...♗c7! 22 ♖ac1 ♖h8!!**

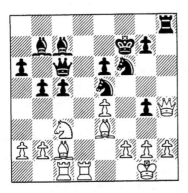

Aah!!

**23 ♕xh8 ♘g6!**

Suddenly the queen is trapped and White is in trouble!

**24 ♕d8 ♗xd8 25 ♖xd8 b4 26 ♘e2 ♘xe4 27 ♖cd1 ♘e5 28 ♖b8 ♘f6 29 ♘f4 g5 30 ♖xb7+ ♕xb7 31 ♘d3 ♘xd3 32 ♗xd3 ♘e4 33 ♖c1 a5 34 g3 ♕d5 35 ♗xe4 ♕xe4 36 ♖xc5 ♕b1+ 37 ♔g2 a4 38 ♖xg5 ♕e4+ 39 ♔g1 e5 40 ♖h5 ♕b1+ 41 ♔g2 ♕xb2 42 ♖h7+ ♔e6 43 ♗c5 ♕c2 44 ♖h6+ ♔f7 45 ♗d6 ♕c6+ 0-1**

> ## Game 77
> ### Gelfand-Dreev
> *Biel 1995*

**1 d4 d5 2 c4 c6 3 ♘c3 ♘f6 4 ♘f3 e6 5 e3 ♘bd7 6 ♗d3 dxc4 7 ♗xc4 b5 8 ♗d3 ♗b7 9 0-0 a6 10 e4 c5 11 d5 ♕c7 12 ♗c2 ♗e7 13 dxe6 fxe6 14 ♘g5 ♕c6 15 f4**

With this move, White avoids the time-consuming win of the exchange and takes the opportunity instead to support the e4-e5 central push.

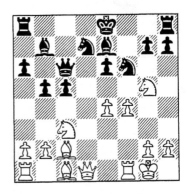

**15...h6**

15...0-0!? is interesting, as 16 e5 fails to 16...♕xg2+ mate!

**16 ♘f3 0-0-0 17 ♕e2 ♖hf8**

Dreev suggests 17...♔b8 here. 17...b4 18 e5 bxc3 19 exf6 ♗xf6 20 bxc3 ♘b6 21 ♗d2 ♘d5 22 ♕e1 is then slightly better for White according to Gelfand.

**18 e5 ♘d5 19 ♘xd5 ♕xd5 20 a4 b4 21 ♗e3?!**

21 ♖d1! ♕c6 22 a5! g5 23 fxg5 hxg5 24 ♗xg5 ♖xf3 (24...♗xg5 25 ♘xg5 ♘xe5 26 ♗e4) 25 ♗xe7 ♖g8 26 ♖d6 ♕c7 27 ♗e4 ♘xe5 28 ♖xe6 is given by Gelfand as clearly better for White.

**21...♘b6 22 ♘d2 ♕c6 23 ♘b3? ♘c4 ½-½**

A strange draw offer as Black has a wonderful position!

In the games so far in this section White has tried to coax his opponent Black back to the main line by offering him the chance to play ...c5-c4. We shall now consider the hard-line approach where White seeks to make Black pay for omitting ...c5-c4.

### Game 78
### Kozul-Beliavsky
*Slovenia 1995*

1 d4 ♘f6 2 c4 c6 3 ♘c3 d5 4 e3 e6
5 ♘f3 ♘bd7 6 ♗d3 dxc4 7 ♗xc4 b5
8 ♗d3 a6 9 e4 c5 10 d5 ♕c7 11 0-0
♗b7 12 b3

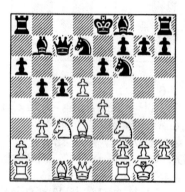

I have changed the move order of this game slightly (the actual sequence was 11 b3 ♗b7 12 0-0) to get a convenient diagram! This move has two main points: it ensures that a future ...c5-c4 by Black will split his queenside pawns after b3xc4 ...b5xc4, and by thus discouraging ...c5-c4, it maintains the white bishop on d3 and prevents the active deployment of the black king's bishop to d6.

However, by spending a tempo on this consolidating move, White is turning his back on the plan which best suits his position: the central attack via pressure against e6. Although White intends instead to soften up the black queenside with a2-a4, Black has such an obvious and easy target in the d5-pawn that I don't believe that White can be successful.

**12...♗e7**

Kozul-Lalic, Croatia 1995, saw the risky 12...c4 13 bxc4 bxc4 14 dxe6 fxe6 15 ♗c2 ♗b4, which seemed okay for Black after 16 ♗d2 (16 ♘a4!?) 16...♗d6 17 ♘d4 ♘c5 18 f4 e5 19 ♘f5 0-0 20 ♕e2 ♘d3 21 ♗xd3 cxd3 22 ♕xd3 ♗b4.

**13 ♗g5**

The more testing 13 a4!? was played in Krasenkov-Timman, European Team Championship, Pula 1997. After 13...exd5 (13...c4!? 14 bxc4 bxc4 15 ♗c2 0-0 16 ♘d4 ♖fe8 17 dxe6 fxe6 18 ♘xe6 ♕e5! was unfathomable in Krasenkov-Se.Ivanov, Augustow 1996) 14 ♘xd5 ♘xd5 15 exd5 0-0 16 axb5 axb5 17 ♖xa8 ♗xa8 18 ♗xb5 ♘f6 19 ♗b2 ♘xd5 20 ♖e1 White was a little better.

**13...0-0 14 ♖c1 ♖ad8! 15 ♗xb5!?**

A very clever spot as 15...axb5 16 ♘xb5 ♕b8 17 d6! nets a pawn (Beliavsky). However, by eating up White's centre, Black finds his way to achieve even a slight edge.

**15...exd5 16 ♗d3 dxe4 17 ♘xe4 ♗xe4 18 ♗xe4 ♘e5 19 ♕e2 ♘xe4 20 ♗xe7 ♘xf3+ 21 gxf3 ♕xe7 22 ♕xe4 ♕g5+ 23 ♕g4 ♕d2 24 ♖xc5 ♕xa2 25 ♕a4 ♕e2 26 ♕e4 ♕d2 27 ♖a1 ♖fe8 28 ♖e5 ♖xe5 29 ♕xe5 ♕d3 30 ♕e4 ♕b5 31 ♕a4 ♕g5+ 32 ♕g4 ♕f6 33 ♖c1 h5 34 ♕xh5 g6 35 ♕g4 ♖d4 36 ♕c8+ ♔h7 37 ♕h3+ ♔g7 38 ♖c8 ♕g5+ 39 ♕g3 ♕f5 40 ♖e8 ♖f4 41 ♔g2 g5 42 ♖e3 ♔g6 43 ♖e8 ½-½**

### Black avoids or delays ...♗b7
*Question 6:* Why delay ...♗b7? I thought the whole point was to get the bishop active on the long diagonal!

*Answer:* Black is trying to be a clever here: by switching the order in which he develops his pieces, Black hopes to prevent White from launching an early attack on e6 or making the e4-e5 thrust. By leaving the bishop on c8 retains the protection of e6. Plans such as d5xe6 followed by ♘d4 or ♘g5, or e4-e5 to open the e-file will be easier for Black to defend against, with e6 defended.

Note that this idea can only be used via the 8...a6 move order. The main line using the delayed ...♗b7 is 8...a6 9 e4 c5 10 d5 c4 11 ♗c2 ♕c7 12 0-0 ♗c5.

The bishop is very active on c5: Black is anticipating d5xe6 f7xe6, opening the f-file, and hopes to link up with the bishop's attack on the f2-pawn by castling and playing ...♘g4.

*Question 7:* How will Black deal with the threat of e4-e5?

*Answer:* After White has taken on e6 Black will block e4-e5 by playing ...♘e5. Since the bishop on c5 pins the pawn on f2 to the king on g1, White will not be able to play a quick f2-f4 to chase away a black piece from e5. If White does not take on e6, then Black can blockade in the centre, as we shall see in the Game 80.

**1 d4 d5 2 c4 c6 3 ♘f3 ♘f6 4 ♘c3 e6 5 e3 ♘bd7 6 ♗d3 dxc4 7 ♗xc4 b5 8 ♗d3 a6 9 e4 c5 10 d5 ♕c7 11 0-0**

11 dxe6 fxe6 12 ♘g5 was well met by 12...♘e5! in Nikolic-Bareev, European Club Cup, Lyon 1994.

**11...c4 12 ♗c2 ♗c5 13 dxe6**

After 13 ♕e2 e5 Black is okay – see the next game.

**13...fxe6**

Now Black would be fine after 14 ♕e2 ♘e5, ready to meet 15 ♗f4 with 15...♘xf3+ 16 ♕xf3 e5 and 15 ♘xe5 ♕xe5 16 ♔h1 with 16...0-0 17 f4 ♕h5. So White needs to act quickly.

**14 e5!**

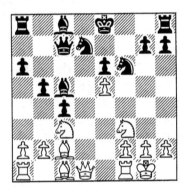

*Question 8:* What? You said e4-e5 wasn't dangerous with the bishop on c8!

*Answer:* In fact e4-e5 is dangerous here, but not for the usual reasons! Since e6 is defended, White cannot attempt anything on the e-file. However, since Black has not placed his bishop on the a8-h1 diagonal, White has many tactical ideas to gain a tempo on the unprotected rook on a8, and this, coupled with White's lead in development, is enough to give him a powerful initiative. To tell you a little secret, the key idea in this line is mine, all mine! I had known about it for two years, but never got a chance to play it. While seconding Joel Lautier for this match, I showed him this idea and lo and behold, he got to use it! 14 e5 had been played before, but it had been dismissed as leading to equality. However, I found something new that gives Black a few headaches.

**14...♘xe5 15 ♗f4! ♗d6**

15...♘xf3+ 16 ♕xf3 ♕b7 17 ♘e4! is very unpleasant for Black.

**16 ♗xe5 ♗xe5 17 ♘xe5 ♕xe5 18 ♖e1 ♕c5**

18...♕c7 19 a4 b4 (19...0-0 20 axb5 is also good for White) 20 ♘d5! ♘xd5 21 ♕xd5 ♖a7 22 ♕h5+! ♕f7 23 ♕c5! is very unpleasant for Black.

**19 ♘e4 ♘xe4 20 ♗xe4!**

Gaining a tempo on the rook on a8!

**20...♖a7 21 b4! ♕g5**

21...♕xb4 22 ♕h5+ gives White excellent play for the two pawns.

**22 f4!!**

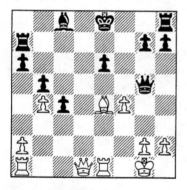

This was my discovery (hence the '!!'). 22...♕xf4 is met by 23 ♕d4! (threatening both 24 ♕xa7 and 24 ♗c6+) 23...♕c7 24 ♖f1!, preventing Black from castling kingside. After 24...♖f8 25 ♖xf8+ ♔xf8 26 ♗xh7, the threat of ♖f1+ is horrific for Black. Since the f4-pawn is immune, Black cannot keep his queen on the fifth rank to stop the disruptive ♕h5+.

**22...♕h4!? 23 g3 ♕d8 24 ♕h5+ ♖f7 25 ♖ad1 ♕b6+ 26 ♔f1 h6**

Horrible, but Black will never get castled otherwise.

**27 ♗g6 0-0 28 ♗xf7+ ♖xf7**

White has an overwhelming game. However, the game was eventually drawn after many adventures! If I had known then what I knew at the end of this match, I would not have been surprised at this outcome, as the match finished level at 4-4 after eight hard-fought draws!

**29 ♕c5 ♕xc5 30 bxc5 ♖c7 31 ♖e5 b4 32 ♖d6 a5 33 c6 a4 34 ♔e1 b3 35 axb3 cxb3 36 ♔d2 ♔f7 37 ♖b5 ♔e7 38 ♖d4 ♖xc6 39 ♖xa4 ♖c2+ 40 ♔e3 ♖xh2 41 ♖a7+ ♔f6 42 ♖xb3 ♖c2 43 ♔d3 ♖c6 44 ♖ba3 ♖d6+ 45 ♔e3 ♗d7 46 ♖3a5 ♖d1 47 ♖c7 ♖d6 48 ♖b7 ♖d1 49 ♖aa7 ♔e7 50 ♖a8 ♖d5 51 ♖g8 ♔f7 52 ♖h8 ♔e7 53 ♖b4 ♖a5 54 ♖d4 ♗c6 55 ♖c4 ♖a3+ 56 ♔d4 ♗d7 57 ♖c3 ♖a4+ 58 ♔e3 ♖a5 59 ♖d3 e5 60 ♖b8 exf4+ 61 gxf4 ♖a7 62 ♖d5 ♗e6 63 ♖db5 ♔f6 64 ♖8b6 g6 65 ♖e5 ♖e7 66 ♔d4 ♔f7 67 ♖d6 ♔f6 68 ♖a5 ♖d7 69 ♖xd7 ♗xd7 70 ♔e4 h5 71 ♖a6+ ♗e6 72 ♖b6 h4 73 ♖a6 h3 74 ♔f3 ♔f7 75 ♔g3 ♗f5 76 ♖a8 ♔f6 77 ♖h8 ♔g7 78 ♖h4 ♗c8 79 ♔f3 ♗f5 80 ♔e3 ♗c8 81 ♔e4 ♗f5+ 82 ♔e5 ♗c8 ½-½**

**Black plays ...e6-e5**

*Game 80*
**Kharitonov-Ivanchuk**
*USSR 1988*

**1 d4 d5 2 ♘f3 ♘f6 3 c4 e6 4 ♘c3**

c6 5 e3 ♘bd7 6 ♗d3 dxc4 7 ♗xc4
b5 8 ♗d3 a6 9 e4 c5 10 d5 c4 11
♗c2 ♕c7 12 0-0 ♗c5 13 ♕e2 e5!

e6 5 e3 ♘bd7 6 ♗d3 dxc4 7 ♗xc4
b5 8 ♗d3 ♗b7 9 0-0 a6 10 e4 c5 11
d5 c4 12 ♗c2 e5

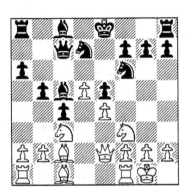

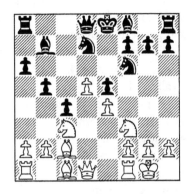

The ideal time for this move. Black's bishop is well placed on c8, covering the exposed f5-square and White's queen is somewhat in the way on e2, blocking the idea of ♘e2-g3.

**14 ♘h4?!**

A mistake according to Ivanchuk. 14 ♘d1 was better, preparing b2-b3.

**14 ... 0-0 15 ♔h1 ♗d4! 16 ♘f5?! ♘c5 17 ♕f3 ♗xf5 18 ♕xf5 ♕c8! 19 ♕f3 ♕g4 20 ♕xg4 ♘xg4 21 ♘d1 f5!**

Ivanchuk already claims a winning advantage here!

**22 exf5 ♘f6 23 ♘e3 ♖ad8 24 a4 ♘xd5 25 axb5 axb5 26 ♖a5 ♘c7 27 ♗d2 ♖a8 28 g4 e4 29 ♔g2 ♘d3 30 ♖b1 ♗xe3 31 fxe3 ♖xa5 32 ♗xa5 ♘d5 33 ♗d2 ♖a8 34 ♔g3 b4 35 ♗xd3 cxd3 36 ♖c1 ♖a2 37 ♖c5 ♖xb2 38 ♖xd5 ♖xd2 39 ♔f4 ♖c2 40 ♔e5 b3 41 ♖d8+ ♔f7 0-1**

---

*Game 81*
**Podgaets-Muhametov**
*Moscow 1995*

---

**1 d4 d5 2 c4 c6 3 ♘c3 ♘f6 4 ♘f3**

By releasing the central tension here instead of playing the main line 12...♕c7, Black accepts that his light-squared bishop will not find activity on the a8-h1 diagonal. He reasons that the piece activity that d5xe6 concedes to him weighs less than the benefits it provides White: the target of the e6-pawn and the potential e4-e5 break. By closing the centre with ...e6-e5, Black removes the point of tension that was the basis of White's attacking ambitions, forcing White to search elsewhere for activity.

**13 ♘e2!**

The structure is similar to that of the Chigorin Ruy Lopez (minus White's c3-pawn and Black's d6-pawn) and there are positional motifs common to both: the transfer of the queen's knight to f5 and the undermining of the black queenside with b2-b3 and even a2-a4. The text prepares b2-b3 without allowing ...b5-b4 and ...c4-c3 with tempo, while taking the knight towards the f5-square that was exposed when Black went ...e6-e5.

**13...♗c5 14 b3! cxb3 15 axb3**

In removing the c4-pawn, White has gained some manoeuvring space for his pieces on the queenside and freed d3 for a white knight which is a stepping stone towards two black queenside weaknesses: c5 and c6 (via b4, supported by a rook on c1). To see the value of the c5-square, imagine White's pawn on b4 and a white knight on c5: from c5, the white knight attacks a6 and the bishop on b7, while allowing White to build up his major pieces behind it on the c-file.

**15...0-0 16 ♘g3 g6**

Weakening the kingside, but the threat of ♘f5 is rather annoying for Black. Perhaps 16...♘e8 would have been better, preparing to meet 17 ♘f5 with 17...♘d6.

**17 ♗h6 ♖e8 18 h3 ♖c8 19 ♕d2 ♗f8 20 ♗xf8! ♖xf8 21 ♖fc1!**

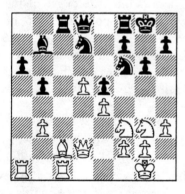

**21...♕e7?**

A bad mistake according to Podgaets who recommends instead 21...♘e8 22 ♗d1! (to activate the bishop via g4!) 22...♖xc1 23 ♖xc1 ♘d6, though he still considers this to be clearly better for White. This is a typical example of what can happen in

this opening. White's pawn wedge on e4 and d5 gives him a clear space advantage and reduces Black's minor pieces to passivity – the bishop on b7 just defends the a6-pawn and prevents White from occupying the c6 outpost with a major piece; the knight on d7 is tied to the e5-pawn; and the knight on d6, while comfortably placed, has limited scope for manoeuvre. White's c-file control also discourages Black's queen from abandoning d8 due to the possibility of ♖c7. Finally, since the dark-squared bishops have been exchanged, Black's dark squares are vulnerable to attack or infiltration by the white queen: White can challenge the blockade on d6 via ♕b4 or instigate kingside threats with ♕h6.

Clearly, the only piece that can challenge the dark-square incursions of the white queen is Black's own queen. Now we begin to see the method that White will adopt to develop an initiative. By creating threats on the dark squares with his queen, White will draw the black queen from its protection of c7, allowing ♖c7. His play is based on a combination of queen, rook and space advantage; he will normally seek the advantage in the middlegame. Consequently, Black must aim to exchange White's active major pieces and head for the endgame. However, it would be wrong to assume that all endings are unfavourable for White. For example, after an exchange of rooks, if White can follow b3-b4 (preventing ...a6-a5-a4) with a transfer of a knight to c5, he will enjoy a certain initiative. Thus White can consider Podgaets's idea of 24 h4.

A preventive move such as 24...h5 doubles the strength of 25 ♕h6, while after 24...♕e7 25 h5 ♖c8 26 ♖xc8+, White can seek to implement the above ending with the annoying h5 thrust as a bonus. It thus seems that Podgaets's assessment is justified.

**22 d6! ♕d8 23 b4!**

Freeing b3 for the light-squared bishop from where it attacks the sensitive f7-pawn. 23...♕b6 24 ♗b3! ♖cd8 24...♖xc1 25 ♖xc1 ♘xe4 26 ♘xe4 ♗xe4 27 ♘g5 ♗a8 28 ♖c7 gives White excellent compensation according to Podgaets.

**23...♕b6 24 ♗b3 ♖cd8 25 ♖e1!**

Calmly reinforcing the e4-pawn and regrouping his rooks to active squares.

**25...♘e8 26 ♖ad1 ♘df6 27 ♘xe5 ♘xd6 28 ♕f4 ♔g7 29 ♖d3 ♘c4 30 ♗xc4 bxc4 31 ♘f5+!**

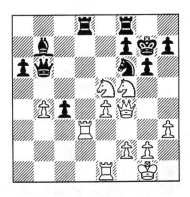

**31...♔h8 32 ♕h6 ♘h5 33 ♖d7! ♕f6 34 ♘d6 ♔g8 35 ♘xb7 ♖de8 36 ♘g4 ♕c6 37 ♘c5 a5 38 e5 axb4 39 ♘e4 ♖e6 40 ♘g5 1-0**

Essentially, as we have seen, the plan of blocking the centre with ...e6-e5 is most successful when Black has not yet committed his light-squared bishop to b7, since then it guards f5

and can also emerge with effect either to g4 or, after a black queenside pawn advance with ...a6-a5 and ...b5-b4, to a6. The most effective version of the ...e6-e5, for Black can be achieved via 8...a6 9 e4 c5 10 d5 c4 11 ♗c2 e5.

*Question 9:* Can't White just avoid ...e6-e5 by taking on e6 as soon as Black plays ...c5-c4?

*Answer:* Aha! Read on!

### Black takes the bishop on d3

**1 c4 c6 2 ♘c3 d5 3 d4 ♘f6 4 e3 e6 5 ♘f3 ♘bd7 6 ♗d3 dxc4 7 ♗xc4 b5 8 ♗d3 a6 9 e4 c5 10 d5 c4 11 dxe6 cxd3**

A key resource if Black was hoping to meet 11 ♗c2 with the blockading 11...e5 rather than the main line 11...♗b7 12 0-0 ♕c7.

**12 exd7+ ♕xd7 13 0-0 ♗b7**

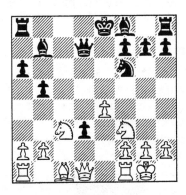

This standard position can also arise from 8...♗b7 9 0-0 a6 10 e4 c5 11 d5 c4 12 dxe6 cxd3 13 exd7+ ♕xd7. Karpov considers that Black can only think of making a draw in this line. However, in practice Black has tended to hold his own comfortably. Generally he will generally sacrifice his pawn on d3, but in contrast to normal lines, he will have the two bishops and a sound pawn structure.

**14 ♖e1**

The drawback to this line is that if White wants, he can force a draw with 14 ♘e5 ♛d4 15 ♘f3 ♛d7 16 ♘e5.

**14...♗e7 15 e5 ♘d5 16 ♘e4 0-0 17 ♛xd3 ♛g4 18 ♘g3**

18 ♘fg5!? is seen in the next game.

**18...f5!?**

This sharp move is an idea of the famous Russian coach Mark Dvoretsky.

**19 ♗d2**

19 exf6 ♗xf6 20 h3 ♘b4! gives Black good counterplay (Chernin).

**19...♖ad8 20 ♛b3 ♔h8 21 h3 ♛g6 22 ♖ac1! f4 23 ♘e4 ♘e3 24 ♗xe3 ♗d5!**

24...♗xe4 25 ♗c5 ♖d3 26 ♛xd3 ♗xd3 27 ♗xe7 would have provided White with excellent play for the sacrificed queen according to Chernin.

**25 ♗c5! ½-½**

This amazing queen sacrifice (25 ♛c3 ♗xe4 is very good for Black) is White's only way to play. Peter Wells suggests that after Chernin's recommendation of 25...♗xb3 26 ♗xe7 or 26 axb3!? ♗xc5 27 ♘xc5, intending e5-e6, White may even be slightly better.

*Game 83*
**Piket-Shirov**
*Aruba (match) 1995*

**1 d4 d5 2 c4 c6 3 ♘c3 ♘f6 4 ♘f3**

e6 5 e3 ♘bd7 6 ♗d3 dxc4 7 ♗xc4 b5 8 ♗d3 ♗b7 9 0-0 a6 10 e4 c5 11 d5 c4 12 dxe6 cxd3 13 exd7+ ♛xd7 14 ♖e1 ♗e7 15 e5 ♘d5 16 ♘e4 0-0 17 ♛xd3 ♛g4 18 ♘fg5!?

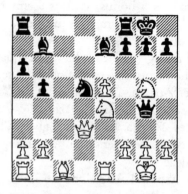

An interesting Karpov idea, threatening ♘f6+!

**18...♖fd8! 19 h3 ♛h5 20 ♘g3**

Piket also suggests 20 e6!? or 20 ♗d2.

**20...♛g6 21 ♛xg6 hxg6 22 a3 ♖ac8 23 ♘f3 b4?!**

Perhaps a mistake. Piket suggests 23...♔f8 or 23...♘b6. White does develop a certain amount of pressure in the game.

**24 ♗g5 f6 25 exf6 gxf6 26 ♗d2 ♔f7 27 axb4 ♗xb4 28 ♖a4 ♗xd2 29 ♘xd2 g5 30 ♘c4 ♔g6 31 ♖e6 ♔f7 32 ♖e1 ♔g6 33 b3 ♘f4 34 ♘e3 ♖c5 35 ♖b4 ♖b5 36 ♖xb5 axb5 37 ♖c1 ♖d3 38 ♖c7 ♗xg2 39 ♘xg2 ♘xh3+ 40 ♔f1 ♖xb3 41 ♘e4 ♖b1+ 42 ♔e2 ♖b2+ 43 ♔e1 f5 44 ♖c6+ ½-½**

It seems therefore that White may be able to keep a nagging plus in these lines, although White players hoping for a direct attack may be disappointed by their endgame nature!

### Summary

Dreev's queenside castling plans (Games 75 and 77) are particularly worthy of attention, while 8...a6 9 e4 c5 10 d5 c4 11 ♗c2 e5!? may also be worth a try if Black wishes to establish a blockade in the centre.

**1 d4 d5 2 c4 c6 3 ♘f3 ♘f6 4 ♘c3 e6 5 e3 ♘bd7 6 ♗d3 dxc4 7 ♗xc4 b5 8 ♗d3**

**8...♗b7**

    8...a6 9 e4 c5 10 d5 *(D)*

        10...♕c7 11 0-0 c4 12 ♗c2 ♗c5

            13 dxe6 – *Game 79*; 13 ♕e2 – *Game 80*

        10...c4 11 dxe6 cxd3 12 exd7+ ♕xd7 13 0-0 ♗b7 – Games 82 and 83

        (by transposition)

**9 0-0 a6 10 e4 c5 11 d5 ♕c7**

    11...c4 *(D)*

        12 ♗c2 e5 – *Game 81*

        12 dxe6 cxd3 13 exd7+ ♕xd7 14 ♖e1 ♗e7 15 e5 ♘d5

        16 ♘e4 0-0 17 ♕xd3 ♕g4

            18 ♘g3 – *Game 82*; 18 ♘fg5 – *Game 83*

**12 dxe6**

    12 ♗c2 ♗e7 13 dxe6 fxe6 14 ♘g5 ♕c6 *(D)*

        15 ♕f3 h6 16 ♕h3 hxg5 17 ♕xh8+ ♔f7 18 ♕h3 g4 19 ♕h4 ♘e5

          20 f4 – *Game 75*; 20 ♖d1 – *Game 76*

        15 f4 – *Game 77*

    12 b3 – *Game 78*

**12...fxe6** – *Game 74*

        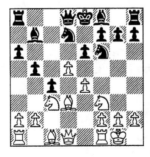

*10 d5*        *11...c4*        *14...♕c6*

# CHAPTER NINE

## Meran Variation with 8...♗b7: White Alternatives

**1 d4 d5 2 c4 c6 3 ♘f3 ♘f6 4 ♘c3 e6 5 e3 ♘bd7 6 ♗d3 dxc4 7 ♗xc4 b5 8 ♗b3 ♗b7**

Until recently, both of the lines examined in this chapter, 9 e4 and 9 a3, might have been considered the main lines of the Meran, but in the last couple of years, they have both dropped out of fashion as White players have concentrated on 9 0-0.

The first part of this chapter (Games 84-90) is concerned with 9 e4 (Games 91-95 focus on 9 a3) so let us start with an overview of this move.

**9 e4**

is a logical move: it achieves White's basic aim of freeing his dark-squared bishop by opening the c1-h6 diagonal. However, there is a drawback:

**9...b4! 10 ♘a4 c5**

After 9 e4, Black had to act to challenge White's centre straightaway. Black wants to play ...c6-c5, but obviously the b-pawn would hang if this were played immediately and 9...a6 is obvious but too slow: 10 e5! ♘d5 11 ♘xd5 cxd5 12 0-0 is very pleasant for

White. By a process of elimination we therefore arrive at 9...b4, which permits ...c6-c5 by freeing the c-pawn from the job of defending the b-pawn. Since 9...b4 attacks the knight on c3 White has no time to use his central trumps immediately. Another good side-effect is that White's knight is forced offside to the a4-square, weakening his support of e4.

**11 e5 ♘d5**

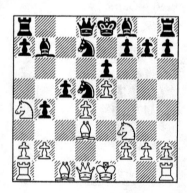

*Question 1:* What is White aiming for here?

*Answer:* White's strength is his central pawn structure and in particular his pawn on e5, which attacks Black's weakened central dark squares and provides an outpost for a white knight on d6. This pawn also gives White attacking chances on the kingside, as it takes away the defensive square f6 from the black knights: thus g4 and h5 are free for the white queen, while h7 also lacks its usual protection. If White plays on the kingside with ♘g5 and ♕h5 (attacking h7 and f7) he may be able to cause Black grave danger.

However, White can only divert his pieces to the wing if his centre is absolutely secure. Black must therefore keep the pressure on White's central pawns. Thus his c5-pawn is very important: Black can play ...c5xd4, destroying the base of White's pawn centre and preventing ♘g5 due to the loose pawn on e5.

*Question 2:* What are Black's aims?

*Answer:* Black's wants to develop without allowing White to whip up kingside play. If he is successful in this, then White's centre will switch from being an attacking weapon to an easy target for Black's pieces. An interesting feature of this line is the position of the pawn on a7.

*Question 3:* Well, what about it?

*Answer:* Black's queenside structure with the b-pawn on b4 is common in queen's pawn openings, but usually it arises after Black has played ...a7-a6 and ...b7-b5 and White undermined the queenside with a2-a4. Black never normally plays ...b5-b4 on his own initiative without provocation by a2-a4. Here, Black does have the compensation of having forced the white knight offside to a4, but White has

kept his pawn on a2 and the black a-pawn has not moved.

*Question 4:* Wow! Big deal!

*Answer:* This may seem insignificant, but it plays a major part in every single variation. White gains the possibility of a2-a3 to attack Black's queenside, while the absence of a pawn on a6 gives White ♗b5 to attack the knight on d7 or embarrass the black king on e8.

Now it's time to get down to specific moves. We shall first of all consider the main line, 12 0-0 (Games 84-88) before moving on to 12 ♘xc5 (Game 89) and 12 dxc5 (Game 90).

> ### Game 84
> ### Yakovich-Giorgadze
> *Yerevan Open 1996*

**1 d4 d5 2 c4 c6 3 ♘c3 ♘f6 4 e3 e6 5 ♘f3 ♘bd7 6 ♗d3 dxc4 7 ♗xc4 b5 8 ♗d3 ♗b7 9 e4 b4 10 ♘a4 c5 11 e5 ♘d5 12 0-0 a6?**

We examine this inferior line to show the power of White's play if left unchecked. The correct 12...cxd4 is considered in Games 85-88.

**13 ♘g5! cxd4 14 ♘xe6! fxe6 15 ♕h5+ ♔e7 16 ♗g5+ ♘5f6 17 ♖fe1! ♕e8 18 exf6+ gxf6 19 ♖xe6+!! ♔xe6 20 ♕g4+!**

20 ♖e1 would have been met by 20...♘e5. The text forces the king to move farther afield.

**20...♔d6**

20...♔f7 21 ♗c4+ ♔g7 22 ♗d2+ ♕g6 23 ♕xd7 wins, as Yakovich shows.

**21 ♕xd4+ ♔c7 22 ♖c1+ ♔b8 23 ♗f4+ ♘e5 24 ♘b6!**

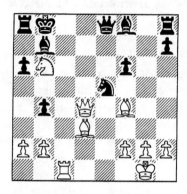

The key move in the attack, threatening ♘d7+ winning the black queen.

**24...♖a7 25 ♘d7+ ♔a8 26 ♘b6+ ♔b8 27 ♘d7+ ♔a8 28 ♗e3 1-0**

After a teasing little repetition, the finish. Black resigned as 28...♘c6 29 ♖xc6 ♕xe3 30 ♘b6+ ♔b8 31 ♕d8+ leads to mate. A gem of a game!

> ## Game 85
> ## Piket-Kramnik
> *Amsterdam 1993*

**1 d4 d5 2 c4 c6 3 ♘c3 ♘f6 4 ♘f3 e6 5 e3 ♘bd7 6 ♗d3 dxc4 7 ♗xc4 b5 8 ♗d3 ♗b7 9 e4 b4 10 ♘a4 c5 11 e5 ♘d5 12 0-0 cxd4 13 ♖e1**

For 13 ♘xd4!? see Games 87 and 88.

**13...g6!!**

After ...c5xd4, White gained the extra possibility of ♘xd4, allowing the white queen to come to g4, attacking g7 and e6, or h5, attacking f7. 13...g6 sets up the ideal defensive structure against a queen on g4 (the pawn on g6 and bishop on g7, defending the dark squares), while also taking the h5-square from White's queen. Furthermore, it also shields h7 from the bishop on d3 along the b1-h7 diagonal,

which takes the sting out of ♘g5.

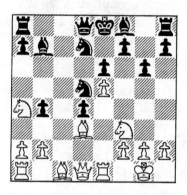

**14 ♗g5**

14 ♗d2!? is seen in the next game.

**14...♕a5 15 ♘xd4 a6!!**

Despite their active positions, White's pieces are not coordinating to create one big threat, but rather a series of 'mini-threats'. For example, 15...♗g7 would have been awkwardly met by 16 ♗b5! The calm 15...a6 prevents ♗b5 and asks White to find another idea.

**16 ♖c1 ♗g7 17 ♘c6 ♗xc6 18 ♖xc6 0-0 19 ♗c4!?**

White attacks the knight on d5 now that it has lost the support of the bishop on b7. Now 19...♘xe5 loses the queen to 20 ♖c5! (that knight on a4 comes in useful at last!) and 19...♗xe5 20 ♘c5! ♘xc5 21 ♖xe5 ♘d7 22 ♖e1 ♖fc8 23 ♗xd5 ♕xd5 24 ♕xd5 exd5 25 ♖d6 ♘c5 26 ♖xd5 ♘e6 27 ♗f6 was pleasant for White in Piket-M.Gurevich, Belgium 1993. However, Black has another resource.

**19...h6! 20 ♗xd5!**

The sharpest attempt. 20 ♗h4 ♘5b6 is about equal according to Piket, while 20 ♗d2 ♘xe5! 21 ♖c5 ♕xc5 22 ♘xc5 ♘xc4 is a good version of the queen sacrifice, which Piket assesses as slightly better for Black.

**20...♕xd5 21 ♕xd5 exd5 22 ♗f6**

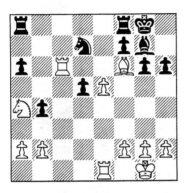

**22...♘xe5!!**

Quite amazing! After 23 ♖xe5, Black stresses the weakness of White's back rank with 23...♖ac8!! 24 ♗xg7 ♖xc6 25 ♗xh6! (stopping ...♖c1+) 25...g5! 26 ♗xg5 f6! 27 ♖xd5 fxg5 28 ♖xg5+ ♔h7 29 f3 ♖d8, when despite White's temporary material edge, Black has the better prospects due to White's rather sad knight on a4. All this analysis is by Piket.

**23 ♗xe5 ♖ae8! 24 f4 f6 25 ♘b6 fxe5 26 ♘xd5 exf4 27 ♖xe8 ♖xe8 28 ♖xg6 ♔h7 29 ♖xa6 ♖e2 30 ♔f1 ♖xb2 31 ♘xf4 ½-½**

---

### Game 86
## Alterman-Dreev
*Manila Olympiad 1992*

---

**1 d4 d5 2 c4 c6 3 ♘f3 ♘f6 4 ♘c3 e6 5 e3 ♘bd7 6 ♗d3 dxc4 7 ♗xc4 b5 8 ♗d3 ♗b7 9 e4 b4 10 ♘a4 c5 11 e5 ♘d5 12 0-0 cxd4 13 ♖e1 g6 14 ♗d2!?**

*Question 5:* This looks rather strange! What's the point?

*Answer:* Since Black is putting his bishop on the h8-a1 diagonal, White attacks the pawn whose protection the bishop will abandon: the b4-pawn.

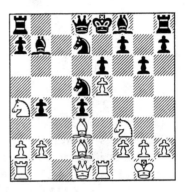

**14...♗g7 15 ♗b5!**

This move marks the start of a very sharp tactical plan which pushes Black's position to the limit. Again, White uses the fact that Black's dark-squared bishop is not covering the f8-a3 diagonal any more: by pinning the knight on d7 to the king on e8, White threatens to dramatically activate his knight on a4 with ♘c5!

**15...a6! 16 ♘c5! axb5 17 ♘xb7 ♕b6 18 ♘d6+ ♔e7!**

The best choice, as 18...♔f8 19 ♘g5! ♘xe5 20 ♖xe5 ♗xe5 (20...♕xd6 21 ♕f3! ♗f6 22 ♖xd5 exd5 23 ♗b4! wins) 21 ♘dxf7 is rather grim for Black, as Stohl points out.

*Question 6:* I'm sorry, but even after 18...♔e7 this position looks losing!

*Answer:* Stay calm! The knight on d6 is a dangerous piece, but it is not secure – Black is threatening to destroy its support with ...♘xe5. White also has few pieces in this attack – little else apart from the knight and the pawn on e5 – and not much time to bring up the reserves; he must attack now or ...♘xe5 will net another pawn. Moreover, it is very difficult for White to involve his major pieces as Black's solid centre makes such a good barrier.

**19 ♗g5+!**

The most dangerous continuation, forcing the black king back to the back rank. 19 ♘g5 was tried in an earlier game between Stohl and Sakaev in Dortmund 1992, but 19...♖hf8! 20 ♘xh7 (20 ♘xe6 fxe6 21 ♗g5+ ♗f6! 22 exf6+ ♔xd6 wins according to Stohl), and now Stohl's 20...♘xe5! 21 ♘e4 (21 ♘xf8 ♕xd6 22 ♘h7 ♖h8 23 ♘g5 ♘d3 wins) 21...f5! 22 ♘xf8 (22 ♘eg5 ♖fd8 23 f4 ♘e3 24 ♗xb4+ ♔e8 looks good for Black) 22...fxe4 23 ♘xg6+ ♘xg6 24 ♕g4 ♔f7 is slightly better for Black.

**19...♔f8 20 ♖c1!**

The most incisive continuation, grabbing the open c-file and bringing an extra unit into the attack. 20 ♘xd4 ♘xe5 21 ♘5xb5 h6 22 ♗h4 ♘c4 23 ♘xc4 ½-½ occurred in Yakovich-Novikov, Yerevan 1996.

**20...h6!**

A vital strengthening move. The immediate 20...♘xe5 fails to 21 ♘xe5 ♕xd6 22 ♖c6 trapping the queen, as 22...♕b8 23 ♘d7+ forks king and queen. This would not be a problem if Black could give up his queen for good material compensation with 22...♕xe5 23 ♖xe5 ♗xe5. However, here 24 ♕e1! is nasty: 24...♗g7 (24...♗f6 25 ♗xf6 ♘xf6 26 ♕e5! ♔g7 27 g4 h6 28 h4 wins, as does 24...f6 25 ♖xe6 ♔f7 26 ♖xe5 fxe5 27 ♕xe5) 25 ♕c1!, threatening ♖c8+, when 25...♖e8 fails to 26 ♕c5+ ♔g8 27 ♖c8! and 25...♗f6 26 ♗h6+ is also bad.

**21 ♗h4**

**21...♔g8?**

Now was the time for 21...♘xe5. The difference is that after 22 ♘xe5 ♕xd6 23 ♖c6, the queen sacrifice 23...♕xe5 24 ♖xe5 ♗xe5 was quite promising for Black in Hjartarson-Akopian, World Team Championship, Lucern 1993. Without the threat of ♗h6, Black's king is perfectly safe.

Instead of 23 ♖c6 Alterman suggests 23 ♗g3 ♕e7 24 h4 to soften up the black kingside, but after 24...h5! 25 ♕f3 ♔g8 Black has very good prospects as 26 ♘xg6 fxg6 27 ♕xd5 exd5 28 ♖xe7 d3 29 ♖d7 ♗xb2 30 ♖c6 d2 is by no means worse for Black.

The text is a bad mistake since it gives White a crucial opportunity to reinforce the pride of his position: the knight on d6.

**22 ♗g3 ♔h7 23 ♘xf7 ♖hf8 24 ♘d6 ♘f4 25 ♕d2?!**

25 ♖e4! was cleaner and would have given White a decisive advantage.

**25...♘h5 26 ♘xd4 ♘xg3 27 hxg3 ♗xe5 28 ♘xe6 ♗xd6 29 ♘xf8+ ♖xf8 30 ♖e6 ♖f6 31 ♖ce1 ♕c5 32 ♖1e3 h5 33 ♖e2 ♔g7 34 ♖e1 ♔f7 35 ♕e2 ♘e5 36 ♖xd6 ♖xd6 37**

♕xe5 ♕xe5 38 ♖xe5 ♖d2??

38...♖d1+ 39 ♔h2 ♖d2 would have made a draw according to Alterman.

**39 b3! ♖d1+ 40 ♔h2 ♖d2 41 f3 ♖xa2 42 ♖xb5 ♖a1 43 ♖xb4 g5 44 ♖b8 1-0**

---

### Game 87
### I.Sokolov-Chernin
*Wijk aan Zee 1991*

---

**1 d4 d5 2 c4 c6 3 ♘c3 ♘f6 4 e3 e6 5 ♘f3 ♘bd7 6 ♗d3 dxc4 7 ♗xc4 b5 8 ♗d3 ♗b7 9 e4 b4 10 ♘a4 c5 11 e5 ♘d5 12 0-0 cxd4 13 ♘xd4!?**

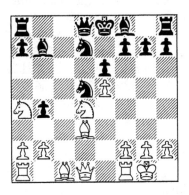

**13...♘xe5 14 ♗b5+ ♘d7 15 ♖e1**

*Question 7:* What does White have for the sacrificed pawn?

*Answer:* He seems to have a lot of compensation: his rook is well-placed on the half-open e-file; his bishop on b5 pins the knight unpleasantly; and sacrifices such as ♘xe6 are in the air. Black suffers from a considerable lag in development and, to make matters worse, has to deal with the threat of ♘c6, attacking the black queen while allowing ♕xd5!

And yet nothing seems to work for White! The problem again is the queen's knight which contributes nothing to White's play in the centre and on the queenside. This is an attack where pieces will have to be sacrificed to open up Black's solid structure; there is an urgent need for reserves to support the initial sacrifices and the offside knight on a4 seems to ruin all these attempts!

**15...♖c8!**

The first cool move, covering the c6-square and thus preventing ♘c6.

**16 ♕h5**

The second big threat arises: by pinning the pawn on f7 to the king on e8 along the h5-e8 diagonal, White instigates the threat of ♘xe6 or ♖xe6+!

The unsound but aesthetic 16 ♕xd5?! gave Black an endgame plus in Piket-M.Gurevich, Ostend 1991, after 16...exd5 17 ♖e1+ ♗e7 18 ♘xe7 ♔d8! 19 ♗d2 ♕a5 20 ♗c6 ♖e8! 21 ♗xb7 ♖xe7 22 ♖xe7 ♔xe7 23 ♗xa8 ♕xa4.

**16...g6! 17 ♕e2**

The aggressive 17 ♕e5 is considered in the next game.

**17...a6!**

Amazingly enough, this is not the only good defence in this position! Dreev has played 17...♕e7!?, which leads to an unclear ending after 18 ♗g5 ♕xg5 19 ♘xe6 ♕xg2+ 20 ♔xg2 ♘f4+ 21 ♔f1 ♘xe2 22 ♖ad1 fxe6 23 ♗xd7+ ♔f7 24 ♗xc8 ♗xc8 25 ♔xe2 ♗a6+ 26 ♔f3 ♗b7+, as in Nadera-Dreev, Manila Olympiad 1992.

However, the text gives Black a better ending!

**18 ♗xa6 ♗xa6 19 ♕xa6 ♗g7! 20 ♗g5 ♘c7!!**

The position seems difficult, but Chernin finds an amazing resource.

**21 ♕a5**

21 ♕b7 ♖b8 22 ♗xd8 ♖xb7 23 ♗xc7 ♖xc7 24 ♘b5 ♖c2 was very pleasant for Black in Vyzmanavin-Novikov, Moscow 1990, while the violent 21 ♘xe6 fxe6 22 ♖xe6+ ♔f7! 23 ♗xd8 ♘xa6 24 ♖e7+ ♔f6 25 ♖xd7 ♖hxd8 just wins for Black according to Chernin.

**21...♖a8!**

White cannot play 22 ♕xb4 as then Black wins a piece with the tactic 22...♕xg5.

**22 ♗xd8 ♖xa5 23 ♗xc7 ♖xa4 24 ♖ed1 ♘f6 25 ♗e5 0-0 26 a3 ♘d5 27 ♗xg7 ♔xg7 28 ♘c2 bxa3 29 ♖xa3 ♖c4 30 ♘e3 ♘xe3 31 ♖xe3 ♖c2 32 b3 ♖d8 33 ♖a1 ♖a8 34 ♖ee1 ♖xa1 35 ♖xa1 ♖b2 36 h4 ♖xb3 37 g3 h6 38 ♖a5 ♔f6 39 ♔g2 ♖d3 40 ♖a7 ♖d6 41 ♔f3 e5 42 ♖a8 ♖d3+ 43 ♔e4 ♖d4+ 44 ♔e3 ♔f5 45 ♖a7 f6 46 ♖h7 h5 47 ♖g7 ♖g4 48 ♖h7 ♖b4 49 ♔f3 e4+ 50 ♔e2 ♖b2+ 51 ♔e3 ♖b3+ 52 ♔e2 ♖b2+ 53 ♔e3 ♖b3+ 54 ♔e2 ♔g4 55 ♖h6 ♔h3 56 ♖xg6 ♖f3 57 ♖h6 ♔g2 58 ♖xh5 ♖xf2+ 59 ♔e3 f5 60 ♖g5 ♔f1 61 g4 ♖f3+ 62 ♔d4 e3 63 ♖xf5 ♖xf5 64 ♔xe3 ♖f8 0-1**

---

1 ♘f3 d5 2 d4 ♘f6 3 c4 e6 4 ♘c3 c6 5 e3 ♘bd7 6 ♗d3 dxc4 7 ♗xc4 b5 8 ♗d3 ♗b7 9 e4 b4 10 ♘a4 c5 11 e5 ♘d5 12 0-0 cxd4 13 ♘xd4!? ♘xe5 14 ♗b5+ ♘d7 15 ♖e1 ♖c8! 16 ♕h5 g6! 17 ♕e5

The most aggressive continuation, keeping the pressure on e6 while attacking the rook on h8.

**17...♕f6! 18 ♕e4?!**

18 ♘f3 ♗g7 is the main line and seems sufficient for Black: 19 ♗xd7+ ♔xd7 20 ♕e2 only gave White a draw in Akopian-Dokhoian USSR Championship 1991, after 20...♕e7 21 ♕b5+ ♔c7 22 a3 ♗b8 23 axb4 a6 24 ♕a5 ♕xb4 25 ♕xb4 ♘xb4 26 ♗f4+ ♔a7 27 ♗e3+ ♔b8 28 ♗f4+.

**18...♖c7!**

An excellent defensive move: 18...♗g7? was absolutely destroyed in Mikhalchisin-Lanc, Trnava 1988, by 19 ♘xe6 fxe6 20 ♗g5!, when 20...♕f7 (20...♕xg5 21 ♕xe6+ ♔f8 22 ♕xd7 ♘f4 23 ♖e8+ wins) 21 ♕xe6+ ♕xe6 22 ♖xe6+ ♔f7 23 ♗xd7 ♖c7 24 ♖d6! gave White a clear advantage.

**19 ♕g4 ♗e7 20 ♗h6 a6!**

*see following diagram*

White's problem is that his opponent can easily chase back the white pieces from their advanced positions.

**21 ♗xd7+ ♔xd7! 22 ♖ad1 ♔c8!**

Putting the king to safety. White's desperate sacrifice now flounders on the weakness of his back rank.

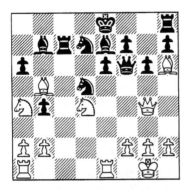

**23 ♘xe6 fxe6 24 ♖xe6 ♕f5 25 ♕xf5 gxf5 26 ♖xd5 ♗xd5 27 ♘b6+ ♔b7 28 ♘xd5 ♖d8 29 ♖e5 ♗f8 30 ♗g5 h6 31 h4 hxg5 32 ♘xc7 ♖d1+ 33 ♔h2 ♗d6! 0-1**

> ## Game 89
> ## Bareev-Kramnik
> ## *Dortmund 1995*

**1 d4 d5 2 c4 c6 3 ♘c3 ♘f6 4 e3 e6 5 ♘f3 ♘bd7 6 ♗d3 dxc4 7 ♗xc4 b5 8 ♗d3 ♗b7 9 e4 b4 10 ♘a4 c5 11 e5 ♘d5 12 ♘xc5**

With this capture White rids his position of the offside knight in a4, while clearing away some of the defences around the black king. However, these exchanges free Black's position.

**12...♘xc5 13 dxc5 ♗xc5 14 0-0**

*Question 8:* Wait! Are you crazy? White can play 14 ♗b5+ here!!

*Answer:* Aha, and now 14...♔e7.

*see following diagram*

*Question 9:* Yes, but I've forced the black king to move! It's exposed, in the centre, vulnerable to attack...

*Answer:* At first sight it feels bad to move the king and lose the right to castle. However, the key thing about Black's position is its solidity, especially in the central area: it will take something special to break past the knight on d5, supported by the bishop on b7 and the pawn on e6. White also has no pieces in the attack: there is the bishop on b5, and... nothing else! In fact the bishop is simply loose on b5, and Black threatens ...♕b6, hitting the bishop and the f2-pawn. White has only a temporary initiative; Black will soon play ...h7-h6, to stop anything coming to g5, play his king's rook to d8 and then slip his king back to f8 and absolute safety. Since White has no body of pieces to support his one check, his temporary initiative is doomed to slip away without trace.

**14...h6!**

Black must be very careful. As Kholmov demonstrates, 14...0-0 is asking for disaster: 15 ♗xh7+ ♔xh7 16 ♘g5+ ♔g6 (16...♔g8 17 ♕h5 ♖e8 18 ♕xf7+ ♔h8 19 ♕h5+ ♔g8 20 ♕h7+ ♔f8 21 ♕h8+ ♔e7 22 ♕xg7+ is mate) 17 ♕c2+ f5 18 exf6+ ♔xf6 19 ♕xc5 ♖c8 20 ♕xf8+!! ♔xf8 21 ♘h7+ neatly finishes Black off. Consequently, with his calm move, Black prevents ♗xh7+

tricks and prepares to castle.

**15 ♘d2!? 0-0 16 ♘e4 ♗d4!**

The passive 16...♗e7 would allow White to attack the kingside with 17 ♕g4! By attacking the e-pawn that White has left unprotected with his knight manoeuvre, Black makes sure that his opponent cannot simply prosecute his ideas at his own pace.

**17 ♘d6 ♗c6 18 ♗h7+ ♔xh7 19 ♕xd4 f6! 20 a3**

20 ♗d2 fxe5 21 ♕xe5 ♕d7 was played in Gagarin-Muhametov, Potsdam 1994, when Gagarin claims an edge for White after 22 ♘c4!? ♖f5 23 ♕g3 ♖af8 24 ♘e5 ♕e8 25 ♖fc1 ♗b5 26 f3, but does not look terrifying.

**20...fxe5 21 ♕e4+ ♔g8 22 ♕xe5 ♕f6 ½-½**

---

### Game 90
### Yusupov-Kramnik
*Horgen 1995*

---

**1 d4 d5 2 c4 c6 3 ♘c3 ♘f6 4 e3 e6 5 ♘f3 ♘bd7 6 ♗d3 dxc4 7 ♗xc4 b5 8 ♗d3 ♗b7 9 e4 b4 10 ♘a4 c5 11 e5 ♘d5 12 dxc5**

This used to be considered a tricky move order, but it seems now to make

no difference!

**12...♘xc5! 13 ♗b5+**

13 ♘xc5 ♗xc5 transposes to Game 89 above.

**13...♘d7 14 ♗g5 ♕a5!**

14...♗e7 loses, as Wells points out, to 15 ♘c5! ♗xg5 16 ♗xd7+ ♔f8 17 ♗xe6!

**15 ♗xd7+**

15 ♘d4 ♗a6! 16 ♗c6 ♖c8 17 ♖c1 b3+! was horrific for White in C.Hansen-Shirov, Biel 1992.

**15...♔xd7**

This position was originally assessed as better for White, but as Kramnik shows, Black can consolidate, as White has no way to get at the black king.

**16 0-0 ♗e7 17 b3 h6! 18 ♗xe7 ♔xe7 19 ♘d2 ♘f4 20 ♘c4 ♕d5 21 ♕xd5 ♗xd5 22 ♘e3 ♖hc8 23 ♖fe1 ♗e4 24 f3 ♗g6 25 ♘c4 ♘d3 26 ♖ed1 ♖d8 27 a3 bxa3 ½-½**

We shall now turn our attention to the quieter 9 a3.

---

### Game 91
### Karpov-Kramnik
*Dortmund 1995*

---

**1 d4 d5 2 c4 c6 3 ♘c3 ♘f6 4 e3 e6 5 ♘f3 ♘bd7 6 ♗d3 dxc4 7 ♗xc4 b5 8 ♗d3 ♗b7 9 a3**

As we know, Black ideally wants to play ...c6-c5, but first he has to protect b5 with ...a7-a6 or try ...b5-b4. 9 a3 is directed against both of these two ideas. White will meet 9...a6 with 10 b4, clamping down on c5; while by attacking b4, he also hopes to make ...b5-b4 a little less tempting, since by delaying e3-e4, he reserves the e4-square for his queen's knight.

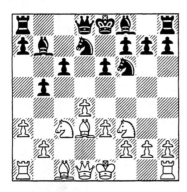

*Question 10:* Oh I see. It doesn't sound earth-shattering!

*Answer:* No, it isn't, but this is one of those annoying lines that can give White a nice safe edge if Black is unwary or slightly careless.

**9...b4! 10 ♘e4**

After 10 axb4 ♗xb4, Black easily achieves ...c6-c5. 10 ♘e4 is the move which has revitalised this variation.

**10...♘xe4**

10...a5 is rather risky – see Games 92-95.

**11 ♗xe4 bxa3! 12 bxa3 ♗d6**

With a series of accurate moves Black has solved the problem of his b-pawn and he is now not far from playing ...c6-c5. The slight drawback to his plan is that he has brought the white light-squared bishop to e4, which temporarily prevents ...c6-c5 by pinning the c6-pawn to the bishop on b7, and that he has opened the b-file, which gives White the chance to play ♖b1 to harass the bishop on b7 along the b-file, but these factors don't seem to be sufficient for White to be able to do any real damage.

**13 ♗d2 ♖b8 14 ♕a4!?**

The sharpest continuation. 14 0-0

0-0 15 ♗b4 c5! was equal in Karpov-Kramnik, Monaco (rapidplay) 1996.

**14...c5 15 ♗xb7 ♖xb7 16 dxc5 ♗xc5 17 ♗a5 ♕b8 18 ♖d1 0-0 ½-½**

Chandler analyses 19 ♖xd7!? ♕e8! 20 ♘e5 ♖b1+ (20...♗d6 21 0-0 ♗xe5 22 ♖fd1 ♖xd7 is equal and is safer) 21 ♔e2 ♖xh1 22 ♗c3 ♕c8 23 ♕g4 g6 24 ♘xg6 ♕a6+! 25 ♔d2! hxg6 26 ♕xg6+! fxg6 27 ♖g7+ ♔h8 28 ♖f7+ with a draw by repetition!

The previous game was not too thrilling, but it is a very effective equaliser for Black. It is certainly preferable to 10...a5, which results in a position that could arise from 8...b4 9 ♘e4 (Chapter 11) but with extra moves a2-a3 and ...a7-a5 thrown in. As we shall see, this should be nice for White as he has the chance to open the a-file with a3xb4 at some stage.

*Game 92*
**Greenfeld-Khenkin**
*Israel 1995*

**1 ♘f3 ♘f6 2 c4 c6 3 ♘c3 d5 4 d4 e6 5 e3 ♘bd7 6 ♗d3 dxc4 7 ♗xc4 b5 8 ♗d3 ♗b7 9 a3 b4! 10 ♘e4 a5 11 ♘xf6+**

11 0-0 can be seen in Game 95.

**11...♘xf6 12 e4 ♗e7 13 ♕e2! ♘d7**

Black's sharp alternatives here, 13...c5 and 13...♕b6, are considered in Games 93 and 94 respectively.

**14 0-0 0-0 15 ♖e1!? ♕c7**

15...♖e8 16 ♗f4 c5 17 ♗b5 is good for White according to Greenfeld, but 15...c5 is critical. After 16 d5, Greenfeld gives 16...♘b6 17 dxe6 fxe6 as unclear, but 18 ♗e3 followed by consolidation with ♖ac1 and ♖ed1 must give

White a slight edge due to Black's exposed queenside. 16...exd5 17 exd5 Re8 18 ♗b5! and 17...♘f6 18 ♗f4! Re8 19 ♕c2 ♗xd5 20 ♗xh7+ ♔h8 21 Rxe8+ ♕xe8 22 Re1 both favour White according to Greenfeld.

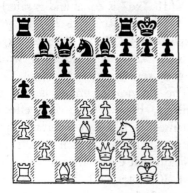

**16 e5! Rfe8 17 ♘g5 ♗xg5 18 ♗xg5 ♘f8 19 ♕h5?**

A mistake. 19 Rac1!, to prevent the freeing ...c6-c5, would have given White an overwhelming position according to Greenfeld.

**19...c5! 20 Rac1 ♕d7 21 Rxc5 Rec8 22 axb4 Rxc5 23 bxc5 ♕xd4 24 ♕e2 ♕xc5 25 h4 ♕d5 26 ♕f1 h6 27 ♗e7 ♘g6 28 ♗xg6 ½-½**

To counter 13 ♕e2, Black players have recently been trying some very radical solutions.

> ### Game 93
> ### Karpov-Shirov
> *Linares 1994*

**1 d4 d5 2 c4 c6 3 ♘f3 ♘f6 4 ♘c3 e6 5 e3 ♘bd7 6 ♗d3 dxc4 7 ♗xc4 b5 8 ♗d3 ♗b7 9 a3 b4! 10 ♘e4 a5 11 ♘xf6+ ♘xf6 12 e4 ♗e7 13 ♕e2! c5!?**

Thematic in a way, since it is part of

the Semi-Slav tradition not to mind losing the right to castle. However, this is usually done when White has played e4-e5 and Black has blocked the central files with an immovable knight on d5. Here, with the e4-pawn restricting the knight on f6, Black's task is much more difficult.

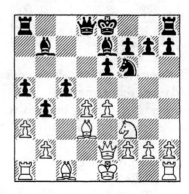

**14 ♗b5+ ♔f8 15 dxc5 ♗xc5**

15...♗xe4 16 ♗e3 is slightly better for White according to Karpov.

**16 ♗d3 h6 17 0-0 g5**

17...g6 18 ♗f4 ♔g7 19 ♗e5 is rather nasty for Black according to Karpov.

**18 ♗e3 ♗xe3 19 ♕xe3 ♔g7 20 ♘e5!**

White is making good use of the e5-square!

**20...♘d7 21 ♘c4 ♕e7 22 ♕d4+ e5 23 ♕d6 ♕xd6 24 ♘xd6 ♘c5 25 ♗c4 Rhd8 26 ♘f5+ ♔g6 27 f3 ♘a4 28 Rf2 ♘b6 29 ♗b5 ♗c8 30 axb4 axb4 31 Rxa8 ♘xa8 32 ♘e7+ ♔g7 33 ♘d5 ♗e6 34 ♘xb4 Rb8 35 ♗c6 Rxb4 36 ♗xa8 Ra4 37 ♗b7 Ra1+ 38 Rf1 Ra4 39 Rf2 Ra1+ 40 Rf1 Ra4 41 ♗c6 Rb4 42 Rf2 Rc4 43 ♗d5 ♗xd5 44 exd5 Rd4 45 b3 Rd1+ 46 Rf1 Rxd5 47 b4 ♔f6 48 Rb1 ♔e6 49 b5 ♔d7 50 b6 ♔c8 51 b7+ ♔b8 52**

♖b6 ♖d4 53 ♔f2 h5 54 ♔e3 g4 55 ♖f6 ♖d7 56 ♖f5 ♖xb7 57 ♖xh5 ♖b3+ 58 ♔f2 gxf3 59 gxf3 f6 60 h4 ♔c7 61 ♖h6 ♖b6 62 h5 ♔d7 63 ♖g6 ♔e6 64 h6 ♖b7 65 ♔g3 ♖b1 66 ♔h2 ♖b7 67 ♔h3 ♖b1 ½-½

---

### Game 94
### Bareev-Dreev
*Russia 1996*

---

1 d4 d5 2 c4 c6 3 ♘f3 ♘f6 4 ♘c3 e6 5 e3 ♘bd7 6 ♗d3 dxc4 7 ♗xc4 b5 8 ♗d3 ♗b7 9 a3 b4! 10 ♘e4 a5 11 ♘xf6+ ♘xf6 12 e4 ♗e7 13 ♕e2! ♕b6!? 14 0-0 c5 15 axb4! cxb4

15...axb4 16 ♖xa8+ ♗xa8 17 ♗b5+ ♔f8 18 d5 exd5 19 exd5 ♗xd5 20 ♖e1 ♕b7 21 ♘e5 is clearly better for White according to Bareev.

16 d5 exd5 17 ♗e3 ♗c5 18 ♗xc5 ♕xc5 19 ♖ac1 ♕b6 20 ♗b5+ ♔f8 21 e5 ♘e8 22 ♖fe1 ♘c7? 23 e6! ♘xe6 24 ♘e5

With the threat of ♘d7+, forking king and queen.

24...♔g8 25 ♘xf7 ♔xf7 26 ♖c6!

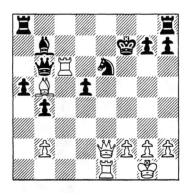

26...♕d8 27 ♕xe6+ ♔f8 28 ♖d6 1-0

The other plan with 0-0 and e4-e5 also looks very promising here!

---

### Game 95
### Gavrilov-Novikov
*Riga Open 1995*

---

1 d4 d5 2 c4 e6 3 ♘f3 ♘f6 4 ♘c3 c6 5 e3 ♘bd7 6 ♗d3 dxc4 7 ♗xc4 b5 8 ♗d3 ♗b7 9 a3 b4! 10 ♘e4 a5 11 0-0 ♗e7 12 ♘xf6+ ♘xf6 13 e4 0-0 14 e5 ♘d7 15 ♗e4 ♖b8 16 axb4! axb4 17 ♕c2 h6 18 ♗e3

Gavrilov shows that the freeing 18...c5 fails tactically due to 19 ♗xb7 ♖xb7 (19...cxd4 20 ♗xh6 ♖xb7 21 ♗f4 is best but still bad) 20 dxc5 ♘xc5 21 ♗xc5 ♕c8 22 ♖a5! (the difference!)

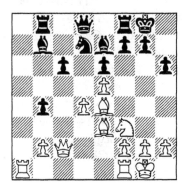

18...♘b6 19 ♘d2 ♘d5 20 ♘b3 ♕b6?! 21 ♗d2 ♖fd8 22 ♖fc1 ♖a8 23 ♖xa8 ♖xa8 24 ♘c5 ♗c8 25 ♕b3 ♖a5 26 ♕g3 ♔h8 27 ♕h3 ♗f8 28 ♗b1 ♘e7 29 g4 ♔g8 30 ♕d3 ♘g6 31 ♘b3 ♖d5 32 h4 ♗e7 33 h5 ♘f8 34 ♕c4 ♗a6 35 ♕xc6 ♕xc6 36 ♖xc6 ♗e2 37 ♗e4 ♖d7 38 f3 ♗d1 39 ♘a5 ♖xd4 40 ♗e3 ♖d7 41 ♖c8 ♗a4 42 ♗c6 ♖d3 43 ♗f2 ♖d1+ 44 ♔g2 ♖c1 45 ♖xf8+ ♔xf8 46 ♗xa4 ♖a1 47 b3 ♖a2 48 ♔g3 f6 49 ♘c6 ♖xa4 50 ♘xe7 ♔xe7 51 bxa4 b3 52 ♗c5+ 1-0

## Summary

At the moment Black seems to be holding his own quite comfortably after both 9 e4 b4 10 ♘a4 c5 and 9 a3 b4! 10 ♘e4 ♘xe4. One thing, however: don't touch 9 a3 b4 10 ♘e4 a5.

**1 d4 d5 2 c4 c6 3 ♘f3 ♘f6 4 ♘c3 e6 5 e3 ♘bd7 6 ♗d3 dxc4 7 ♗xc4 b5 8 ♗d3 ♗b7**

**9 e4**

    9 a3 b4 10 ♘e4

        10...♘xe4 – *Game 91*

        10...a5

            11 ♘xf6 ♘xf6 12 e4 ♗e7 13 ♕e2 *(D)*

                13...♘d7 – *Game 92*

                13...c5 – *Game 93*

                13...♕b6 – *Game 94*

            11 0-0 – *Game 95*

**9...b4 10 ♘a4 c5 11 e5 ♘d5 *(D)* 12 0-0**

    12 ♘xc5 – *Game 89*; 12 dxc5 – *Game 90*

**12...cxd4**

    12...a6 – *Game 84*

**13 ♖e1**

    13 ♘xd4 ♘xe5 14 ♗b5+ ♘d7 15 ♖e1 ♖c8 16 ♕h5 g6

        17 ♕e2 – *Game 87*; 17 ♕e5 – *Game 88*

**13...g6 *(D)* 14 ♗g5**

    14 ♗d2 – *Game 86*

**14...♕a5 – *Game 85***

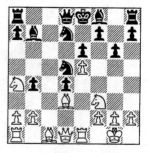

     *13 ♕e2*           *11...♘d5*           *13...g6*

# CHAPTER TEN

## Meran Variation with 8...a6: Old Main Line – 9 e4 c5 10 e5

---

**1 d4 d5 2 c4 c6 3 ②f3 ②f6 4 ②c3 e6 5 e3 ②bd7 6 ♗d3 dxc4 7 ♗xc4 b5 8 ♗d3 a6 9 e4 c5 10 e5**

The variation with 9 e4 c5 10 e5 is the most aggressive way for White to play, and is a direct attempt to refute, or at least exploit the inconveniences of, Black's move order with 8...a6.

*Question 1:* How is that?

*Answer:* With 8...♗b7, Black only plays ...c6-c5 once he has placed his bishop on the a8-h1 diagonal. Consequently Black always has piece cover of the d5-square; e4-e5 can never really inconvenience him since he can always play his knight to d5 without any bother. However, in the 8...a6 9 e4 line, Black has to rush ...c6-c5 without first developing his light-squared bishop. When White plays 10 e5 attacking the knight on f6, 10...②d5 is poor since after 11 ②xd5 Black must recapture with a pawn on d5, blocking the a8-h1 diagonal and leaving him with a rather shaky position.

Black's only chance is to fight fire with fire and play

**10...cxd4**

Black counters the threat against his knight on f6 attacking White's knight on c3. 11 exf6 bxc3 gives Black a good game. Usually, White replies with **11 ②xb5**

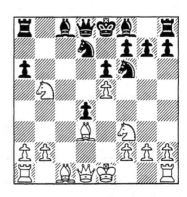

*Question 2:* Why?

*Answer:* Rather than allow Black just to take White's knight on c3, White makes a 'desperado' sacrifice to get as much as he can for the knight before it succumbs to the inevitable.

Now things can get a little confusing. The main line here has historically been 11...②xe5, while both

---

11...♘g4 and 11...axb5 12 exf6 ♛b6 have also had a lot of theory devoted to them. However in the last couple of years, there have been virtually no games played with these lines, since a completely new main line has emerged. It is so new in fact that Peter Wells' magisterial *The Complete Semi-Slav* (published in 1994) contains virtually no mention of it!

Consequently, I have concentrated almost exclusively on this new line and will just give a summary (almost a history lesson!) of the other lines.

**11...axb5 12 exf6 gxf6!?**

12...♛xf6?? (12...♘xf6 13 ♗xb5+ followed by 14 ♘xd4 or ♛xd4 wins a pawn) 13 ♗g5 traps the queen.

*Question 3:* I can see that 13 ♗xb5 loses a piece to 13...♛a5+, but can't White simply play 13 ♘xd4, regaining his pawn and leaving him with a clearly better pawn structure?

*Answer:* This is a crucial question. Let us take a look at the stem game for this line.

*Game 96*
**Alterman-Chernin**
*Groningen (PCA Qualifier) 1993*

**1 d4 d5 2 c4 c6 3 ♘c3 ♘f6 4 e3 e6 5 ♘f3 ♘bd7 6 ♗d3 dxc4 7 ♗xc4 b5 8 ♗d3 a6 9 e4 c5 10 e5 cxd4 11 ♘xb5 axb5**

Black's alternatives here are considered in Game 100.

**12 exf6 gxf6**

The old 12...♗b7 is the subject of Game 99.

**13 ♘xd4 ♛b6!!**

The key move that has revitalised

this variation. Alterman showed the way to play against 13...♗b7 in a game against Har Zvi in Israel 1993: 14 ♗e3! (White's idea is not to castle, but to develop by playing the king to e2. This avoids giving Black any counter-play against the white king by pressuring g2 after castling) 14...♗xg2 (14...♖g8 is simply met by 15 ♛h5! ♖xg2 16 ♔e2! with a clear advantage for White according to Alterman) 15 ♖g1 ♗d5 16 ♗xb5 ♛c7 17 ♛d3 ♛xh2 18 ♗xd7+ ♔xd7 19 ♛b5+ ♔d8 20 ♘c6+ ♔c7 21 ♗b6+ with a very big attack. White developed his play so quickly in the game above because he was able to maintain his knight on d4, where it is is ideally placed on d4 because it attacks all the loose light squares in Black's position: it can threaten a sacrifice on e6, and it supports ♗xb5.

Chernin's 13...♛b6 puts pressure on the knight and intends to increase this by playing ...♗c5, which forces White to take early measures to bolster his knight. The second and very crucial point is that by leaving the light-squared bishop on c8, Black robs the force from ♗xb5. In the 13...♗b7 line, once the black queen left d8, ♗xb5 threatened ♗xd7+, drawing the black king into the firing line of the white queen. Here ♗xd7+ is simply met by the recapture on d7 with the bishop. 13...♕b6 thus destabilises White's strength (his d4-knight) and neutralises one of his major threats (♗xb5, aiming for ♗xd7+). Coupled with the open lines this enables Black to quickly whip up a ferocious initiative. **14 ♗e3**

14 ♗xb5 is met by 14...♗b4+ 15 ♔f1 e5! 16 ♗xd7 ♗xd7 with a strong initiative, while 14 ♗e4 is met by the surprising 14...♖a4! 15 ♗e4 ♗c5 with compensation according to Chernin. Finally, 14 ♘xb5 ♗b7 15 0-0 ♖g8 gives a huge attack.

**14...♗b4+! 15 ♔f1 ♗c5! 16 ♗xb5 e5 17 ♗xd7+ ♗xd7 18 ♕f3 ♕a6+ 19 ♘e2 ♖g8!? 20 ♗xc5 ♗c6 21 ♕h5 ♗xg2+ 22 ♔e1 ♗xh1 23 ♕xh7 0-0-0!**

Black is just winning but the finish is very nice!

**24 ♖c1 ♔b8 25 ♕xf7 ♗d5 26 ♕h5 ♕d3 27 ♕h4 ♗c4 0-1**

28 ♕xc4 ♕d2+ 29 ♔f1 ♕d1+!! 30 ♖xd1 ♖xd1+ is mate!

Consequently, White players have shunned 13 ♘xd4 in favour of 13 0-0, putting the king into safety first!

*Game 97*
**Gelfand-Shirov**
*Linares 1997*

**1 d4 d5 2 c4 c6 3 ♘c3 ♘f6 4 ♘f3 e6 5 e3 ♘bd7 6 ♗d3 dxc4 7 ♗xc4 b5 8 ♗d3 a6 9 e4 c5 10 e5 cxd4 11 ♘xb5 axb5 12 exf6 gxf6 13 0-0 ♕b6!**

At the cost of a pawn and his pawn centre, White has greatly loosened Black's structure – e4-e5xf6 has doubled Black's f-pawns, while ♘xb5 has reduced Black's queenside to an isolated b-pawn. Black's king, in contrast to White's, lacks a haven on either wing and will have to take its chances in the centre behind the f7, f6, e6 cluster. Due to his large range of weaknesses, it is difficult for Black to consolidate his extra pawn, so he should seek instead to generate activity.

**14 ♕e2!**

Attacking the pawn on b5. 14 ♗e4 ♗b7 15 ♗xb7 ♕xb7 16 ♘xd4 ♖g8 17 f3 ♘e5 17...♘e5 18 ♕e2 ♗c5 19 ♗e3 ♖d8 20 ♖ad1 ♘c4 21 ♗f2 ♕b6! was equal, Kamsky-Kramnik, Linares 1994

**14...♗a6**

Black's wants to keep hold of some queenside light squares by keeping the b-pawn on b5. The alternative 14...b4! is seen in the next game.

**15 ♖d1!**

This move has been causing Black problems. White's removes the rook from the f1-a6 diagonal and takes the sting out of Black's idea of ...♘xd3.

**15...♗c5**

15...♘c5 is mentioned by Romanov and now 16 ♘xd4 ♘xd3 17 ♕xd3.

Although Black has won the bishop pair, it is at the cost of his extra pawn and a couple of tempi. By exchanging off the bishop on d3, Black reduces his opponent's ability to use the queenside light squares to attack the black king. However, the exchange of Black's knight further loosens his own position. In particular, the kingside dark squares – f6, for example – are much easier to attack. Black's problem is that although he has plenty of open lines for his pieces, and can thus activate them easily, it is a difficult for him to coordinate them.

After 17 ♕xd3, White intends to set up his ideal attacking formation: queen on the g-file (stopping Black's counterplay with ...♖g8 and preventing ...♗e7 due to ♕g7), bishop to e3 and queen's rook to the c-file.

**16 a3! ♗b7!? 17 ♗xb5 ♖g8 18 b4?!**

This seems a trifle rushed to me. 18 ♗f4!? looks interesting, preparing to retreat the bishop to g3 and deal with Black's pressure against g2.

**18...♗e7 19 ♖xd4!?**

19 ♗f4 is still worth a try here.

**19...♕xd4! 20 ♘xd4 ♗xg2!**

Amazingly White has no way to get out of this with a material advantage: 21 ♗xd7+ ♔xd7 22 ♕b5+ fails to 22...♗c6+!

**21 ♕e3 ♗h3+ 22 ♔h1 ♗g2+ 23 ♔g1 ♗h3+ 24 ♕g3!?**

Very brave, sacrificing a pawn for chances with his passed pawn.

**24...♖xg3+ 25 hxg3 ♗xb4 26 ♗b2 ♗c5 27 a4 e5 28 ♘c6 ♔f8 29 a5 ♘b8 30 ♖c1 ♗d6 31 ♘xb8 ♖xb8 32 a6 ♖xb5 33 a7 ♖a5 34 ♖a1 ♖xa7 35 ♖xa7 ♔g7 36 ♔h2 ♗e6 37 ♖a8 ♗c5 38 ♔g1 h5 39 ♗c1 ♔g6 40 ♖h8 ♗g4 41 ♔g2 ♔g7 42 ♖b8 ♗e6 43 ♖b5 ♗d4 44 ♖b8 ½-½**

*Game 98*
**De Sousa-N.Eliet**
*French Championship 1996*

1 c4 c6 2 d4 d5 3 ♘c3 ♘f6 4 e3 e6 5 ♘f3 ♘bd7 6 ♗d3 dxc4 7 ♗xc4 b5 8 ♗d3 a6 9 e4 c5 10 e5 cxd4 11 ♘xb5 axb5 12 exf6 gxf6 13 0-0 ♕b6 14 ♕e2! b4!

This is Black's best chance: by playing the pawn to b4, Black weakens his grip over the queenside light squares even more, but by occupying b4, he at least creates the chance of defending the d4-pawn with ...♗c5 without having the bishop driven away.

**15 ♖d1 ♗c5! 16 ♗f4**

16 ♗xh7 ♗a6 (16...♖xh7 loses the exchange to 17 ♕e4!) 17 ♗d3 e5!? is extremely murky. Black will retreat the bishop to e7 and attack the light squares with ...♘c5. White should stop this by transferring the king's knight to b3 or e4 via d2.

**16...♗b7 17 ♗b5 ♖d8 18 ♖ac1 ♖g8 19 ♗g3 ♔f8 20 ♕c4 ♗d5 21 ♕d3 ♗xf3 22 gxf3 ♘e5 23 ♕e2 d3 24 ♗xd3 ♘xd3 25 ♖xd3 ♗xf2+ 26 ♔g2 ♗d4 27 ♖c4 e5 28 ♕d2 f5 29 ♔f1 ♖a8 30 ♖xb4 ♕a6 31 ♕e2 f4 32 ♗f2 ♕g6 33 ♖bxd4 exd4 34 ♗xd4 ♖e8 35 ♗c5+ ♔g7 36 ♕d2 ♕f5 37 ♖d5 ♕h3+ 38 ♕g2+ ♕xg2+ 39 ♔xg2 ♔f6+ 40 ♔f1 ♖a8 41 a3 ♔e6 42 ♖d6+ ♔e5 43 ♖d2 ½-½**

We shall now take a rapid look through the older lines that used to fashionable in this variation.

> **Game 99**
> **Csiszar-Sploshrov**
> *Budapest Open 1996*

**1 d4 d5 2 c4 e6 3 ♘c3 c6 4 e3 ♘f6 5 ♘f3 ♘bd7 6 ♗d3 dxc4 7 ♗xc4 b5 8 ♗d3 a6 9 e4 c5 10 e5 cxd4 11 ♘xb5 axb5 12 exf6 ♗b7!?**

An interesting little idea.

**13 fxg7**

Very natural, but I wonder if 13 ♘xd4 is possible here, hoping to transpose to Alterman-Har Zvi in the notes to Game 96 after 13...gxf6 14 ♗e3!

**13...♗xg7 14 0-0 0-0 15 ♖e1**

The greedy 15 ♗xb5 ♘c5 16 ♗f4 e5!? 17 ♗g3 ♘e6!, intending ...e5-e4, gave Black good compensation in Sakaev-Belikov, USSR 1990.

**15...♘c5!?**

15...♕b6 16 ♖e1 ♗d5 17 h4!, intending h4-h5-h6, was dangerous for Black in Shabalov-Kishnev, USSR 1988. The text is often dismissed as bad, but it is not quite clear.

**16 ♗xh7+! ♔xh7 17 ♘g5+ ♔g8!?**

This is the point! 17...♔g6 18 ♕g4 f5 19 ♕g3! ♔f6 20 ♕e5+ ♔g6 21 ♕xc5 is very unpleasant for Black.

**18 ♕h5 ♖e8 19 ♕xf7+ ♔h8 20 ♖e5?**

This is not the best. Unfortunately for Black, White seems to be able to obtian an advantage with 20 b4! ♕d5 21 f3, when 21...d3 22 bxc5 d2 23 ♗xd2 ♕xd2 24 ♕h5+ ♔g8 25 ♖ad1 ♕c2 26 ♖d7! ♕xc5+ 27 ♔h1 is very dangerous for Black.

**20...♕e7 21 ♕h5+ ♔g8 22 ♕h7+ ♔f8 23 ♘xe6+ ♕xe6 24 ♖f5+ ♕xf5 25 ♕xf5+ ♔g8 26 ♗f4 ♖ac8 27 h4 d3 28 h5 ♗e4 29 ♕g4 ♔h7 30 f3 ♖g8 31 ♕h3 ♗xf3 32 g4 ♗xb2 33 ♖f1 ½-½**

On move 41 after a time scramble that left both score-sheets illegible!

The final idea is a line that theoretically always seems to be doing fine, but is rather difficult to handle.

---

### Game 100
### Bareev-Yusupov
*Linares 1993*

---

**1 d4 d5 2 c4 c6 3 ♘c3 ♘f6 4 e3 e6 5 ♘f3 ♘bd7 6 ♗d3 dxc4 7 ♗xc4 b5 8 ♗d3 a6 9 e4 c5 10 e5 cxd4 11 ♘xb5 ♘xe5**

By eliminating White's pawn on e5, Black makes sure that he keeps his kingside pawn structure intact.

11...♘g4 12 ♘d6+! ♗xd6 13 exd6 ♛a5+ 14 ♕d2! ♕d5 15 ♕g5! ♕xg5 16 ♗xg5 ♘c5 17 ♗e2 f6 18 ♗d2 e5 19 0-0 was good for White in Greenfeld-D.Gurevich, Beersheva 1994.

**12 ♘xe5 axb5 13 ♗xb5+ ♗d7 14 ♘xd7 ♛a5+ 15 ♗d2 ♛xb5 16 ♘xf8 ♔xf8**

Still the most popular, although Lukacs's 16...♖xf8 deserves a mention and brought him a good win against Ibragimov in Budapest 1992 after 17 a4 ♛c4 18 b3 ♛d3 19 ♕e2!? ♛xb3 20 0-0 ♖xa4 21 ♕e5 ♘d7! 22 ♕xg7 ♖xa1 23 ♖xa1 ♛b2! 24 ♖a8+ ♔e7 25 ♗g5+

♔d6 26 ♖a6+ ♔d5! 27 h4 ♛b1+ 28 ♔h2 ♛b8+ and now White should have played for the draw with 29 ♔g1.

**17 b3 ♘d5**

17...♔e7 was rehabilitated by Bykhovsky against Greenfeld in Kfar-Sava 1995, when 18 a4 ♛d5 19 0-0 ♖hc8 20 b4 ♘e4 21 b5 ♖c4! 22 b6 ♘xd2 23 ♕xd2 ♖axa4 24 ♖xa4 ♖xa4 25 ♖b1 ♖a8 26 ♕c2 ♛d6! 27 ♕xh7 ♖b8 29 b7 ♛d5 gave Black a fine game.

**18 a4 ♛d3**

To stop White from castling. 19 ♗b4+ fails because of 19...♘xb4.

**19 ♕e2 ♛xb3 20 0-0 ♛c2 21 ♖fc1 d3 22 ♕e1 ♛b2 23 ♖c4?!**

23 a5 would have been better according to Yusupov.

**23...♖b8 24 a5 ♔e7 25 a6 ♖b5?!**

25...♖hc8 26 ♖xc8 ♖xc8 27 a7 ♖a8 28 ♖b1 ♛d4 29 ♖b7 ♔d6! would have given Black a clear advantage according to Yusupov.

**26 ♖cc1 ♛d4 27 ♖cb1 ♖xb1 28 ♕xb1 ♖b8 29 ♕c1 ♖a8 30 ♖a5 ♖a7 31 ♕a3+ ♔f6 32 ♖a4 ♛b6 33 ♕xd3 g6 34 ♗h6 ♛b2 35 h4 ♔e7 36 g3 ♕c3 37 ♕b5 ♛c7 38 ♕b2 ♖a8 39 a7 f6 40 ♗f4 ♘xf4 41 ♖xf4 e5 42 ♖a4 ♔f7 43 ♕d2 ♔g7 44 ♕e3 ♛b7 45 ♕c5 ♖d8 46 ♖a1 ♖a8 47 ♔h2 ♔g8 48 g4 ♛e4 49 ♖a4 ♛b7 50 g5 fxg5 51 hxg5 h6 52 gxh6 ♔h7 53 ♖a3 ♕f7 54 ♕e3 ♛b7 55 ♔g3 ♛c7 56 ♖a6 ♕f7 57 ♔h2 ♛b7 58 ♖a5 ♕c7 59 ♖a6 ♛b7 60 ♕d3 ♕f7 61 ♕e3 ½-½**

White's main alternative to the craziness of 11 ♘xb5 is to play instead 11 ♘e4, an old move that was recently resurrected by the Spanish player Pablo San Segundo.

---

> ## Game 101
> ## San Segundo-Vera
> *Alcobendas 1994*

**1 d4 ♘f6 2 c4 e6 3 ♘f3 d5 4 ♘c3 c6 5 e3 ♘bd7 6 ♗d3 dxc4 7 ♗xc4 b5 8 ♗d3 a6 9 e4 c5 10 e5 cxd4 11 ♘e4**

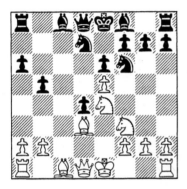

### 11...♘d5

This seems like Black's best reply. 11...♘xe4 12 ♗xe4 ♗b4+ 13 ♗d2 ♗xd2+ 14 ♕xd2 ♖b8 15 ♕xd4 gives White a small plus.

### 12 0-0 ♕c7!?

This is the most logical way to meet this line. Black makes use of the fact that the knight on e4 blocks the e-file to nip off White's e-pawn and go two pawns up. But it's very risky! 12...h6 13 a4 b4 14 ♗c4 (14 ♗c2!?, intending ♕xd4) 14...♗b7 15 ♕xd4 ♕b6 16 ♖d1 ♖c8 17 a5 ♕xd4 18 ♖xd4 ♘c5 19 ♘d6+ ♗xd6 20 exd6 0-0 21 ♗d2 was a touch better for White in Korchnoi-Gelfand, Madrid 1996.

### 13 ♗g5 ♘xe5 14 ♘xe5 ♕xe5 15 ♖e1

Vera suggests that 15 f4 ♕b8 16 f5 would have been dangerous.

### 15...♕b8

At the Linares Open in 1995, Dmitri Gurevich played 15...♕c7 against San Segundo, when 16 ♖c1 ♕d7 17 ♗b1 ♗b4 18 ♕xd4 0-0 19 ♘f6+ ♘xf6 20 ♕xb4 ♖d8 21 ♗xf6 gxf6 22 ♖c3 ♕d4 23 ♕a3 was very dangerous but not conclusive. Vera also suggests 15...♗b7!? 16 ♘f6+ gxf6 17 ♖xe5 fxe5, sacrificing the queen to blunt White's initiative.

### 16 ♖c1 ♕b6 17 ♕g4 ♗b7 18 a4 ♗b4 19 ♖e2 bxa4 20 ♗h4 ♔f8?

The decisive mistake after which Black seems to be lost. 20...0-0, however, does not look too bad for Black: 21 ♘f6+ ♘xf6 22 ♗xf6 g6 23 ♗xd4 ♕d8 24 ♕f4 ♗d6 25 ♕h6 e5 26 ♖e3 exd4 27 ♖h3 ♖e8 28 ♕xh7+ ♔f8 29 ♗xg6 ♕f6 'unclear' is Vera's analysis, but this looks good for Black to me.

### 21 ♘g5 ♖e8 22 ♕h5 g6 23 ♗xg6!

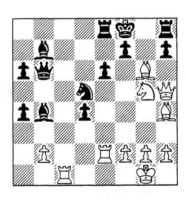

### 23...fxg6 24 ♕f3+ ♔g7 25 ♕f7+ ♔h6 26 ♖xe6 ♗c6 27 h3 ♖ef8 28 ♖cxc6 ♖xf7 29 ♘xf7+ ♔g7 30 ♖xb6 ♔xf7 31 ♖xa6 ♖c8 32 ♖e4 ♖c1+ 33 ♔h2 ♗d6+ 34 ♖xd6 1-0

This line thus deserves further investigation as a more sensible and measured approach to the 8...a6 9 e4 c5 10 e5 cxd4 variation!

---

## Summary

If you don't mind unbalanced pawn structures then this chapter is for you! Black is not doing badly at all in general, but it obviously takes a special type of player (like Shirov!) to thrive in this sort of situation. The older lines with 11...♘xe5 are theoretically healthy, although it can be a little daunting in a practical game to face two connected passed pawns!

**1 d4 d5 2 c4 c6 3 ♘f3 ♘f6 4 ♘c3 e6 5 e3 ♘bd7 6 ♗d3 dxc4 7 ♗xc4 b5 8 ♗d3 a6**

**9 e4 c5 10 e5 cxd4** *(D)* **11 ♘xb5**
     11 ♘e4 – *Game 101*
**11...axb5**
     11...♘xe5 – *Game 100*
**12 exf6** *(D)* **gxf6**
     12...♗b7 – *Game 99*
**13 ♘xd4**
     13 0-0 ♕b6 14 ♕e2 *(D)*
          14...♗a6 – *Game 97*
          14...b4 – *Game 98*
**13...♕b6** – *Game 96*

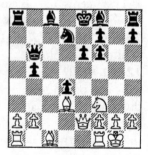

*10...cxd4*       *12 exf6*       *14 ♕e2*

# CHAPTER ELEVEN

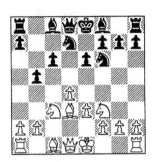

## Meran Variation: Systems with an Early ...b5-b4

**1 d4 d5 2 c4 c6 3 ♘f3 ♘f6 4 ♘c3 e6 5 e3 ♘bd7 6 ♗d3 dxc4 7 ♗xc4 b5 8 ♗d3**

In this chapter we focus on lines with an early ...b5-b4 for Black.

*Question 1:* How does this system arise?

*Answer:* There are two move orders. 8...b4 leads directly into the ...b5-b4 complex. By delaying the development of the bishop on c8, Black gains a variety of extra possibilities, though it is not clear how good these are! The most common move order, however, is 8...♗b7 9 0-0 b4. We shall discuss the significance of this move order later, but suffice it to say that this does give White a couple of extra possibilities: he can play 9 e4 (when 9...b4 was seen in Games 84-90) or 9 a3 (when 9...b4 was the subject of Games 91-95).

*Question 2:* What is the point of ...b5-b4?

*Answer:* With this advance Black moves the b-pawn from its attacked square on b5 to the safe b4-square. It also gains a tempo on the knight on c3, disturbing White's piece set-up and allowing Black to play ...c6-c5 with the greatest possible speed. However, by playing ...b5-b4, Black loses some control over the queenside light-squares: he gives away the c4-square (which is a particularly nice square for a white knight) and the a4-square. Moreover, unlike in the 8...♗b7 9 e4 b4 10 ♘a4 line, Black does not force White's queen's knight offside, as it can come to the centre with ♘e4.

First, let us see what happens if Black plays the straightforward but rather inflexible 8...♗b7 9 0-0 b4 10 ♘e4 ♘xe4.

---

*Game 102*
**Sadler-Bisby**
*Isle of Man Open 1995*

---

**1 d4 d5 2 c4 c6 3 ♘c3 ♘f6 4 e3 e6 5 ♘f3 ♘bd7 6 ♗d3 dxc4 7 ♗xc4 b5 8 ♗d3 ♗b7 9 0-0 b4 10 ♘e4 ♘xe4!? 11 ♗xe4**

The exchange on e4 has blocked

White from pushing e3-e4. Moreover, by forestalling ♘xf6+, Black keeps his queen's knight on d7, where it supports the ...c6-c5 break. The drawback of the exchange is that it brings the white bishop to the h1-a8 diagonal, making it less easy for Black to achieve ...c6-c5 quickly.

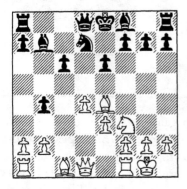

**11...♗e7 12 ♕a4!? ♕b6 13 ♗d2?!**

After this, White has no advantage. During the postmortem, I was rather confused as I had seemed to get nothing whilst playing the only moves! Then Peter Wells showed me 13 ♘d2! The knight is headed for c4, and as a bonus, it will arrive with tempo by attacking the queen on b6. Moreover, after ...♘f6, the bishop on e4 can retreat to f3 and maintain White's pressure along the h1-a8 diagonal. White will then develop his dark-squared bishop on b2-b3 and ♗b2, making sure of course that his queen does not get trapped on a4! In fact, ♘d2 would also not be bad on the 12th move as well.

In the game, I was struggling.

**13...0-0 14 ♖fc1 ♖fc8 15 ♖c4 ♘f6?!**

A slightly nervous move. 15...a5 16 ♖ac1 ♕a7!, threatening ...♘b6, would

have forced 17 ♕d1 c5! with a slight edge for Black.

**16 ♗xb4 ♘xe4 17 ♗xe7 ♕xb2 18 ♖f1 a5? 19 ♖c2 ♕b5 20 ♕a3 ♕d5 21 ♖fc1 ♖c7 22 ♗c5 ♗c8 23 ♘e5 f6 24 ♘c4 ♘xc5 25 ♘b6 ♕e4 26 ♘xa8 ♖a7 27 ♘b6 1-0**

More often than not Black plays this line with the immediate 8...b4.

### Game 103
### Yakovich-Sveshnikov
*Yerevan Open 1996*

**1 d4 d5 2 c4 c6 3 ♘c3 ♘f6 4 e3 e6 5 ♘f3 ♘bd7 6 ♗d3 dxc4 7 ♗xc4 b5 8 ♗d3 b4 9 ♘e4 ♘xe4**

9...♗b7 10 ♘xf6+ gxf6!? 11 e4 c5 12 ♗e3 ♕b6 13 ♖c1 0-0-0!? 14 0-0 ♔b8 was the rather outrageous attempt in Yakovich-Filippov, Perm 1997. After 15 ♕e2 ♖g8 16 ♖fd1 f5!? 17 ♗f4+ ♗d6 18 ♗xd6+ ♕xd6 19 dxc5 ♘xc5 20 ♗b1 Black's position was very loose. Black's other alternatives, 9...c5 and 9...♗e7, are considered in Games 104-105 and 106-109 respectively.

**10 ♗xe4 ♕b6!?**

10...♗b7 11 0-0 would have transposed to the game above, but by using the flexible (8...b4) move order, Black hopes to improve on that line. By protecting the attacked c6-pawn with the queen, he frees his light-squared bishop to come to the a6-f1 diagonal to cover the c4-square. His aim is then to move his rook from a8 and break with ...c6-c5.

**11 ♕a4!?**

11 0-0 seems sensible and if 11...♗a6 then 12 ♖e1 ♖c8 13 a3 is troublesome for Black.

**11...♗b7 12 ♘d2 ♖c8 13 a3 c5!**

This novelty seems to equalise quite comfortably, so White definitely needs something earlier.

**14 dxc5 ♗xc5 15 axb4**

Or 15 0-0 bxa3 16 bxa3 ♕a6!

**15...♗xb4 16 0-0 ♖c7!**

The key defensive move.

**17 ♗xb7 ♕xb7 18 ♘b3 0-0 19 ♖d1 ♖b8 20 ♗d2 h6 21 ♘a5 ♕b5 22 h3 ♗xd2 23 ♕xb5 ♖xb5 24 ♖xd2 ♘f6 25 ♖a4 ♘d5 26 ♘c4 ♔f8 27 ♔f1 ♔e7 28 ♔e2 f6 29 g3 ♖bc5 30 ♘a3 ♖b7 31 ♖c4 ♖bc7 32 ♖xc5 ♖xc5 33 ♘c2 a5 34 h4 g5 35 hxg5 hxg5 36 e4 ♘c7 37 ♘e3 ♘b5 38 ♔d1 ♘d6 39 ♖d4 ♖e5 40 f3 f5??**

When this happens, it really is heartbreaking.

**41 ♖xd6 fxe4 42 fxe4 ♖xe4 43 ♖d3 ♔f6 44 ♔d2 ♖b4 45 ♔c3 ♔e5 46 ♘c4+ ♔e4 47 ♖e3+ ♔f5 48 ♘xa5 ♖b8 49 ♘c4 ♔g4 50 b4 ♔h3 51 ♘d6 g4 52 ♘e4 ♔g2 53 ♔c4 ♖c8+ 54 ♔d4 ♖b8 55 ♖b3 ♖b5 56 ♘c5 1-0**

A more aggressive and consistent continuation for Black is 9...c5. He has already safeguarded his b-pawn, so why not play ...c6-c5 immediately?

*Game 104*
**Ivanchuk-Oll**
*Biel Interzonal 1993*

**1 c4 e6 2 d4 ♘f6 3 ♘f3 d5 4 ♘c3 c6 5 e3 ♘bd7 6 ♗d3 dxc4 7 ♗xc4 b5 8 ♗d3 b4 9 ♘e4 c5**

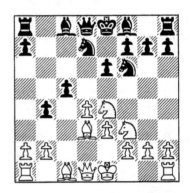

**10 ♘xf6+**

After 10 0-0, Piket's 10...♕b6! is best. By putting pressure on d4, Black stops White from setting up his attacking structure after e3-e4 ...c5xd4, ♘xd4 as the queen on b6 defends the pawn on d4. After 11 ♘xf6+ gxf6 12 b3 cxd4! (the right time, as 12...♗b7 13 ♗b2 cxd4 14 ♗xd4 is annoying for Black) 13 exd4!? (13 ♘xd4 ♗c5 is fine for Black) 13...♗b7 14 ♖e1 ♗d6 15 ♗e4 ♗xe4 16 ♖xe4 ♕b7 Black had equalised in Bareev-Piket, Dortmund 1995.

**10...gxf6**

10...♘xf6 11 ♘e5!, with ideas of ♗b5+ and ♕f3, is difficult for Black.

**11 ♗e4!?**

11 0-0 ♕b6! transposes to the note to White's 10th move and 11 e4!? is considered in the next game.

**11...♖b8 12 0-0 f5 13 ♗c6 ♕c7**

Trying to drive the white bishop from the long diagonal. 13...♖b6!? is also possible.

**14 d5**

On 14 ♘e5, Oll gives 14...♗g7 15 ♗xd7+ ♗xd7 16 ♘xd7 ♕xd7 17 dxc5 ♕xd1+ 18 ♖xd1 ♖c8 19 ♗d2 a5 with equality.

**14...♗g7 15 e4 fxe4 16 ♖e1!?**

An interesting idea. Lugovoi-Sveshnikov, Novgorod Open 1995, continued instead 16 ♘g5 0-0 17 ♗xd7 ♗xd7 18 ♘xe4 c4! 19 ♖e1 ♖b5 20 ♗h6!? ♗xh6 21 ♘f6+ ♔g7 22 ♕d4 ♔g6 23 h4 ♕f4! 24 h5+ ♔g7 25 ♘e8+ ♔g8 26 ♘f6+ ♔h8 27 ♕xf4 ♗xf4 28 ♘xd7 ♖d8 29 dxe6 fxe6 and Black was winning. I think he always had that one under control!

**16...exd5!**

16...0-0 17 ♖xe4 exd5 18 ♗xd5 with ♗f4 to follow is very good for White according to Oll.

**17 ♕xd5**

17 ♗xd5 ♘f6! 18 ♗xe4 0-0 is unclear according to Oll.

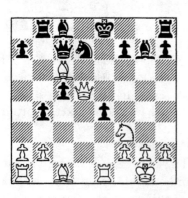

**17...0-0 18 ♕xe4 ♖b6 19 ♗a4 ♖e6 20 ♗f4 ♖xe4 21 ♗xc7 ♖xe1+ 22 ♖xe1 ♗xb2 23 ♗d6 ♖d8 24 ♗c7 ♖f8 25 ♗d6 ½-½**

Neither side can avoid the repetition.

*Game 105*
**Akesson-Ingbrandt**
*Stockholm (Rilton Cup) 1997*

**1 d4 d5 2 c4 c6 3 ♘f3 ♘f6 4 ♘c3 e6 5 e3 ♘bd7 6 ♗d3 dxc4 7 ♗xc4 b5 8 ♗d3 b4 9 ♘e4 c5 10 ♘xf6+ gxf6 11 e4!? cxd4 12 ♘xd4 ♗c5 13 ♗e3!?**

This is very risky. Black has not yet committed his light-squared bishop, which detracts from the strength of ♗b5. 13 ♘b3 would have been safer.

**13...♕b6! 14 ♗c2!? ♗a6**

Stopping White from castling kingside.

**15 ♗a4!**

Now the fun begins! White's first threat is 16 ♗xd7+ ♔xd7 17 ♘b3+ winning a piece.

**15...♖d8 16 ♖c1!**

**16...0-0**

White threatened 17 ♖xc5 ♕xc5 18 ♘c6! ♕c4 19 ♘xd8 0-0 20 ♕g4+ ♔h8 21 ♗h6! ♖g8 22 ♘xf7+ mate. 16...b3!? (intending ...♗b4+) is tempting, to meet 17 ♖xc5, not with 17...♕xc5 when 18 ♘c6 ♕c4 19 axb3! is strong, but with 17...bxa2!?

After 18 ♘c2 ♕xb2, I really don't know what is going on!

**17 ♗xd7 ♖xd7**

Or 17...b3!? 18 ♖xc5 ♕xc5 (18...bxa2!?) 19 ♕g4+ ♔h8 20 ♘xe6!, and now 20...♕b4+ 21 ♗d2 fxe6!? (to stop ♕g7+ mate; 21...♕xd2+!? 22 ♔d2 ♖xd7+ 23 ♔c1 seems better for White) 22 ♗xb4 bxa2. Here 23 ♕d1 fails to 23...♖xd7 24 ♕a1 ♖fd8, when 25 ♕xa2 ♖d1+ is mate, but 23 ♔d2 ♖xd7+ 24 ♔c3! (24 ♔c2 ♗d3+ 25 ♔b3 ♗b1!! followed by ...a2-a1♕!) 24...♖c8+ 25 ♔b3 ♗c4+ 26 ♔a3 does the trick for White.

**18 ♖xc5!**

It took me a while to believe that 18...♕xc5 loses to 19 ♕g4+ ♔h8 20 ♘xe6! Black has no checks and cannot deal with the double threat of ♕g7+ mate and ♗xc5.

**18...f5**

Black's last chance was 18...b3.

**19 exf5 ♕xc5 20 ♕g4+ ♔h8 21 ♘xe6! ♕e5 22 ♘xf8 ♖d8 23 ♘d7!**
**1-0**

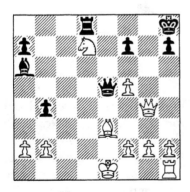

23...♖xd7 loses to 24 f6!, threatening ♕xd7 and ♕g7+ mate.

Well it worked, but it certainly was risky! There is still plenty of life in this system for Black!

**1 d4 ♘f6 2 c4 c6 3 ♘c3 d5 4 ♘f3 e6 5 e3 ♘bd7 6 ♗d3 dxc4 7 ♗xc4 b5 8 ♗d3 b4 9 ♘e4 ♗e7**

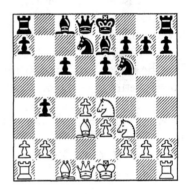

This quiet move introduces the main line of the 8...b4 variation.

**10 ♘xf6+ ♘xf6 11 e4 ♗b7 12 ♕e2!**

It is now time to discuss move orders! Black players who play the main line of this variation usually prefer to reach it via 8...♗b7 9 0-0 b4 10 ♘e4 ♗e7 11 ♘xf6+ ♘xf6. The flexibility of 8...b4 is of no use in the main line, since Black wants his bishop on b7 in all cases. Moreover, 8...b4 9 ♘e4 ♗e7 10 ♘xf6+ ♘xf6 11 e4 ♗b7 gives White the possibility of delaying castling with 12 ♕e2!

*Question 3:* Can't Black just castle here?

*Answer:* 12...0-0 13 e5! ♘d7 14 ♕e4! (14 h4!?) 14...g6 15 ♗h6 ♖e8 is not pleasant for Black after 16 h4!? or the more sober 16 0-0. Black must therefore play 12...♘d7 to anticipate 13 e5. However, after 13 0-0 0-0, Black has lost all chance of playing the lines that arise after 12 0-0 0-0 13 ♕e2 c5!?

*Question 4:* How does the 8...♗b7 move order help?

*Answer:* After 8...♗b7 9 0-0, White has already castled. Consequently, after 9...b4 10 ♘e4 ♗e7 11 ♘xf6+ ♘xf6 12 e4, he cannot play ♕e2 before Black castles, and after 12...0-0 13 ♕e2, Black can play the most active lines with 13...c5.

**12...♘d7 13 e5?!**

This, however, tries for too much. 13 0-0 was better – see the next game.

**13...c5!**

Preparing castling by preventing ♕e4.

**14 dxc5 0-0 15 0-0?! ♘xc5 16 ♗c4 ♖c8 17 ♗f4 ♘a4!**

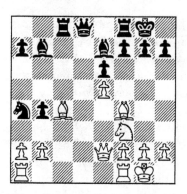

A typical idea in this system. The knight is impossible to remove from a4, since b2-b3 would concede an outpost on c3. White must live with the annoying pressure against b2.

**18 ♖fd1 ♕a5 19 ♖d2 ♖fd8! 20 ♖xd8+**

The natural 20 ♖ad1 would have

lost a pawn to 20...♘xb2! 21 ♖xb2 ♖xd1+ 22 ♕xd1 ♖xc4.

**20...♖xd8 21 ♖c1 h6 22 h3 ♘b6**

Regrouping the knight now that it has done its duty.

**23 ♗b3 ♘d5 24 ♗d2 ♕b6 25 ♖c2 a5 26 ♕c4 ♗f8 27 ♕g4 ♘e7! 28 ♗e3 ♕b5 29 ♖c5 ♕e2 30 ♖xa5 ♘f5 31 ♗b6 ♖c8 32 ♔h2 ♖c1 33 ♗e3 ♖a1 34 ♘d4 ♕f1 35 ♘xf5 exf5 36 ♗xf7+ ♔h8 0-1**

A nice game from Piket.

*Game 107*
**Levin-Antunes**
*Seville Open 1994*

**1 d4 d5 2 c4 c6 3 ♘c3 e6 4 ♘f3 ♘f6 5 e3 ♘bd7 6 ♗d3 dxc4 7 ♗xc4 b5 8 ♗d3 b4 9 ♘e4 ♗e7 10 ♘xf6+ ♘xf6 11 e4 ♗b7 12 ♕e2! ♘d7 13 0-0 0-0**

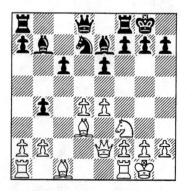

On d7, his knight is well-placed to support ...c6-c5 since d4xc5 ...♘xc5 hits the bishop on d3. However, Black has less control over the d5-square, so it is easier for White to meet ...c6-c5 with the central thrust d4-d5.

**14 ♖d1**

Very natural, but White could bor-

row from another variation and play
14 ♖e1!? to meet 14...c5 with 15 d5
exd5 16 exd5, hitting the bishop on e7.
For a more detailed discussion of this
idea, see the game Greenfeld-Khenkin
(Game 92).

**14...♕c7 15 ♗e3 ♖ac8 16 ♗a6?!**

Very passive. 16 ♖ac1 had to be better.

**16...♕b6 17 ♗xb7 ♕xb7 18 ♖ac1
c5 19 dxc5 ♘xc5 20 e5 ♘a4! 21
♗g5 h6 22 ♗xe7 ♕xe7 23 h3 ♕b7
24 ♕d2 a5 25 a3 b3 26 ♕d4 ♕b5
27 ♘e1 ♘b6 28 ♖xc8 ♖xc8 29 ♘d3
♘d5 30 a4 ♖c4 31 axb5 ♖xd4 32
♔f1 ♘f4 33 b6 ♘xd3 34 b7 ♖b4 35
♖xd3 ♖xb7 36 ♔e2 a4 37 ♖d8+ ♔h7
38 ♖a8 ♖b4 39 ♔e3 g5 40 ♖a7 ♔g6
41 g3 h5 42 ♔d3 h4 43 ♔c3 hxg3
44 fxg3 ♖e4 45 ♔d3 ♖xe5 46 ♖xa4
♖e1 47 ♖b4 ♖g1 48 ♖xb3 ♖xg3+ 49
♔c4 ♖xb3 0-1**

The final two games deal with the
main line position that arises when
White has already committed himself
to early castling.

| *Game 108* |
| :---: |
| **Lautier-Piket** |
| *Monaco (match) 1996* |

**1 d4 d5 2 c4 c6 3 ♘f3 ♘f6 4 ♘c3
e6 5 e3 ♘bd7 6 ♗d3 dxc4 7 ♗xc4
b5 8 ♗d3 ♗b7 9 0-0 b4 10 ♘e4
♗e7 11 ♘xf6+ ♘xf6 12 e4 0-0 13
♕e2 c5**

*see following diagram*

The most testing move. 13...♘d7
would have transposed to the previous
game.

**14 dxc5!**

This is inconvenient for Black, as
14...♗xc5? 15 e5! ♗xf3 (15...♘d5 16
♗xh7+!) 16 ♕xf3 ♘d5 17 ♕e4 g6 18
♗h6 ♖e8 19 ♗b5 ♖e7 20 ♗g5! wins
the exchange.

**14...♖c8!?**

14...♘d7!?, to recapture on c5 with
the knight, was slightly better for
White in Stohl-Novikov, Ostrava
1995, after 15 c6! ♗xc6 16 ♗e3 ♗b7
17 ♖ac1 ♕a5 18 ♗b5 (18 ♘d4!?)
18...♖ad8 19 ♘d4! (19...♗xe4 with 20
♗c6!). This is nothing huge for White
but he is just a touch better.

**15 ♗d2!?**

This was improvised at the board
and is quite sneaky. Serper's suggestion of 15 ♖d1 ♖xc5 16 ♗e3 ♖a5 17
♘d2! looks good, so I would love to
know what Piket had in mind!

**15...♗xc5?**

This falls into the same trap that
Black had previously avoided! 15...a5
16 a3 (16 ♖ac1!?) 16...bxa3 17 ♖xa3
♖xc5 is suggested as unclear by Piket.

**16 e5 ♗xf3 17 ♕xf3 ♘d5 18 ♕e4
g6 19 ♗h6 ♖e8 20 ♗b5 ♖e7 21 ♗g5
♕b6 22 ♗xe7 ♘xe7**

Despite White's extra exchange, it is

no easy matter to win this position since Black is so solid.

**23 ♗d7 ♖d8 24 ♖ad1 ♘f5 25 ♗a4 ♖xd1 26 ♗xd1 ♗d4 27 b3 ♕c5 28 ♗g4 ♘e7 29 ♗f3 ♘d5 30 ♕h4 ♘c3 31 ♕d8+ ♔g7 32 ♕f6+ ♔g8 33 ♕d8+ ½-½**

Like the other seven games in this match, the game was drawn!

Now the most aggressive try for White, and the one favoured by most of the top players: 13 e5.

*Game 109*
**Beliavsky-Anand**
*Reggio Emilia 1991*

**1 d4 d5 2 c4 c6 3 ♘c3 ♘f6 4 e3 e6 5 ♘f3 ♘bd7 6 ♗d3 dxc4 7 ♗xc4 b5 8 ♗d3 ♗b7 9 0-0 b4 10 ♘e4 ♗e7 11 ♘xf6+ ♘xf6 12 e4 0-0 13 e5 ♘d7 14 ♗e4**

Preventing ...c6-c5 by pinning the pawn to the bishop on b7.

**14...♖b8**

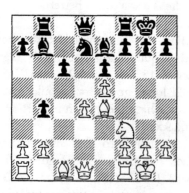

Defending the bishop to allow ...c6-c5.

**15 ♕c2**

The *ECO* recommendation of 15 ♗c2 is rather mystifying here! However, 15 ♗e3 seems very sensible. Jelen-Furlan, Bled 1992, continued 15...c5 16 ♗xb7 ♖xb7 17 d5. White had a slight edge after 17...exd5 18 ♕xd5 ♕b6 19 ♗g5 ♖e8 20 ♗xe7 ♖xe7 21 ♖ac1 ♖c7 22 ♖fd1 ♘f8 23 ♘d2.

**15...h6 16 ♗e3 c5! 17 ♗xb7 ♖xb7 18 dxc5**

Gelfand has suggested that 18 ♕e4 ♕a8 19 ♖fd1 is slightly better for White here, but it's not that much. Instead 18 ♖fd1 ♕c8 19 dxc5 ♘xc5 20 ♖ac1 ♖d8! 21 ♕c4 (21 ♖xd8 ♕xd8 22 ♗xc5 ♖c7! is equal according to Gelfand) 21...♖xd1 22 ♖xd1 a5 23 ♖c1 ♖d7 was level in Karpov-Antunes Tilburg 1994.

**18...♘xc5 19 ♖fd1 ♕b8 20 ♕c4**

20 ♗xc5 ♖c8 21 ♗xa7 ♖xc2 22 ♗xb8 ♖xb8 23 ♖ab1 ♖a8 24 ♘d4 ♖c5 25 ♖a1 g5 gives Black good compensation for the pawn according to Anand, who is a frequent advocate of the Semi-Slav.

**20...♘d7 21 ♕e4 ♖c8 22 ♖d2 ♖bc7 23 ♖ad1 ♖c4 24 ♖d4 ♘b6 25 ♕g4 ♔f8 26 ♕e4 ♔g8 27 ♕g4 ♖xd4 28 ♖xd4 ♔f8 29 ♕h5 ♕c7 30 h4 ♗c5 31 ♖d2 ♗xe3 32 fxe3 ♘d5 33 ♔f2 ♕c5 34 ♘d4 ♘f6 35 ♕f3 ♕xe5 36 ♖d1 ♔g8 37 ♕f4 ♕d5 38 ♖a1 e5 39 ♕f5 ♖c4 40 b3 exd4 0-1**

## Summary

These systems are still quite fresh and unexplored and they could well prove to be a nasty surprise for an unprepared White player.

**1 d4 d5 2 c4 c6 3 ♘f3 ♘f6 4 ♘c3 e6 5 e3 ♘bd7 6 ♗d3 dxc4 7 ♗xc4 b5 8 ♗d3**

**8...♗b7**

    8...b4 9 ♘e4

        9...♘xe4 – *Game 103*

        9...c5 10 ♘xf6+ gxf6 *(D)*

            11 ♗e4 – *Game 104*

            11 e4 – *Game 105*

        9...♗e7 10 ♘xf6+ ♗xf6 11 e4 ♗b7 12 ♕e2 ♘d7 *(D)*

            13 e5 – *Game 106*

            13 0-0 – *Game 107*

**9 0-0 b4 10 ♘e4 ♘xe4**

    10...♗e7 11 ♘xf6+ ♘xf6 12 e4 0-0 *(D)*

        13 ♕e2 – *Game 108*

        13 e5 – *Game 109*

**11 ♗xe4 – *Game 102***

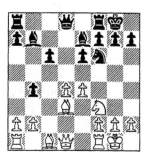

    *10...gxf6*          *12...♘d7*          *12...0-0*

# CHAPTER TWELVE

## Meran Variation:
## Odds and Ends

**1 d4 d5 2 c4 c6 3 ♘f3 ♘f6 4 ♘c3 e6 5 e3 ♘bd7 6 ♗d3**

In this chapter, we take a brief look at some of the unusual variations of the Meran. The first three games with White's other bishop retreats after 6...dxc4 7 ♗xc4 b5, i.e. 8 ♗e2 (Games 110 and 111) and 8 ♗b3 (Game 112). We then move on to a discussion of Black's solid 6...♗d6 (Games 113-116).

Game 110
**Aleksandrov-Yagupov**
*Russia 1996*

**1 d4 d5 2 c4 c6 3 ♘c3 ♘f6 4 e3 e6 5 ♘f3 ♘bd7 6 ♗d3 dxc4 7 ♗xc4 b5 8 ♗e2 a6 9 e4!?**

Piket's 9 0-0 worked successfully against Kaidanov in Groningen 1993 after 9...c5 10 d5 exd5 11 ♘xd5 ♗b7 12 ♘xf6+ ♕xf6 13 a4 b4 14 e4 h6 15 ♗c4 ♘b6 16 e5 ♕g6 17 ♗d3 with a slight initiative for White. The idea of 9 0-0 is to avoid the lines in the game, meeting 9...♗b7 with 10 e4 and 11 e5.
**9...b4 10 e5 bxc3 11 exf6 ♘xf6!**

The simplest. 11...cxb2 12 fxg7 bxa1♕ 13 gxh8♕ looks fun, but actually it is just horrible for Black!
**12 bxc3 ♗d6 13 ♕a4!?**

13 ♘d2!? has not been scoring well recently. Tunik-Savchenko, St Petersburg 1996, continued 13...0-0 14 ♘c4 ♗e7 15 ♘e5 ♕c7 16 ♗f3 ♗b7 17 ♖b1 ♖a7 18 0-0 c5! 19 ♗f4 ♕c8 20 dxc5 ♗xc5 and Black was fine. 13 0-0 is considered in the next game.

**13...♗d7 14 ♘e5 c5! 15 ♘xd7 ♕xd7 16 ♕xd7+ ♔xd7 17 ♗f3 ♖ab8 18 dxc5 ♗xc5 19 ♗f4 ♖b6 20 0-0 ♘d5!**

This move equalises according to Yagupov.

**21 ♖fd1 ♗d6 22 ♗xd6 ♖xd6 23 c4 ♘c3 24 ♖dc1 ♖d3 25 ♖c2 ♖b8 26 ♔f1 ♘a4 27 c5 ♖d4 28 ♖e1 ♔c7 29 g3 ♖b5 30 ♖e5 ♖b2 31 ♖ee2 ♖bb4 32 ♔g2 ♖bc4 33 c6 ♘c5 34 ♖b2 ♖c1 35 ♖ec2 ♖xc2 36 ♖xc2 ♘d3 37 ♔f1 ♘b4 38 ♖b2 ♖c4 39 ♗e2 ♖c1+ 40 ♔g2 a5 41 a3 ♘xc6 42 ♗a6 ♔d6 43 ♖b7 ♘e5 44 ♗b5 ♖c7 45 ♖b8 h5 46 a4 ♖c2 47 h3 ♖c5 48 ♖d8+ ♔e7 49 ♖a8 ♘c4 50 h4 ♘d6 51 ♖a7+ ♔f6 52 ♖xa5 ♖d5 53 f3 g6 54 ♔f2 ♔g7 55 ♔g2 e5 56 ♔f2 ♔h6 57 g4 f6 58 ♔g3 hxg4 59 fxg4 ♘e4+ 60 ♔f3 ♘c3 61 ♔e3 ♘xa4 ½-½**

*Game 111*
**Gabriel-Slobodjan**
*Bad Homburg 1996*

**1 ♘f3 d5 2 c4 c6 3 d4 ♘f6 4 ♘c3 e6 5 e3 ♘bd7 6 ♗d3 dxc4 7 ♗xc4 b5 8 ♗e2 a6 9 e4 b4 10 e5 bxc3 11 exf6 ♘xf6! 12 bxc3 ♗d6 13 0-0**

**13...♕c7!**

The most accurate, side-stepping the pin with ♗g5 and preparing ...c6-c5 as quickly as possible.

**14 ♗d3 c5 15 ♗g5 ♗b7 16 ♖e1 ♘d7!**

Preparing kingside castling when Black will have no problems.

**17 ♗e4 0-0 18 ♗xb7 ♕xb7 19 ♖b1 ♕c6 20 ♘e5 ♗xe5 21 dxe5 ♖fb8 22 ♗e7 ♖xb1 23 ♕xb1 ♖b8 24 ♕c1 ♘xe5 25 ♖xe5 ♕c7 26 ♖xc5 ♕xe7 27 ♖c4 g6 28 h3 ♕d6 ½-½**

*Game 112*
**Ilincic-Kosic**
*Belgrade 1996*

**1 d4 d5 2 c4 c6 3 ♘f3 ♘f6 4 ♘c3 e6 5 e3 ♘bd7 6 ♗d3 dxc4 7 ♗xc4 b5 8 ♗b3**

I tried this move once myself, but didn't like it! The bishop is not well placed here since dreams of sacrifices on the a2-g8 diagonal are likely to remain just that.

**8...b4 9 ♘e2 ♗b7 10 ♘f4 ♗d6 11 ♘g5 ♗xf4! 12 exf4 0-0 13 0-0 c5 14 ♗e3?!**

14 ♖e1 was better, but White's position is not impressive anyway.

**14...♗a6 15 ♖e1 c4!**

Black now stands very well, but loses it near the time control.

16 ♗c2 ♗b7 17 f5 exf5 18 ♗xf5
♘b6 19 ♕c2 g6 20 ♗h3 ♖e8 21
♖ad1 ♕d5 22 ♘f3 ♗c6 23 b3 c3 24
♘e5 ♗b7 25 a3 a5 26 axb4 axb4 27
♘d3 ♕b5 28 ♘c5 ♗d5 29 ♗g5
♖xe1+ 30 ♖xe1 ♖e8 31 ♕c1 ♘e4 32
♘xe4 ♖xe4 33 ♖xe4 ♗xe4 34 ♕f4
♕e8 35 ♕d6 ♘d5 36 ♗d7 ♕a8 37
f3 ♗d3 38 h4 c2 39 ♗c6 ♕a1+ 40
♔h2 c1♕ 41 ♗xc1 ♕xc1 42 ♗xd5
♕e1 43 ♕b8+ ♔g7 44 ♕e5+ ♕xe5+
45 dxe5 f6 46 f4 fxe5 47 fxe5 g5
48 ♔g3 ♔g6 49 ♔f3 ♔f5 50 e6 ♗b5
51 hxg5 ♔xg5 52 ♔e4 1-0

## Game 113
## Lalic-Nogueiras
*Moscow Olympiad 1994*

1 d4 d5 2 c4 e6 3 ♘c3 c6 4 e3 ♘f6
5 ♘f3 ♘bd7 6 ♗d3 ♗d6

**7 e4!?**

Critical. An early e3-e4 forces Black
to play lines involving the capture on
e4 and denies him the variations arising from 7 0-0 0-0 8 e4 dxc4 9 ♗xc4 e5
(Game 116), as 7 e4 dxc4 8 ♗xc4 e5 9
dxe5 ♘xe5 10 ♘xe5 ♗xe5 11 ♕xd8
♔xd8 12 ♗xf7 is good for White.

**7...dxe4 8 ♘xe4 ♘xe4 9 ♗xe4 c5!?**

9...♗b4+ is seen in the next game
and 9...h6! in Game 115.

**10 0-0 ♕c7 11 ♗c2! b6?!**

11...0-0 was safer, but then perhaps
12 dxc5 to meet 12...♘xc5 with 13 b4
and 14 c5, gaining queenside space.

**12 d5! e5 13 ♖e1 0-0 14 ♘g5 ♘f6
15 ♕d3 g6 16 ♕f3 ♕e7 17 ♕c3!**

Fine play by Lalic: the black position is now ripe to be opened by f2-f4

**17...♘h5 18 f4 f6 19 fxe5 fxe5 20
♘e4 ♗f5 21 ♗g5 ♕d7 22 ♗a4 ♕xa4
23 ♘xd6 e4 24 ♗e7 ♖fe8 25 ♘xe8
♖xe8 26 d6 ♘f4 27 ♕e5 ♘d3 28
♕d5+ ♔g7 29 ♖xe4 ♕c2 30 ♖f1 1-0**

## Game 114
## Illescas-Prie
*Linares Zonal 1995*

1 d4 d5 2 c4 c6 3 ♘f3 ♘f6 4 ♘c3
e6 5 e3 ♘bd7 6 ♗d3 ♗d6 7 e4!?
dxe4 8 ♘xe4 ♘xe4 9 ♗xe4 ♗b4+
10 ♗d2 ♗xd2+ 11 ♕xd2 c5!?

This may be too simplistic.

**12 0-0-0 ♕c7 13 d5 exd5 14 cxd5
♕d6 15 ♗c2 0-0 16 ♖he1 ♘f6 17
♘e5!**

This is nice for White: he has a large
spatial advantage and a passed d-pawn.

17...♗g4 18 f3 ♗h5 19 g4 ♗g6 20
♗xg6 hxg6 21 g5 ♘d7 22 ♘c4 ♕a6
23 b3 ♘b6 24 ♕a5 ♖fd8 25 ♕xa6
bxa6 26 d6 ♔f8 27 ♘e5 ♖ac8 28
♖e4 ♘d7 29 ♖h4 ♔g8 30 f4 ♘f8 31
d7 ♖c7 32 ♖d6 ♘xd7 33 ♖h3 f6 34
gxf6 gxf6 35 ♘xg6 ♔g7 36 ♘e7
♖e8 37 ♘d5 ♖b7 38 ♖e3 ♖xe3 39
♘xe3 ♘b6 40 ♔d2 ♔g6 41 ♔e2 ♖h7
42 ♘f1 ♖h3 43 ♔f2 a5 44 ♖c6 a4
45 bxa4 ♖a3 46 ♖xc5 ♘xa4 ½-½

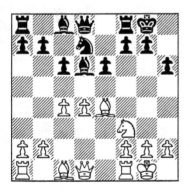

Game 115
**Sherbakov-Shabanov**
*Russian Ch., Elista 1996*

1 d4 d5 2 c4 c6 3 ♘f3 ♘f6 4 ♘c3 e6
5 e3 ♘bd7 6 ♗d3 ♗d6 7 e4 dxe4 8
♘xe4 ♘xe4 9 ♗xe4 h6! 10 0-0 0-0

A key position. Black will play ...e6-
e5 to liquidate White's d4-pawn. The
prophylactic ...h7-h6 was necessary as
9...0-0 10 0-0 e5? would have lost a
pawn to 11 dxe5 ♘xe5 12 ♘xe5 ♗xe5
13 ♗xh7+ ♔xh7 14 ♕h5+.
11 ♗c2 e5 12 ♖e1 ♗b4 13 ♗d2
♗xd2 14 ♕xd2 exd4 15 ♕xd4 ♕b6
16 ♕c3 a5 17 ♖ad1 ♘f6 18 ♖d6
♕b4 19 ♕e5! ♕xc4 20 ♗d3 ♕g4 21
h3 ♕h5 22 ♕g3!!

Black is powerless against the twin
threats of ♖xf6 and ♖e5.
22...♘d5 23 ♖e5 f5 24 ♖g6 ♖f7 25
♖e8+ ♔h7 26 ♘e5 ♖c7 27 f4 1-0

Game 116
**Lautier-Anand**
*London (rapidplay) 1995*

1 d4 ♘f6 2 c4 c6 3 ♘c3 d5 4 e3 e6
5 ♘f3 ♘bd7 6 ♗d3 ♗d6 7 0-0 0-0 8
e4 dxc4 9 ♗xc4 e5

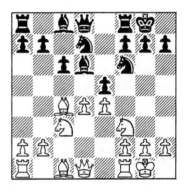

**10 ♗g5 ♕e7 11 ♖e1!?**
11 d5 is also possible, meeting
11...♘b6 with 12 ♗b3.
**11...exd4 12 ♘xd4?**
This leads to disaster. White must
play 12 e5! ♘xe5 13 ♘e4. For the two
pawns, White has pins on the e-file
and the h4-d8 diagonal. Natural moves
all fail: 13...♗e6 loses to 14 ♘xe5
♗xe5 15 f4!; while 13...♗f5 14 ♘xd6!
♘xf3+ 15 ♕xf3 ♕xd6 16 ♕xf5 and
13...♗g4 14 ♕xd4! ♘xf3+ 15 gxf3 ♗e5
16 ♘xf6+ gxf6 17 ♖xe5! fare no better.
**12...♘e5 13 ♗f1 ♗c5!**
Suddenly f2 is looking really weak.
14 ♘a4 ♗g4 15 ♕d2 ♗b4 16 ♘c3
♖ad8! 17 ♗e3 c5 18 ♘f5 ♗xf5 19
♕c2 ♗g6 0-1

## Summary

8 ♗e2 may be worth an occasional try as a surprise weapon, while Black players in a solid mood may wish to give 6...♗d6 a whirl.

**1 d4 d5 2 c4 c6 3 ♘f3 ♘f6 4 ♘c3 e6 5 e3 ♘bd7 6 ♗d3**

**6...dxc4**
> 6...♗d6
>> 7 e4 dxe4 8 ♘xe4 ♘xe4 9 ♗xe4 *(D)*
>>> 9...c5 – *Game 113*
>>> 9...♗b4+ – *Game 114*
>>> 9...h6 – *Game 115*
>> 7 0-0 0-0 8 e4 dxc4 9 ♗xc4 – *Game 116*

**7 ♗xc4 b5 *(D)* 8 ♗e2**
> 8 ♗b3 – *Game 112*

**8...a6 9 e4 b4 10 e5 bxc3 11 exf6 ♘xf6 12 bxc3 ♗d6 *(D)* 13 ♕a4**
> 13 0-0 – *Game 111*

**13...♗d7 – *Game 110***

*9 ♗xe4*

*7...b5*

*12...♗d6*

# CHAPTER THIRTEEN

## 6 ♕c2 ♝d6:
## 7 ♝e2 and 7 ♝d3

1 d4 d5 2 c4 c6 3 ♘f3 ♘f6 4 ♘c3 e6 5 e3 ♘bd7 6 ♕c2 ♝d6

6 ♝d3 is a straightforward move with clear aims. By contrast, 6 ♕c2 is a shadowy 'half-move' whose aims are linked as much with Black's development plans as White's own.

By delaying committing the light-squared bishop, White discourages the immediate 6...dxc4, as after 7 ♝xc4 b5, White has the useful extra move ♕c2 in comparison with the 6 ♝d3 line.

6...♝d6 is the normal response. This develops another piece, enabling ...0-0, while supporting ...e6-e5.

Now White faces a crucial choice between two main moves, 7 ♝e2 and 7 ♝d3 (the less common 7 g4 and 7 b3 are discussed in the (next chapter). We shall first examine how Black has been neutralising 7 ♝e2.

1 d4 d5 2 c4 e6 3 ♘c3 c6 4 e3 ♘d7

5 ♘f3 ♘gf6 6 ♕c2 ♝d6 7 ♝e2 0-0 8 0-0 ♖e8

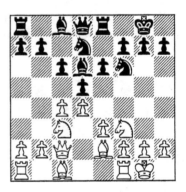

*Question 1:* What is the idea here?

*Answer:* White's basic aim remains the same in all lines after 5 e3: he wants to push e3-e4 to gain central space and free his dark-squared bishop. 8...♖e8 dissuades 9 e4 as 9...♘xe4 10 ♘xe4 dxe4 11 ♕xe4 e5! is a good riposte for Black.

Now that Black has stopped the early e3-e4, he will seek to solve his only positional problem: his inactive light-squared bishop on c8. He can do this in two ways:

1) He can release the central tension with ...d5xc4 and then play ...e6-e5, opening the c8-h3 diagonal for his bishop. The rook on e8 supports the e-pawn's advance to e4, attacking White's knight on f3.

2) He can fianchetto the bishop with ...b7-b6 and ...♗b7, and then open the long diagonal with ...c6-c5.

Note that 8...dxc4 9 ♗xc4 transposes to the line 7 ♗d3 0-0 8 0-0 dxc4 9 ♗xc4 considered in Games 120-124.

**9 ♖d1**

By putting the rook on the d-file opposite the queen on d8, White dissuades Black from playing ...d5xc4 and ...e6-e5.

**9...♕e7**

So Black removes his queen from the d-file and supports ...e6-e5 again.

**10 a4**

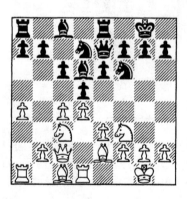

*Question 2:* What is White trying to do here?

*Answer:* White cannot play 10 e4 because of 10...♘xe4 11 ♘xe4 dxe4 12 ♕xe4 e5, so what is he to do? Think of what I said earlier: that this system often seems more concerned with anticipating Black's development than furthering White's own.

*Question 3:* Too subtle for me!

*Answer:* White has spotted that when Black tries to develop his bishop with 10...b6, then 11 e4! is possible as 11...dxe4 12 ♘xe4 ♘xe4 13 ♕xe4 e5 is no longer a solution as c6 is hanging!

*Question 4:* Can't Black just play 13...♗b7 with good chances?

*Answer:* White would have an edge here as Karpov proved against Kamsky in their match in Elista 1996. After 14 ♗f4! ♗xf4 15 ♕xf4 c5 16 ♕c7! ♖ab8 17 b4! we can see that a2-a3 also helps support this space-gaining push. Karpov assesses the position after 17...♖ec8 18 ♕f4 ♗xf3 19 ♗xf3 cxd4 (19...cxb4 20 axb4 ♖xc4 21 ♖xa7 ♖d8 22 b5 ♕b4 23 ♗c6 ♘f6 24 ♕c7 is clearly better for White according to Karpov. Fine preparation!) 20 ♕xd4 as slightly better for White.

*Question 5:* Right, so Black should break with 10...dxc4 11 ♗xc4 e5 then?

*Answer:* Wrong! Then 12 ♘g5! is annoying. But now you can guess why Black plays his next move!

**10...h6! 11 h3**

*Question 6:* Not again! Why?

*Answer:* Again White is anticipating Black's plan: after ...d5xc4 and ...e6-e5, ...e5-e4 unleashes the attack of the black dark-squared bishop on the h2-pawn. 11 h3 protects White's kingside and so draws the attacking potential from Black's plan. Remember that the inclusion of h2-h3 and ...h7-h6 does not help Black to play ...b7-b6!

**11...dxc4!**

No more subtlety: Black goes for his plan!

**12 ♗xc4 e5 13 ♘h4!**

A typical idea. White tries to exploit

the weakened kingside light squares.

**13...♘f8!**

Preventing ♘g6 and preparing to take the white knight if it lands on f5.

**14 dxe5**

14 ♘f5 ♗xf5 15 ♕xf5 e4! leaves the white queen a little uncomfortable.

**14...♕xe5! 15 ♘f3 ♕e7**

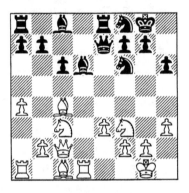

The position is about equal.

**16 ♗d2 ♗d7 17 ♖ac1 ♖ad8 18 e4 ♘g6 19 ♗e3 ♗b8 20 ♖d2 ♗c8 21 ♖xd8 ♖xd8 22 ♖d1 ♖e8 23 ♗f1 b6 24 b4 ♔f8 25 ♘d4 ♕e5 26 g3 ♕h5 27 ♕e2 ♕xe2 28 ♗xe2 ♗d7 29 ♔g2 ♗c7 30 f3 ♘e7 31 ♗f2 g5 32 ♖c1 ♗e5 33 ♗d3 ♖d8 34 ♘ce2 ♘h5 35 ♗a6 ♗e8 36 ♖d1 ♖d6 37 ♖c1 ♗d7 38 ♗c4 f5 39 exf5 ♘xf5 40 ♘xf5 ♗xf5 0-1**

This is Black's most reliable equaliser and has contributed to a loss of faith in 7 ♗e2. So what about 7 ♗d3. How does this help White?

---

**Game 118**
**Dautov-Shirov**
*German Bundesliga 1996*

---

**1 d4 d5 2 c4 c6 3 ♘f3 ♘f6 4 ♘c3 e6 5 e3 ♘bd7 6 ♕c2 ♗d6 7 ♗d3**

**0-0 8 0-0 ♕e7**

The first point of 7 ♗d3 is that the fianchetto of the light-squared bishop is not easy to achieve as 8...b6 9 e4 dxe4 10 ♘xe4 ♘xe4? loses a pawn to 11 ♗xe4, forking the h7- and c6-pawns. The text aims for a similar build-up to the previous game.

However, 8...h6!? is interesting, simply removing the h-pawn from the attack of the queen and bishop. In the game Spraggett-Bacrot, Enghien 1997, Black already stood well after 9 ♖d1 ♕e7 10 c5!? ♗b8!? 11 e4 e5 12 cxd5 ♘xd5 13 ♗f1 ♘xc3 14 bxc3 e4. Another try is 8...♖e8 to meet 9 e4 with 9...dxc4 10 ♗xc4 e5!? as 11 ♘g5 ♖f8 does not seem to lead anywhere.

Black's other major choices in this position, 8...e5 and 8...dxc4, are considered in Games 119-124.

**9 c5!**

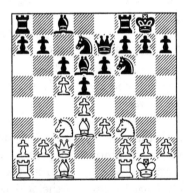

This, together with the next move, gives the 7 ♗d3 line its venom.

**9...♗c7 10 e4 dxe4 11 ♘xe4**

The point of White's play is to restrict Black's choices and hinder his development. This plan stops both of Black's central breaks. By occupying the e4-square, White prevents ...c6-c5 break. Unfortunately for Black, ...e6-e5 is also impossible: 10...e5 11 exd5 cxd5 12 ♗g5! e4 13 ♘xd5! ♘xd5 14 ♗xe7 exd3 15 ♕xd3 ♘xe7 16 d5! was a disaster in Dautov-Ribli, German Bundesliga 1996, while 11...e5 12 ♘xf6+ ♘xf6 (12...♕xf6+ 13 ♗xh7+) 13 dxe5 ♗xe5 14 ♖e1! is also awful.

*Question 6:* Black does get the d5-square though!

*Answer:* That is true, but it is just one square for one piece. It cannot be used to launch an attack or to free Black's game. The gains White makes far outweigh the concession of d5.

**11...h6 12 ♖e1**

Making sure that Black cannot stage a breakout with ...e6-e5.

**12...♖d8 13 a3 ♘xe4 14 ♗xe4 ♘f6 15 ♗d3 ♗d7 16 b4 ♗e8 17 ♕e2 ♘d5 18 ♕e4! ♘f6 19 ♕h4 ♖d5 20 g4 ♗d8 21 g5 ♘h7 22 ♗e4 ♘xg5 23 ♘xg5 ♖xg5+ 24 ♗xg5 ♕xg5+ 25 ♕xg5 hxg5 26 b5?**

According to Dautov, 26 ♖ad1! ♖d8 27 ♖d3 ♗f6 28 ♖ad1! a6 29 f4! would have consolidated the white position, leaving him with a clear advantage.

**26...♗f6 ½-½**

So how should Black react to this new threat? He has several options. The most common is to play 8...dxc4 9 ♗xc4, transposing back into the less highly regarded lines of the ♗e2 complex (Games 120-124). However, first we take a look at an independent line.

> ## Game 119
> **Karpov-Kramnik**
> *Las Palmas 1996*

**1 d4 d5 2 c4 c6 3 ♘f3 ♘f6 4 ♘c3**

e6 5 e3 ♘bd7 6 ♕c2 ♗d6 7 ♗d3 0-0 8 0-0 e5

*Question 7:* Why does Black play 8...e5?

*Answer:* After this move, White can give Black an isolated queen's pawn with 9 cxd5 cxd5 10 dxe5 ♘xe5 11 ♘xe5 ♗xe5. In return for this concession, Black frees his position and activates his pieces: he has opened the c8-h3 diagonal for his bishop. Moreover, White's kingside is rather short of defensive pieces as both his light-squared bishop and queen are in attacking positions on the b1-h7 diagonal.

**9 cxd5! cxd5 10 e4! exd4!?**

The sharpest move. Kramnik tried 10...dxe4 11 ♘xe4 ♘xe4 12 ♗xe4 h6 against Karpov in Vienna 1996, but after 13 ♗e3! exd4 14 ♗h7+! ♔h8 15 ♗xd4 ♘f6 16 ♗f5! ♗xf5 17 ♕xf5, White had some unpleasant pressure.

**11 ♘xd5 ♘xd5 12 exd5 h6 13 ♘xd4 ♕h4 14 ♘f3 ♕h5 15 ♗h7+ ♔h8 16 ♕f5!**

A very bold idea that was first played in I.Sokolov-Piket, Nussloch 1996. In that game Black replied with 16...♕xf5 17 ♗xf5 ♘f6, but after 18 ♗c2! ♗g4 (18...♘xd5 19 ♖d1 ♘b4 20

♗b3 ♗c7 21 ♗e3 ♘c6 22 ♗c5! wins a pawn as Sokolov shows) 19 ♗b3, White simply had an extra pawn in the ending.

**16...g5!!**

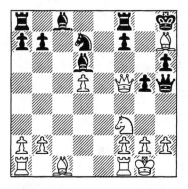

An outrageous reply that defies calculation. Suddenly, White has problems with his bishop on h7 as the threat is ...♔g7 and ...♘f6!

**17 h4**

17 ♗e3!? is met by 17...♔g7 18 ♗d4+ f6 19 ♕e6 ♗b8! with the threat of ...♘e5 and ...g5-g4.

**17...♘b6 18 ♕f6+ ♔xh7 19 ♕xd6 ♗g4 20 ♘h2 ♖ad8 21 ♕b4 ♗f5 22 hxg5 ♘xd5 23 ♕xb7 hxg5 24 ♕b3 ♖h8 25 ♕f3 g4 26 ♕g3 ♘f6 27 f3 ♖d3 28 ♘xg4 ♗xg4 29 fxg4 ♕g6?**

The first mistake according to Kramnik. 29...♕c5+ 30 ♕f2 ♕xf2+ was better, when the game Grabliauskas-Fridman, European Team Championship, Pula 1997, finished 31 ♖xf2 ♘xg4 32 ♖f3 ♖d1+ 33 ♖f1 ♖d5 34 b4 ½-½.

**30 ♕c7 ♔g8 31 ♗f4**

31 g5 would have been clearly better for White according to Kramnik.

**31...♖h4 32 ♗g3 ♖xg3 33 ♕xg3 ♕h6 34 ♕f3 ♖h1+ 35 ♔f2 ♕d2+ 36**

♔g3 ♕d6+ 37 ♔f2 ♕d2+ 38 ♔g3 ♕d6+ 39 ♔f2 ½-½

We now turn our attention to the lines after 8...dxc4 9 ♗xc4. The following game is a classic for this line and shows the dangers that Black can face.

---

*Game 120*
**Karpov-Shirov**
*Biel 1992*

---

**1 d4 d5 2 c4 c6 3 ♘c3 ♘f6 4 e3 e6 5 ♘f3 ♘bd7 6 ♕c2 ♗d6 7 ♗e2 0-0 8 0-0 dxc4 9 ♗xc4 b5**

With this move Black frees b7 for the light-squared bishop with gain of tempo. In typical Meran fashion he will play his bishop to the long a8-h1 diagonal and seek to quickly achieve ...c6-c5 to activate it fully. This is the most aggressive system against the 6 ♕c2 ♗d6 7 ♗d3 systems. The main drawback of 9...b5 is that Black weakens his queenside squares – c5 in particular – a couple of moves before he is ready to repair the damage with ...c6-c5. White's general strategical aim must be to prevent ...c6-c5 in order to keep the light-squared bishop passive behind the c6-pawn. White has five basic ways of achieving this:

1) To establish a knight on e4 via ♘g5-e4, attacking c5.

2) To clamp down on c5 by playing b2-b4.

3) To keep attacking the b5-pawn, meeting ...a7-a6 with a2-a4 so that ...c6-c5 loses the b5-pawn.

4) To play b2-b3 and ♗b2 so that after ...c6-c5, White can activate his dark-squared bishop against the black

king's position by d4xc5.

5) To play e3-e4, forcing ...e6-e5 and creating central counterplay to distract Black from achieving ...c6-c5.

The solid 9...♕e7 is considered in Game 124.

**10 ♗e2 ♖e8**

The more natural 10...♗b7 is the subject of Games 121-123.

**11 ♖d1 ♕c7 12 b3 e5 13 h3 ♗b7 14 ♗b2 a6 15 dxe5 ♘xe5 16 a4 ♖ad8?**

This natural move is a serious mistake. Arlandi-Illescas, Lisbon Zonal 1993, improved with 16...♘g6! when 17 ♘g5 can be met by 17...♗e5!, preventing the white knights from coming to e4.

**17 ♘g5! ♕e7 18 ♘ce4 ♘xe4 19 ♘xe4 ♗b4 20 ♘g3!**

A wonderful positional idea. The teasing threat of ♘f5 is quite irritating and if Black anticipates it with 20...♕e6 then 21 ♖xd8+ ♖xd8 22 ♕e4 is very unpleasant. Karpov sees things that no one else can!

**20...f6 21 ♗xe5 ♕xe5 22 ♗d3! h6 23 ♗g6!**

White's advantage has been transformed from a plus due to Black's weak queenside dark squares to an attack on Black's weak kingside light squares! How did that happen?

**23...♖f8 24 ♘f5 c5 25 axb5 axb5 26 ♖a7 ♕c7 27 ♘h4 ♖xd1+ 28 ♕xd1 ♖a8 29 ♕g4 ♕c6 30 ♖xb7 ♕xb7 31 ♕e6+ ♔h8 32 ♗e4 1-0**

A magnificent game.

## Game 121
## Gelfand-Kramnik
*Dos Hermanas 1997*

**1 d4 ♘f6 2 c4 e6 3 ♘f3 d5 4 ♘c3 c6 5 e3 ♘bd7 6 ♕c2 ♗d6 7 ♗d3 0-0 8 0-0 dxc4 9 ♗xc4 b5 10 ♗e2 ♗b7 11 ♖d1**

The offbeat 11 ♗d2 is considered in the next game and 11 a3 in Game 123, while 11 e4 is simply met by 11...e5.

**11...♕c7**

Here too 12 ♗d2 is possible, threatening 13 b4 to clamp down on c5, as 13...♗xb4 14 ♘xb5! is good for White.

**12 b3**

Black is ready to meet 12 e4 with 12...e5.

**12...a6!**

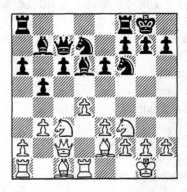

Equalising immediately according to Gelfand, but 13 a4 seems the more critical test here.

13 ♘e4 ♘xe4 14 ♕xe4 c5 15 ♕h4 ♘f6 16 ♗b2 ♕e7 17 dxc5 ½-½

## Game 122
## Karpov-Gelfand
### Dos Hermanas 1997

1 d4 d5 2 c4 c6 3 ♘c3 ♘f6 4 e3 e6 5 ♘f3 ♘bd7 6 ♕c2 ♗d6 7 ♗d3 0-0 8 0-0 dxc4 9 ♗xc4 b5 10 ♗e2 ♗b7 11 ♗d2!?

An unusual move order.

11...♖c8!? 12 ♖fd1 b4 13 ♘e4 ♘xe4 14 ♕xe4 ♕e7 15 a3 bxa3 16 bxa3 ♘f6 17 ♕h4 c5

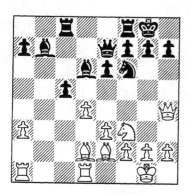

Black has equalised.

18 dxc5 ♗xc5 19 ♗b4 a5 20 ♗xa5 ♗xa3 21 ♗d3 ♗c5 22 ♘e5 h6 23 h3 ♖a8 24 ♗c3 ♘e4 25 ♕xe7 ♗xe7 26 ♗d4 ♗h4 27 g3 ♗f6 28 h4 ♖xa1 29 ♗xa1 ♖a8 30 ♗d4 ♖a2 31 ♖a1 ♖d2 32 ♗xe4 ♗xe4 33 ♘c4 ♖c2 34 ♘a3 ♖c6 35 ♗xf6 gxf6 36 ♘b5 e5 37 ♘a7 ♖c5 38 ♔h2 h5 39 g4 hxg4 40 ♔g3 f5 41 h5 ♔h7 42 ♖a6 ♖c1 43 ♔h4 ♖f1 44 ♖f6 ♖xf2 45 ♘c8 ♗d5 46 ♘d6 ♖h2+ 47 ♔g5 g3 48 ♘xf5 ♗e6 49 ♘xg3 ♖g2 50 ♔h4 ♖h2+ 51 ♔g5 ♖g2 52 ♔h4 ♔g7 53 ♖f1 ♖h2+ 54 ♔g5 ♖g2 55 ♔h4 f6 56 ♘f5+

♔h7 57 e4 ♗d7 58 h6 ♖e2 59 ♘d6 ♔g6 60 ♔g3 ♖e3+ 61 ♖f3 ♖e1 62 ♔g2 ♖d1 63 h7 ♔xh7 ½-½

Enough of all this subtlety; here is one of my games!

## Game 123
## Grivas-Sadler
### Cannes Open 1995

1 d4 d5 2 c4 c6 3 ♘f3 ♘f6 4 ♘c3 e6 5 e3 ♘bd7 6 ♕c2 ♗d6 7 ♗e2 0-0 8 0-0 dxc4 9 ♗xc4 b5 10 ♗e2 ♗b7 11 a3

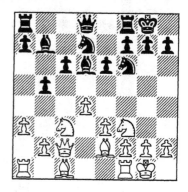

By drawing the sting from ...b5-b4, White hopes to play e3-e4 and keep his centre solid.

11...♖e8! 12 e4 e5 13 ♗g5 h6 14 ♗h4 exd4 15 ♘xd4 ♕b8!

16 ♗g3 is met by 16...♗xg3 17 hxg3 c5! when 18 ♘dxb5 a6! wins a piece, as the white pawn on a3 prevents the knight from retreating there!

16 ♘f3 a5 17 e5!? ♗xe5 18 ♘xe5 ♕xe5 19 ♗f3 b4 20 axb4 axb4 21 ♖xa8 ♗xa8 22 ♘a4 c5 23 ♗xf6 ♕xf6 24 ♗xa8 ♖xa8 25 b3 ♕c6 26 ♖c1 ♖e8 27 h3 ♖e5! 28 ♕d2 ♖g5 29 f3 ♖d5 30 ♕e3 ♖e5 31 ♕f2 ♕d5 32 f4 ♖e8 33 ♘xc5 ♘xc5 34 ♖xc5

♕xb3 35 ♖b5 ♕c4 36 ♖c5 ♕d3 37 ♖c7 b3 38 ♖b7 ♖e2 39 ♕b6 ♕g3 0-1

We shall now move on to Black's main alternative to 9...b5: 9...♕e7.

> ### Game 124
> **Ruzele-Cifuentes**
> *Groningen Open 1996*

1 d4 d5 2 c4 c6 3 ♘c3 ♘f6 4 e3 e6 5 ♘f3 ♘bd7 6 ♕c2 ♗d6 7 ♗e2 0-0 8 0-0 dxc4 9 ♗xc4 ♕e7

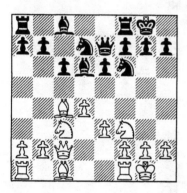

9...♕e7 is a flexible move. Although its main purpose is to support ...e6-e5 followed by a quick ...e5-e4, Black retains the option of using queenside plans instead.

**10 h3**

This is the most critical test of Black's plan.

*Question 8:* Why can't Black just play 10...e5?

*Answer:* Then 11 ♗b3 is awkward as 11...e4 loses a pawn to 12 ♘g5!, while 11...h6 12 ♘h4!, intending ♘g6 and ♘f5, contains unpleasant threats.

**10...c5!? 11 dxc5 ♗xc5 12 e4 ♗d6 13 ♘b5! ♘e5 14 ♘xe5 ♗xe5 15 f4 ♕c5+ 16 ♔h1!?**

16 ♔h2 ♗d7 17 b4!? was played in Ruzele-Cifuentes, Groningen 1996, and now 17...♕c8 18 ♘xa7 ♖xa7 19 fxe5 ♗b5 20 ♗e3 ♕xc4 21 ♕xc4 ♗xc4 22 ♗xa7 was slightly better for White according to Ruzele.

**16...♗d7 17 b4 ♕c8 18 ♘xa7 ♖xa7 19 fxe5 ♗b5 20 ♗e3 ♕xc4 21 ♕xc4 ♗xc4 22 ♗xa7 ♗xf1 23 ♖xf1 ♘xe4 24 ♖c1 h5 25 b5 ♖d8 26 a4?!**

26 ♔h2! first was better according to Ruzele, when 26...♖d2 27 a4 h4 28 a5 g5 29 ♖e1 ♘c3 30 a6 is very good for White.

**26...h4! 27 ♔h2**

27 ♖c4 ♖d1+ 28 ♔h2 ♖e1 29 a5 g5 30 a6 ♘g3 is not very pleasant!

**27...g5 28 ♖e1 ♘c3 29 ♗e3 ♘xa4 30 ♗xg5 ♖d4 31 ♖c1 ♖b4 32 ♗f6 b6 33 ♖c8+ ♔h7 34 ♖h8+ ♔g6 35 ♖g8+ ♔h6 36 ♖h8+ ♔g6 37 ♖g8+ ♔h6 38 ♖g7 ♘c3 39 ♖xf7 ♘d5 40 ♖f8 ♘xf6 41 ♖xf6+ ♔g7 42 ♖xe6 ♖xb5 43 ♖e8 ♖b4 44 ♔g1 ♖f4 45 e6 ♖e4 46 e7 ♔f6 47 ♖b8 ♖xe7 48 ♖xb6+ ♔g5 49 ♖b5+ ♔g6 50 ♔f2 ♖a7 51 ♖e5 ♖f7+ 52 ♔e3 ♖f6 53 ♖e4 ♔g5 54 ♖g4+ ♔h5 55 ♖f4 ♖g6 56 ♖f8 ♖g3+ 57 ♔f4 ♔h6 58 ♖h8+ ♔g7 59 ♖xh4 ♖xg2 60 ♖g4+ ½-½**

## Summary

7 ♗d3 0-0 8 0-0 is the most critical test for Black after 6 ♕c2 ♗d6. If Bacrot's 8...h6 does not fulfil its early promise then 8...dxc4 9 ♗xc4 b5 is looking very sound at the moment.

**1 d4 d5 2 c4 c6 3 ♘f3 ♘f6 4 ♘c3 e6 5 e3 ♘bd7 6 ♕c2 ♗d6**

**7 ♗d3**

> 7 ♗e2 0-0 8 0-0 *(D)*
>> 8...♖e8 – *Game 117*
>> 8...dxc4 9 bxc4 – Games 120-124 (by transposition)

**7...0-0 8 0-0 dxc4**

> 8...♕e7 – *Game 118*
> 8...e5 – *Game 119*

**9 ♗xc4 *(D)* b5**

> 9...♕e7 – *Game 124*

**10 ♗e2 ♖e8**

> 10...♗b7 *(D)*
>> 11 ♖d1 – *Game 121*
>> 11 ♗d2 – *Game 122*
>> 11 a3 – *Game 123*

**11 ♖d1** – *Game 120*

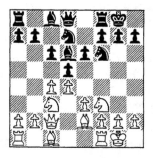

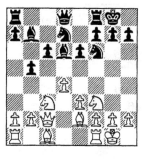

| *8 0-0* | *9 ♗xc4* | *10...♗b7* |
|---|---|---|

# CHAPTER FOURTEEN

## Odds and Ends

1 d4 d5 2 c4 c6 3 ♘f3 ♘f6 4 ♘c3 e6

In this chapter, we briefly examine lines I just couldn't fit in anywhere else! The first two games deal with White's rarer possibilities after 6 ♕c2 ♗d6 and the last two with 5 g3 and 5 ♕b3 respectively.

1 d4 d5 2 c4 c6 3 ♘c3 ♘f6 4 ♘f3 e6 5 e3 ♘bd7 6 ♕c2 ♗d6 7 g4!?

This amazing idea was the brainchild of Alexander Shabalov. It is perhaps surprising to see it relegated to a tiny place in this book, but after this game White is in desperate need of a big improvement.

7...♗b4!

By pinning the white knight on c3, Black provides a square on e4 for his knight on f6 after White plays g4-g5. Although Black loses a tempo with ...♗b4, he claims that g2-g4 is a greater concession if White cannot launch an immediate attack. Note that 7...♘xg4 is met by 8 ♖g1 with awkward play on the g-file.

8 ♗d2 ♕e7 9 a3 ♗xc3 10 ♗xc3 b6! 11 ♗d3 ♗a6!

Black prepares to exchange off one of White's bishops and thus deprive him of the two bishops.

12 ♕a4 dxc4 13 ♕xa6 cxd3 14 ♕xd3 0-0 15 g5 ♘d5 16 ♗d2 f5! 17 0-0-0 c5 18 ♔b1 b5!

Despite the thrust g2-g4-g5, White has no hint of a kingside attack. The text sacrifices a pawn to open lines for

Black's pieces on the queenside.
**19 ♕xb5 ♖ab8 20 ♕a5 ♖b3 21 ♔a2
♖fb8 22 ♖b1 e5 23 ♖hc1 ♕e6 24
♔a1 exd4 25 ♖xc5 ♘xc5 26 ♕xc5
♘c3 27 ♘xd4 ♖xb2 28 ♖xb2**

**28...♕a2+ 0-1**

A very powerful game from Kramnik.

*Game 126*
**Legky-M.Gurevich**
*Bruges 1995*

**1 d4 d5 2 c4 c6 3 ♘f3 ♘f6 4 ♘c3
e6 5 e3 ♘bd7 6 ♕c2 ♗d6 7 b3 0-0
8 ♗d3!?**

If White simply develops with 8
♗e2, then after 8...♕e7 9 0-0 b6, we
are back into similar lines to the previous chapter where White has played
the passive b2-b3. The text is an attempt to do something original.
**8...a6!**

Preparing ...e6-e5 by preventing
♘b5, which would be annoying after
8...e5 9 cxd5 cxd5.
**9 0-0 e5! 10 c5!?**

A risky attempt that turns out well
for Black. 10 cxd5 cxd5 11 dxe5 ♘xe5
was unclear according to Gurevich.

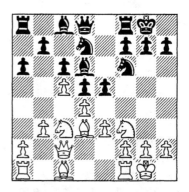

**10...♗c7 11 dxe5 ♘xe5 12 ♘xe5
♗xe5 13 f4 ♗c7 14 ♗b2 ♕e7 15
♘a4?! ♕xe3+ 16 ♔h1 ♖e8 17 ♗xf6
gxf6 18 ♖f3 ♕d4 19 ♗xh7+ ♔f8 20
♖af1 ♗g4 21 ♖3f2 ♖e3 22 ♗f5
♗xf5 23 ♕xf5 ♖ae8 24 ♕h5 f5 25
♘b6 ♗xb6 26 ♕h6+ ♕g7 27 ♕d6+
♔g8 28 cxb6 ♖e1 29 ♕d7 ♕f6 30
g4 ♖1e7 31 ♕xf5 ♕xf5 32 gxf5 ♔g7
33 h4 ♖h8 34 ♖h2 ♔f6 35 h5 ♔xf5
36 h6 f6 37 ♖g1 d4 38 ♖h5+ ♔xf4
39 ♖f1+ ♔g4 40 ♖h2 ♖e3 41 ♖g2+
♖g3 42 ♖xf6 ♖xg2 43 ♔xg2 ♖h7 44
♖d6 c5 45 ♔f2 ♔g5 46 ♖d5+ ♔f4
47 ♖h5 ♔g4 48 ♖xc5 ♖xh6 49 ♔e2
♖xb6 50 ♔d3 ♖d6 ½-½**

*Game 127*
**Topalov-Kramnik**
*Linares 1997*

**1 d4 d5 2 c4 c6 3 ♘f3 ♘f6 4 ♘c3
e6 5 g3!?**

This leads the game into the realms
of the Catalan. Kramnik states that
Black must capture on c4, otherwise
he will just stand worse.
**5...♘bd7 6 ♗g2 dxc4! 7 a4**

Preventing ...b7-b5.
**7...♗e7 8 0-0 0-0 9 e4 e5! 10 dxe5**

♘g4 11 ♗f4 ♕a5 12 e6 fxe6 13 ♕e2 ♘ge5 14 ♘d4 ♘d3!?

A novelty from Kramnik, giving up the e6-pawn in order to activate his light-squared bishop on c8.

15 ♘xe6 ♖f6 16 ♗c7 ♕b4 17 ♘d4?

17 ♘g5 was better according to Kramnik, when 17...♕xb2 18 ♕xb2 ♘xb2 19 f4 with e4-e5 to follow leads to an unclear ending.

17...♗c5 18 ♘c2 ♕xb2 19 ♘d1 ♕b3 20 ♘de3 ♘7e5 21 h3 ♗e6 22 ♔h2 ♖h6 23 ♖ab1 ♗g4!!

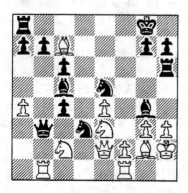

24 ♘xg4 ♘xg4+ 25 ♕xg4 ♕xc2 26 ♕g5 ♘xf2 27 ♖xf2 ♕xf2 28 ♖f1 ♕d4 29 ♗e5 ♕d7 30 ♕c1 ♕e6 31 ♗xg7 ♔xg7 32 ♕g5+ ♖g6 33 ♕xc5 ♕d6 0-1

One of Karpov's favourite standby ideas against the Semi-Slav has been 5 ♕b3. However, Kasparov's treatment in the next game seems very efficient.

*Game 128*
**Karpov-Kasparov**
*Las Palmas 1996*

1 d4 ♘f6 2 ♘f3 d5 3 c4 e6 4 ♘c3 e6 5 ♕b3 dxc4 6 ♕xc4

The actual move order in the game was 4...dxc4 5 ♕a4+ c6 6 ♕xc4, but I have changed it to illustrate the Semi-Slav sequence.

6...b5 7 ♕d3 ♗b7

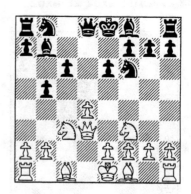

8 a3

8 ♗g5 ♘bd7 9 e3 a6! 10 ♗e2 c5 11 0-0 ♗e7 was just equal in Karpov-Timman, World Championship, Jakarta 1993.

8...a6! 9 e3

After this, Black has no problems. 9 e4 c5 10 e5 is clearly better for White according to Karpov, but I see no problems for Black after 10...cxd4 11 ♘xb5 ♘fd7!? 12 ♘bxd4 ♘xe5! 13 ♘xe5 ♕a5+.

9...c5 10 dxc5 ♗xc5 11 ♕xd8+ ♔xd8 12 ♗d2 ♔e7 13 ♗d3 ♘bd7 14 ♔e2 ♗d6 15 ♖hd1 ♖ac8 16 ♖ac1 ♘b6 17 ♗e1 ♘c4 18 ♖c2 ♗xf3+ 19 gxf3 ♘e5 20 h3 ♘xd3 21 ♖xd3 ♖hd8 22 ♖cd2 ♗c7 23 ♖c2 ♗b6 24 ♖xd8 ♔xd8 25 ♖d2+ ♔e7 26 ♖d1 g6 27 f4 ♖c4 28 f3 ♘d7 29 b3 ♖c6 30 ♘e4 ♖c2+ 31 ♖d2 ♖xd2+ 32 ♗xd2 ♗c5 33 ♘xc5 ♘xc5 34 ♗b4 ♔d6 35 ♔d2 a5 36 ♗xc5+ ♔xc5 37 ♔d3 f6 38 h4 ♔d5 39 b4 axb4 40 axb4 h6 41 e4+ ♔d6 42 ♔e3 e5 43 fxe5+ fxe5 44 ♔f2 ♔e6 45 ♔g2 ½-½

## Summary

All these systems are in need of new ideas for White. For the moment, Black is happy to face them!

**1 d4 d5 2 c4 c6 3 ♘f3 ♘f6 4 ♘c3 e6** *(D)*

**5 e3**

       5 g3 – *Game 127*
       5 ♕b3 – *Game 128*

**5...♘bd7 6 ♕c2 ♗d6** *(D)* **7 g4**

       7 b3 – *Game 126*

**7...♗b4** *(D)* – *Game 125*

    *4...e6*         *6...♗d6*         *7...♗b4*

# INDEX OF COMPLETE GAMES

Printed in the USA
CPSIA information can be obtained
at www.ICGtesting.com
JSHW052200100923
47985JS00002B/3